Oxford Regional Economic Atlas

The United States and Canada

Prepared by the Cartographic Department of
Oxford University Press

Advisory Editors
John D. Chapman, University of British Columbia
John C. Sherman, University of Washington

Second Edition

Prepared with the assistance of Quentin H. Stanford
Don Mills Collegiate Institute, Toronto

OXFORD UNIVERSITY PRESS
1975

Oxford University Press, Ely House, London W.1

GLASGOW   NEW YORK   TORONTO   MELBOURNE   WELLINGTON
CAPE TOWN   IBADAN   NAIROBI   DAR ES SALAAM   LUSAKA   ADDIS ABABA
DELHI   BOMBAY   CALCUTTA   MADRAS   KARACHI   LAHORE   DACCA
KUALA LUMPUR   SINGAPORE   HONG KONG   TOKYO

Oxford Regional Economic Atlas: The United States and Canada
First edition 1967. Reprinted 1968, 1970, 1973

Cased: ISBN 019 894309 1

Paperback: ISBN 019 894308 3

Compiled, drawn, and processed to film by
The Cartographic Department of Oxford University Press

Printed in Great Britain

Maps: Cook Hammond and Kell Ltd, Mitcham, Surrey

Introductory text and Gazetteer: set by The Church Army Press, Oxford and
printed by J. W. Arrowsmith Ltd, Bristol

Acknowledgements

First Edition 1967

Agent-General for the Alberta Government
Agent-General for the British Columbia Government
Agent-General for the Ontario Government
Agent-General for the Québec Government
Dr. T. Armstrong
Association of American Railroads
E. M. Buxton
Canadian Atlantic Provinces Office
Canadian Government Agencies:
    Department of Energy, Mines and Resources, *formerly* Mines and Technical Surveys
    Department of Indian Affairs and Northern Development, *formerly* Northern Affairs and National Resources
    Dominion Bureau of Statistics
    Geological Survey of Canada
    Ministry of Transport
Canadian National Railways, London Office
Canadian Pacific Railways, London Office
Dr. K. M. Clayton
Dr. A. Coleman
Commissioner General, Canadian Corporation for the 1967 World Exhibition
Dr. A. C. Gerlach
C. F. W. R. Gullick
Dr. F. K. Hare
Hydrographic Department, Admiralty, London, U.K.
Professor G. F. Jenks
Kansas Turnpike Authority
Lovell Johns, Ltd.
Mackay School of Mines, University of Nevada
Maine Turnpike Authority
Manitoba Department of Mines and Natural Resources
Map Room, Bodleian Library, University of Oxford
M. Marsden
Meteorological Office, Bracknell, U.K.
Professor R. E. Murphy
National Institute of Oceanography, Wormley, U.K.
New Jersey Highway Authority
New York State Thruway Authority
Office of the High Commissioner for Canada
Ohio Turnpike Authority
Oklahoma Turnpike Authority
Dr. E. R. Oxburgh
Dr. M. E. D. Poore
Rand McNally & Co.
Dr. A. H. W. Robinson
St. Lawrence Seaway Authority
Saint Lawrence Seaway Development Corporation
Service des Arpentages, Ministère des Terres et Forêts
M. A. Shaw
P. E. Smethurst
The Economist Intelligence Unit
United States Government Agencies:

U.S. Civil Aeronautics Board
U.S. Department of the Army: Army Map Service, Corps of Engineers
U.S. Department of Agriculture: Forest Service, Soil Conservation Service
U.S. Department of Commerce: Bureau of the Census, Coast and Goedeti Survey, Weather Bureau
U.S. Department of the Interior: Bureau of Commercial Fisheries, Bureau of Mines, Geological Survey, National Parks Service
U.S. Department of Labor: Bureau of Labor Statistics
U.S. Federal Power Commission
U.S. Interstate Commerce Commission
U.S. Treasury Department: Internal Revenue Service
U.S. Information Service at the United States Embassy, London, U.K.
Professor J. W. Watson
West Virginia Turnpike Commission

Second Edition 1975

Boston Metropolitan Area Planning Council
Communauté Urban de Montréal
Delaware Valley Regional Planning Commission
Denver Regional Council of Governments
Houston-Galveston Area Council
Los Angeles Regional Planning Commission
Metropolitan Washington Council of Governments
Minneapolis/St. Paul Metropolitan Council
New York Regional Plan Association
Northern Illinois Planning Commission
Orange County Planning Commission
Regional Planning Commission of Jefferson, Orleans, and St. Bernard Parishes
Southeast Michigan Council of Governments
Southwestern Pennsylvania Regional Planning Commission

Aviation Statistics Centre, Ottawa
Joyce Berry
Professor Saul B. Cohen
Canadian Arctic Gas Study, Ltd.
Cox Cartographic, Ltd.
Richard Deily, Institute for Iron and Steel Studies
Economics and Statistics Library, University of Oxford
Environmental—Social Program Northern Pipelines, Ottawa
Indian and Northern Affairs, Ottawa
Newbury Drawing Agency, Ltd.
Miklos Pinther
Joan Stanford
Statistics Canada, *formerly* Dominion Bureau of Statistics
The British Petroleum Company, Ltd.
Robert Wharton
United States Atomic Energy Commission

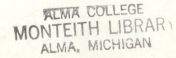

Topics

Contents

Endpapers Population Distribution

*Maps with an asterisk are on a common base map of the United States and Southern Canada at a scale of 1:15.84M or 1″ to 250 miles. The symbols † & ‡ indicate smaller scale versions of the same map at 1:33.94M or 1″ to 535 miles and 1:46.00M or 1″ to 726 miles respectively.

Projection

All the maps, except the urban plans and Alaska (pp. 42/43) are on the same projection. This is a composite projection: South of 55°N it is conical orthomorphic, with origin at 42° N and standard parallels at 35°N and 49° N. The northern portion has been modified by taking the 90°W meridian as straight, and curving the meridians that lie east and west of it inwards; this has the effect of reducing scale errors in the Arctic (to 10% at most). Alaska is on a Lambert conical orthomorphic projection.

Sources

URBAN PLANS pp. 1–7

Authorities: Prof. J. W. Watson, Edinburgh University.
also
Boston: Saul B. Cohen, Clark University.
Chicago: Douglas B. Cargo, University of Chicago.
Denver: Laurence D. Herold, University of Denver.
Detroit: Byran Thompson, Wayne State University.
Houston: J. E. Coffman, University of Houston.
Los Angeles: Howard Nelson, University of California, Los Angeles.
Minneapolis/St. Paul: John Adams, University of Minnesota.
Montréal: Quentin H. Stanford: Don Mills Collegiate Institute.
New Orleans: Patsy Denton, Regional Planning Commission.
New York: Michael P. Marchioni, Hunter College.
Philadelphia: Roman A. Cybriwsky, Temple University.
Pittsburgh: Louis C. Peltier, University of Pittsburgh.
San Francisco: James E. Vance, University of California, Berkeley.
Seattle: Warren Gill, University of British Columbia.
Toronto: Quentin H. Stanford, Don Mills Collegiate Institute.
Vancouver: Warren Gill, University of British Columbia.
Washington, D.C.: Harold Brodsky, University of Maryland.

Sources: *Base Maps:* U.S. Army Map Service, 1:250 000 series: U.S. Geological Survey, 1:24 000 series.
U.S. Dept of Commerce: Bureau of the Census, PC(1) State reports; National Oceanic & Atmospheric Administration Environmental Data Service, Local Climatological Data, 1971; Sectional Aeronautical Charts, 1:500 000, 1973 (*maps*).
Regional Planning Councils *see* Acknowledgements.
see also Urban Plan Legend facing page 1.

TOPOGRAPHIC MAPS pp. 8–45, 128

Sources: *Base Maps:* U.S.A.F. 1:1 000 000 Aeronautical Charts and Operational Navigational Charts 1:1 000 000.
U.S. Bureau of the Census: United States Census of Population, 1960 & 1970.
Dominion Bureau of Statistics *now* Statistics Canada: Census of Canada, 1961 & 1971.
U.S. Geological Survey: Map Showing Extent of Glaciations in Alaska, 1:2 500 000, 1965; Alaska Reconnaissance Topographical Series 1:250 000.
U.S. Civil Aeronautics Board: Airport Activity Statistics, 1971.
Statistics Canada: Air Passenger origin and destination, Domestic Report, 1972.
National Atlas of the United States, 1970.
Atlas of Canada, 1957.
Miscellaneous Road maps.

RELIEF pp. 46–47

Sources: U.S. Naval Oceanographic Office: World Charts.
U.S. Geological Survey: Geologic Map of North America, 1965.
International Hydrographic Bureau, Monaco: Carte générale bathymetric des Océans, 1923.
Hydrographic Office, Admiralty, London, U.K.
National Institute of Oceanography, Wormley, Surrey, U.K.
National Atlas of the United States, 1970.

The National Atlas of Canada, 4th edn., 1973.
N. M. Fenneman. Physical Divisions of the United States (*map*).

SOLID GEOLOGY pp. 48–49

Authorities: U.S. Geological Survey; Dr. E. B. Oxburgh, Oxford University.
Sources: U. S. Geological Survey, Geologic Map of North America, 1965.
Dr. P. King: Evolution of North America, 1959.

PLEISTOCENE GLACIATION AND DRIFT GEOLOGY pp. 50–51

Authority: Prof. K. M. Clayton, East Anglia University.
Sources: Geological Association of Canada: Glacial Map of Canada, 1958.
U.S. Geological Survey: Geologic Map of North America, 1965.
The Geological Society of America: Glacial Map of North America, 1945; Glacial Map of the United States East of the Rocky Mountains, 1959; Pleistocene Eolian Deposits in the United States, Alaska and parts of Canada, 1952 (*map*).
J. L. Hough: Geology of the Great Lakes, 1958.
Science, February 1965: G. Falconer, J. T. Andrews and J. D. Ives, Late Wisconsin End Moraines in Northern Canada.
Geographical Bulletin, Ottawa, May 1962: W. R. Ferrard and R. T. Gujda, Isobases of the Wisconsin Marine Limits in Canada.
U.S.G.S. Professional Papers, 1961: J. H. Feth, Glacial Lakes.
Geological Survey of Canada: Geology and Economic Minerals of Canada, Edit. R. J. W. Douglas, 1970.

SOILS pp. 52–53

Authority: Prof. K. M. Clayton, East Anglia University.
Sources: Atlas Mira, 1965.
U.S. Soil Conservation Service, General Soil Map of the United States (experimental), 1964.
Atlas of Canada, 1957.

POTENTIAL VEGETATION pp. 54–55

Authority: Dr. F. K. Hare, Toronto University.
Sources: A. W. Küchler; Potential Natural Vegetation of the Conterminous United States, 1964 (*map*).
Atlas of Canada, 1957.
World Forestry Atlas, 1951.
Dr. F. K. Hare: A Photo-reconnaissance Survey of Labrador-Ungava (*map*).
B. V. Gutsell: Newfoundland (Modified) (*map*).
Department of Northern Affairs and National Resources: Forestry Regions of Canada (*map*).

RIVER FLOW pp. 56–57

Authority: Prof. J. D. Chapman, University of British Columbia.
Sources: 86th Congress, 1960: Senate Resolution No. 48, Surface Water Resources of the United States.
United States Geological Survey: Circular No. 676, Estimated Use of Water in the United States in 1970.
The National Atlas of Canada, 1970.

SOURCES

LAND USE pp. 58–59

Sources: The National Atlas of the United States, 1970.
International Association of Agricultural Economists: Instituto Geografico De Agostini S.p.A., World Atlas of Agriculture, 1971.

THE NORTH pp. 60–61

Authority: Q. H. Stanford, Don Mills Collegiate Institute, Toronto.

Sources: The Sub-Committee on Science and Technology, Advisory Committee on Northern Development: Science and the North, A Seminar on Guidelines for Scientific Activities in Northern Canada, 1972.
Department of Indian and Northern Affairs: Oil and Gas Activities, edn. 8, 1971; Mines and Mineral Activities, edn. 8, 1971; Canada Showing Location of Indian Bands with Linguistic Affiliations, 1968 (*map*).
Department of Energy, Mines and Resources: North West Canada Transportation Facilities, 1972 (*map*).
Yukon and Northwest Territories Roads and Tracts, 1973 (*map*).
U.S. Bureau of the Census: United States Census of Population, 1970.
Statistics Canada: Census of Canada, 1971.
Mackenzie Valley Pipe Line Research Ltd.: Arctic Oil Pipe Line Feasibility Study, 1974.
Canadian Arctic Gas Study Ltd.: Arctic Gas System Route Map 1974.
U.S. Bureau of Mines: Minerals Yearbook, 1971.
National Atlas of the United States, 1970.
National Atlas of Canada, 4th edn., 1970.

CLIMATIC MAPS pp. 62–71

Authorities: Dr. F. K. Hare, Toronto University; M. Marsden, Sir George Williams University, Montréal.

Sources: U.S. Weather Bureau: Maps and published normals; Mean Daily Solar Radiation, Monthly and Annual, 1964 (*map*); Climatology of the United States, No. 81, Monthly Normals of Temperature, Precipitation, and Heating Degree Days, 1931–1960.
Ministry of Transport, Ottawa: MSS data.
Meteorological Office, Bracknell, U.K.: R.A.F. Form 2215A.
WMO/OMM: No. 117, TP52, Climatological Normals (Clino) for Climat and Climat Ship stations for the period 1931–60.
Canadian Meteorological Memoirs: No. 17, 1964, C. C. Brughner, Distribution of Growing Degree Days in Canada.
M. Marsden: MSS data.
National Atlas of the United States, 1955.
Atlas of Canada, 1957.

DEMOGRAPHIC MAPS pp. 72–77

Authority: Q. H. Stanford, Don Mills Collegiate Institute, Toronto.

Sources: United States Bureau of the Census: Census of Population 1960 & 1970; Census of Population and Housing, 1970; Negro Population in Selected Places and Selected Counties, 1970; General Social and Economic Characteristics, 1970; County and City Data Book, 1972.
United States Department of Health, Education and Welfare: Monthly Vital Statistics Report, Annual Summary for the United States, 1972.

United States Department of Labor: United States Employment and Earnings, Vol. 18, No. 11, May 1972.
United States Statistical Abstract, 1973.
Statistics Canada: Census of Canada, 1966 & 1971; Number of Inhabitants, Population by Ethnic Groups, 1971; Income Distribution by Size in Canada, 1971; Vital Statistics, 1972; The Labour Force, April & October, 1973.
M. V. George, Census Monograph: Internal Migration in Canada, 1961.
The National Atlas of the United States, 1970.

AGRICULTURAL MAPS pp. 78–85

Authorities: Prof. J. C. Sherman, University of Washington; Prof. J. D. Chapman, University of British Columbia.

Sources: United States Department of Agriculture; various statistics.
United States Bureau of the Census: Cotton Production in the United States—Crop of 1963.
Dominion Bureau of Statistics: various statistics.
Prof. G. F. Jenks: Livestock and Livestock Products Sold in the United States, 1959 (*map*).
Pineapple Growers' Association: Pineapple Fact Book, Hawaii, 1965; MSS data.
Department of the Treasury, Bureau of Alcohol, Tobacco and Firearms, ATF PB23.1(4–74): Alcohol, Tobacco and Firearms, Summary Statistics, 1973.
Statistics Canada: Tobacco and Tobacco Products Statistics, 1973.
National Atlas of the United States, 1955.
Atlas of Canada, 1957.

WOOD PROCESSING pp. 86–87

Authority: Q. H. Stanford, Don Mills Collegiate Institute, Toronto.

Sources: Post's Pulp and Paper Directory, 1974.
Directory of Forest Products Industry 1973.
Dept. of the Environment, Canadian Forestry Service: J. S. Rowe, Forest Regions of Canada, Public. No. 1300, 1972.
The National Atlas of the United States, 1970.

COMMERCIAL FISHERIES pp. 88–89

Authority: Q. H. Stanford, Don Mills Collegiate Institute, Toronto.

Sources: F.A.O.: Atlas of Living Resources of the Sea, 1972.
Department of Mines and Technical Surveys, Ottawa: Natural Resources, 1958 (*map*).
U.S. Department of Commerce: Current Fisheries Statistics, No. 5900, 1971; Fishery Statistics of the United States, Statistical Digest No. 64, 1970.
Statistics Canada: Fishery Statistics, New Brunswick, Newfoundland, Northwest Territories, Nova Scotia, Ontario, Prairie Provinces, Prince Edward Island, Québec, 1971; Shipping Reports, Pts. II & III, 1971.
Department of the Army, Corps of Engineers: Waterborne Commerce of the United States, 1972.

FUELS MAPS pp. 90–97

Authorities: Prof. J. D. Chapman, University of British Columbia; Q. H. Stanford, Don Mills Collegiate Institute, Toronto.

Sources: Oxford Regional Economic Atlas: The United States and Canada, 1st. edn., 1967.

United States Department of the Interior: Bituminous Coal and Lignite Distribution, 1969.

United States Bureau of Mines: Preprint from Minerals Yearbook; Coal—Bituminous and Lignite, 1971; Coal—Pennsylvanite Anthracite, 1971; Crude Petroleum and Petroleum Products, 1970; Natural Gas, 1971.

Department of Energy, Mines and Resources, Minerals Branch, Ottawa: Operators List No. 4, Coal Mines in Canada, Jan. 1973; Operator List No. 5, Petroleum Refineries in Canada, 1973; Canadian Minerals Yearbook, 1971; Offshore Exploration, 1973; Electrical Power in Canada, 1971; Main Electrical Transmission Systems and Principal Power Generating Developments, 1971 (*map*).

National Coal Association, Washington: Bituminous Coal Facts, 1972.

Exxon Corpn.: Oil and Gas Atlas, 1972.

The Petroleum Publishing Co.: Oil and Gas Journal, 1970; Oil and Gas Journal Atlas.

Federal Power Commission: Electric Utility Listing by State, Dec., 1969; Steam-Electric Plant Construction Cost and Annual Production Expenses, 1971; Hydroelectric Plant Construction Cost and Annual Production Expenses, 1971; Principal Electrical Facilities, 1971 (*national and regional maps*).

Nuclear Energy International, Washington: Atomic Power, Jan., 1971.

Acres Ltd.: Mid Canada Development Corridor . . . a concept, 1967.

National Atlas of the United States, 1970.

Atlas of Canada, 1957.

MINING AND MINERAL PROCESSING MAPS pp. 98–105

Authorities: Prof. J. D. Chapman, University of British Columbia; Q. H. Stanford, Don Mills Collegiate Institute, Toronto.

Sources: United States Bureau of Mines: Minerals Yearbook, 1970 & 1971; Preprints from Minerals Yearbook, 1971.

United States Atomic Energy Commission: The Nuclear Industry, 1971.

Department of Energy, Mines and Resources, Minerals Resources Division, Ottawa: Minerals Yearbook, 1971; Operators List, No. 1, Primary Iron and Steel, Jan. 1971, No. 2 Metal and Industrial Mineral Mines and processing Plant, 1971.

Engineering and Mining Journal: International Directory of Mining and Mineral Processing Operations, 1973.

Geological Survey of Canada: Mineral Deposits of Canada, 1969 (*map*).

Pit and Quarry Publications Inc.: Portland Cement Plant in the United States, Canada and Mexico, 1973 (*map*).

IRON AND STEEL pp. 106–107

Authority: Q. H. Stanford, Don Mills Collegiate Institute, Toronto.

Sources: Institute for Iron and Steel Studies, Greenbrook, N.J.: Commentaries January, February, March 1973, January–February, 1974; Directory of Iron & Steel Works of the United States & Canada, 1971.

American Iron and Steel Institute: Iron and Steel Producing and Finishing Works of the United States and Canada, 1970.

Engineering and Mining Journal: International Directory of Mining and Mineral Processing Operations, 1973.

Department of Energy, Mines and Resources, Minerals Resources Branch, Ottawa: Operators List No. 1, Primary Iron and Steel, January 1971.

Statistics Canada: Shipping Reports Pts. I and II, 1971.

The St. Lawrence Seaway Authority: Traffic Report of the St. Lawrence Seaway, 1971.

FABRICATED METALS AND MACHINERY pp. 108–109

Authority: Prof. J. D. Chapman, University of British Columbia.

Sources: United States Department of Commerce: County Business Patterns, 1970.

Dominion Bureau of Statistics: Manufacturing Industries in Canada, Section G, Geographical Distribution, 1967.

TRANSPORT EQUIPMENT pp. 110–111

Authorities: Prof. J. D. Chapman, University of British Columbia: Economist Intelligence Unit, London.

Sources: Oxford Regional Economic Atlas: The United States and Canada, 1st. edn., 1967.

Interavia World Directory of Aviation and Astronautics, 1974.

Jane's World Railways, 1974.

Moodie's Industrial Manual, 1973.

'Automotive News' 1973 Review and Reference Edition.

International Shipping and Shipbuilding Directory, 1973.

Scott's Industrial Directories: Ontario Manufacturers, 1972–73; Québec, 1971–72.

Directories of: British Columbia, Trade, 1971; California Manufacturers, 1969; Illinois Manufacturers, 1972; Manitoba Trade, 1974; Michigan Manufacturers, 1971; New England Manufacturers, 1974; Nova Scotia, Manufacturing, 1970–71; Texas Manufacturers, 1970.

CHEMICALS pp. 112–113

Sources: European Chemical News, London, U.K.: Chemical Plant Data, 1970.

TEXTILES pp. 114–115

Authorities: Prof. J. D. Chapman, University of British Columbia; Q. H. Stanford, Don Mills Collegiate Institute, Toronto.

Sources: Oxford Regional Economic Atlas: United States and Canada, 1st. edn., 1967.

Davidson's Blue Books, 1973.

MANUFACTURING pp. 116–117

Authority: Prof. J. D. Chapman, University of British Columbia.

Sources: *see* Fabricated Metals and Machinery.

TOURISM pp. 118–119

Authority: Q. H. Stanford, Don Mills Collegiate Institute, Toronto.

Sources: U.S. Department of the Interior, National Park Service: Number of Tourist Visits and Overnight stays in Areas under the Auspices of the National Park Service during 1973.

SOURCES

U.S. Department of Commerce, 1972 Census of Transportation: Travel during 1972.
U.S. Travel Data Center: 1972 National Travel Expenditure Study.
U.S. Bureau of the Census: Annual Survey of Manufactures 1971.
Statistics Canada: Advance Information, Canada Travel Survey, 1971: Travel, Tourism & Outdoor Recreation—A Statistical Digest, 1972.
Dept. of Trade, Industry and Commerce, Travel Industry Board: The Canadian Tourism Facts Book, 1972.
The National Geographic Society: National Geographic, Feb. 1970, June 1971, Feb. 1974.
The National Atlas of the United States, 1970.
Miscellaneous Road maps.

WATERBORNE COMMERCE pp. 120–121

Sources: Department of the Army, Corps of Engineers: Waterborne Commerce of the United States, Parts I–IV, 1972.
Statistics Canada: Shipping Report, Parts II & III, 1971.
St. Lawrence Seaway Authority: Traffic Report of St. Lawrence Seaway, 1971.

SURFACE COMMUNICATIONS pp. 122–123

Sources: Amtrak Marketing Department: Amtrak Routes, 1973 (*map*).
National Railway Publication Company: The Official Guide of the Railways, Aug. 1972.
Canadian National Railways: Timetable, Oct. 1973–April 1974; Across Canada (*map*).
Canadian Pacific Rail: Timetable, Oct. 1973–April 1974; C.P. Services, 1974 (*map*).

United States Department of Transportation; Federal Highways Administration 1972, Average Daily Traffic on Rural Mileage of the Interstate system of the Travelled-Way (*map*).
Mobil Oil Corpn.: Travel Maps, 1971.

DATES OF RAILROAD CONSTRUCTION pp. 124–125

Authorities: C. F. W. R. Gullick, *formerly* Oxford University; Prof. Saul B. Cohen, Clark University.

Sources: Rand McNally: Handy Railroad Atlas of the United States, 1965.
C. L. Lord and E. H. Lord: Historical Atlas of the United States, 1953.
C. O. Paullin: Atlas of the Historical Geography of the United States, 1932.
Hammond's American History Atlas, 1964.
L. J. Burpee: Historical Atlas of Canada, 1927.
Canadian National Railways: MSS data.

AIR COMMUNICATIONS pp. 126–127

Sources: International Civil Aeronautical Organization, Montréal: Digest of Statistics, No. 166 TF. 1971.
United States Department of Transportation, Federal Aviation Administration, Civil Aeronautics Board: Airport Statistics of Certified Route Air Carriers, June 1971; Handbook of Airline Statistics, 1972; Airman's Information Manual, Airport Directory, 1972.
Statistics Canada: Air Passenger origin and destination, Domestic Report, 1972; Aviation Statistics Centre, Airport Activity Statistics, 1971–1972.
United States Department of Transportation and Canadian Surveys and Mapping Branch: Standard Time Zones of North America, 1971 (*map*).

Abbreviations
used on maps and in the gazeteer

Ala.	Alabama	Ind.	Indiana	Oreg.	Oregon
Alta.	Alberta	Junc(t)., Jnc.	Junction	P.	Pass
Aq.	Aqueduct	Ky.	Kentucky	Pa.	Pennsylvania
Arch.	Archipelago	L.	Lake	P.E.I.	Prince Edward Island
Ariz.	Arizona	La.	Louisiana	Pen., penin.	Peninsula
Ark.	Arkansas	Ldg.	Landing	Pk.	Park, peak
B.	Bay	Man.	Manitoba	Plat.	Plateau
B.C.	British Columbia	Mass.	Massachusetts	Prov. Park	Provincial Park
Br.*br.*	Bridge, branch	Md.	Maryland	Pt(e).	Point(e)
C.	Cape	Mich.	Michigan	Qué.	Québec
Calif.	California	Minn.	Minnesota	R., *r.*	River
Can.	Canada	Miss.	Mississippi	Ra(s).	Range(s)
Cen.	Center, centre	Mo.	Missouri	Res.	Reservoir
Ch., chan.	Channel	Mont.	Montana	R.I.	Rhode Island
Colo.	Colorado	Mt(s)., mtn(s).	Mount(s), mountain(s)	S.	South
Conn.	Connecticut	N.	North	Sask.	Saskatchewan
Cors.	Corners	Nat'l Hist. Park	National Historical Park	S.C.	South Carolina
Cr., *cr.*	Creek	Nat. Mon., N.M.	National Monument	Sd.	Sound
D.C.	District of Columbia	Nat. Park., N.P.	National Park	S.D.	South Dakota
Del.	Delaware	Nat. Rec. Area	National Recreation Area	*Sett.*	Settlement
Des.	Desert	N.B.	New Brunswick	Sprs.	Springs
E.	East	N.C.	North Carolina	St(e).	Saint(e)
Fd.	Fiord	N.D.	North Dakota	Stn.	Station
Fk.	Fork	Nebr.	Nebraska	St. Park	State Park
Fla.	Florida	Nev.	Nevada	Str.	Strait
Ft.	Fort	Nfld.	Newfoundland	Tenn.	Tennessee
G.	Gulf	N.H.	New Hampshire	Tpk.	Turnpike
Ga.	Georgia	N.J.	New Jersey	Va.	Virginia
Gdn.	Garden	N. Mex.	New Mexico	Vt.	Vermont
Harb.	Harbor, Harbour	N.S.	Nova Scotia	W.	West
Hd.	Head	N.W.T.	Northwest Territories	Wash.	Washington
Hts.	Heights	N.Y.	New York	Wis.	Wisconsin
I(s)., *i(s).*	Island(s)	Okla.	Oklahoma	W. Va.	West Virginia
Ill.	Illinois	Ont.	Ontario	Wyo.	Wyoming

Foreword

J. H. Paterson, Professor of Geography, in the University of Leicester

During the hundred years that preceded the ending of World War II in 1945, the peoples of the United States and Canada had broken all previous statistical records for speed and scale of economic development. Never before had there been so rapid an enlargement of the sown area over against the wild, or so immense a movement of settlers from overseas, first to the inhabited core areas and then on to the frontiers; never so great an expansion of railroad mileage against such physical odds. And when the figures for steel production in Carnegie's Pittsburgh were received in steel-making Sheffield in England, they were greeted with sheer disbelief: such was their scale that it seemed as if only Vulcan himself could have matched them.

Even after 1945, with development in full swing over the continental vastness of the Soviet Union, Western Europe achieving new levels of production, and Japan set upon its meteoric rise, Anglo-America still contrived to set fresh records. Its farmers fed the hungry in other lands. It supplied much of the world with farm machinery and commercial aircraft, and to this day leads all other countries in the production of petroleum and bituminous coal. As its railroad services began to atrophy, it developed instead the world's largest network of superhighways. Inevitably, the question has arisen: how has all this been achieved? Was it because of a super-endowment with natural resources? Or was it done by draining off human skills from the rest of the world? Or by some magic of organization or virtue of democracy? And from those questions one is irresistibly drawn on to another: is this primacy permanent or passing? How long is it all likely to last?

In the middle 1800s, when our hundred-year period began, most of the answers to questions like these would have focussed on two things, the political system and the natural endowment. While the system gave rise to such legislative landmarks as the Homestead Acts and the idealistic concept of land granted free to the " actual cultivator," the natural endowment in its turn gave rise to phrases like " limitless resources "; phrases which expressed a confidence that development and the increase of individual wealth could continue indefinitely, because there was enough and to spare for all.

Today we know better. We know that " the system " was abused and that it crushed some and ruined others, ideals notwithstanding. We know that while average wealth has increased and is increasing, averages also imply minima—in this case, the poverty of a minority. And one good reason why the increase of wealth is slow is that resources are in reality far from limitless; that even common resources like water are in short supply; that space itself is a resource; and that the United States (if not, for the present, Canada) is

running out of space in the midst of 9 million square kilometres of it.

It is therefore appropriate that, early on in the *Oxford Regional Economic Atlas of the United States and Canada*, there is a section of topographic maps. They remind us of the dimensions of the stage on which the remarkable Anglo-American drama has been played: it has happened on these plains and mountains, which are no different from those of other lands, and beside these rivers and seas. They also remind us that space for future development is limited. Whatever Anglo-Americans may require or demand in the century ahead must be provided from this natural base—from these lands and no others. Even those limited ventures into imperialism which gave the United States access to resources beyond its shores, in the Philippines and the Caribbean, are now effectively over and cannot be repeated. Today, as never before, Anglo-America must look to its own resources.

So an accurate stock-taking becomes of the utmost importance. What resources do these lands possess: what soils, what minerals, what potential for cultivation? For the answers to these questions, we move into the main body of the Atlas, where patterns of natural conditions and economic development are mapped. And bearing in mind the times, and the population explosion, and the political realities, we shall be particularly concerned to examine those areas which may be thought of as the " reserves," empty now, but holding a potential for future development—northern Canada and Alaska. It is no coincidence that Alaska and the Northwest figure with much greater prominence in this second edition of the Atlas than they did in the first, of 1967. Since that date there have been changes affecting Alaska through, so to speak, both supply and demand. On the supply side, there has been the discovery of the great oil fields of the Arctic Shore and the long arguments among technicians and conservationists about how to get the oil out. On the demand side, there has been the swiftly mounting ecological crisis, the pollution of eastern rivers and lakes, the sprawl of the cities, and the consequent upward revision of the value to the nation of a million and a half square kilometres of Alaska's clean water and untouched land.

Largely empty at present, these " reserves " may well appear to offer ample space and resources for the next generation, and the next after that. But what is their real capacity? Will, for example, the widespread belief that the Canadian North is full of natural wealth merely waiting to be tapped when needed bear detailed examination? Can we take it for granted that there are resources still undiscovered, that capital will be attracted to their exploitation, and labour be provided by Canadians and others eager and willing to work at remote northern sites? On the basis of past experience we can, perhaps, allow ourselves the first of these assumptions; the second and third we cannot. But the first step is to be clear what, so far, is where, and this is a task which the Atlas sets out to fulfil.

It quickly becomes apparent that some part, at least, of Anglo-America's primacy is founded on genuine natural advantages. As examples of these we may take at random the accessibility of the huge Appalachian coal measures, the fertile glacial drifts which give a smooth, cultivable surface to the Agricultural Interior, and the fortuitous penetration of the chain of Great Lakes across the heart of the continent. But none of these of itself created or guaranteed wealth; that depended on the efforts of the inhabitants in organizing coal production and use, in criss-crossing the agricultural areas with railroad tracks, and in linking the Great Lakes by canals.

It therefore becomes important to examine more closely, as the Atlas does, the characteristics of this population, broadly termed Anglo-American because 95 per cent of its 230 million members speak English. To it, Europe has contributed the most numerically, Africa the most tragically (through the shipment of slaves), Asia significantly, Latin America increasingly. The mixture has proved resourceful, hardy (for it has taken hardiness to survive, whether on a cotton plantation, or on a prairie homestead, or in a city ghetto), and successful. But the unmixed elements have also made their contributions—the French of Québec, the Chicanos of the Southwest, and now the blacks and the Indians, asserting ever more emphatically their own cultural distinctiveness. Most of these groups the present Atlas maps; it is safe to predict that the third edition, as and when it is called for, will need to devote even more space to them.

With the second edition of this work in hand, the reader may well find two questions forming in his mind. Firstly, what evidence does it provide that Anglo-American development is still continuing; between 1967 and 1975, how great have the changes been? The answer must be: considerable. To give expression to them, the editors of the Atlas have introduced a range of new maps, as well as updating the others. Consider, as examples, the implications of the map of tourism (pp. 118–9), the greatest " growth industry " of the decade; or the fresh presentation of the chemical industry, with its range of new products; or the map of internal migration from country to town (p. 77), reminding us that, at the last census, over 73 per cent of the population of both countries was classified as urban (and, incidentally, that the Atlas's city maps gain in importance from this fact). These developments may not, as in previous decades, represent the conquest of virgin lands, but they do represent no less significant shifts in the internal economic balance of the continent.

Secondly, however, it may be asked: can a hundred, or a thousand, symbols on a page really tell us anything about these countries? Does it matter that the symbols may, for this second edition, have been moved or enlarged, often by quantities so small as to be invisible to the naked eye?

Clearly, it matters to the cartographer; it is his task and his satisfaction to portray reality as accurately as possible. But the general reader may still need reassuring, and that reassurance can perhaps be offered in the terms of an old geographical axiom, that what concerns us in geography is *the discontinuity of distribution*. We may begin with the impression that we have before us nothing but a page covered with dots. But the dots do not, of course, blanket the *whole* page, and that is precisely the point—it is their uneven distribution on the page that interests us. It raises the question: if here, why not there? And with the asking of that question, we are fairly launched on geographical investigation. Why were all the main railroads except one in the United States (pp. 124–5) built before 1913 while, across the border in Canada, considerable portions of the network were added after that date, and where are these portions? Why is the growing of sorghums so intensive in Kansas and Texas (p. 80), but cut off almost as by a wall at the Colorado and New Mexico state lines? And so on.

On the pages of the second—or, for that matter, the twenty-second edition of this Atlas, a host of similar questions will arouse the curiosity of the reader.

Urban Plans

J. W. Watson, formerly Professor of Geography, in the University of Edinburgh

Scale: Each urban area is shown on the same scale— 1 inch to 6 miles. Each is divided up in the same way to indicate:—

Black: a central business core of multiple stores, office blocks, hotels and passenger stations which, in the case of a metropolitan complex of communities, may be deemed to be the principal commercial centre;

Red: lesser, but significant, business centres, often of secondary cities within the central metropolitan area, or of former towns amalgamated with a city;

Blue: industrial districts, mainly of groups of large-scale plants serving the region or nation as a whole, and excluding service industries related to the city needs only. Isolated industries are shown by conventional squares and areas of industrial wasteland and spoil tips by triangles;

Brown: the built-up area, where urban uses of land predominate; these are chiefly houses, institutions, and streets, but they include playgrounds, cemeteries, transportation yards, and other open spaces used for urban purposes;

Green: major city parks and wooded wastes such as ravines;

Yellow: major military and naval installations.

The data for mapping are based upon reports of city planning boards and industrial commissions; on the U.S. and Canadian Censuses; on the U.S. Army Map Service series, United States 1:250 000 and the U.S. Geological Survey 1:24 000 map series and the Atlas of Canada city maps 1:100 000; on road maps of various oil companies; on aerial photographs; and on personal submissions to the editor. It was not possible to work from a single datum line, although each city has been scrutinized by a local authority in 1974.

The symbols cannot be given identical interpretation on each map. Thus the central business districts of great urban complexes, based on functions central to the whole metropolitan area, are smaller by comparison through the exclusion of services used principally by the central city itself, than business cores of single large cities. Similarly, in the latter, the subsidiary commercial centres may be smaller than those not shown at all in the larger urban complexes. This is seen, too, in district names. In places like Los Angeles and New York, such names have to be kept for what are themselves big communities—often separate cities—whereas in lesser cities they are used for neighbourhoods or suburbs.

This inclusion of slightly differing categories under the same symbol is true of roads, where the names, Freeways, Thruways, Parkways, Turnpikes, Trunk Roads, National Roads, State or Provincial Highways, or major urban thoroughfares, often apply to different classes in different States and Counties. The major roads shown are limited access ones of at least four lanes meant for fast through traffic. They include however, roads with as many as eight lanes. Moreover, some of them have only partially separated, others completely separated junctions, lead-ins and exits. The point is that, for their region and their particular city, they are the rapid-transit thoroughfares.

Still other complications are found in the important institutions; colleges in many a large city are larger than universities in smaller cities. Some cities are built round famous institutions; others may have institutions which are equal in size and repute, but owe their standing as cities to commerce or industry; in the one case the institution has been shown, in the other, it has not. Similarly, differences occur in showing major airports, transportation yards, and fuel depots. Some ports may have oil-storage depots larger than cities which refine oil; in the latter oil-storage is shown as part of the industrial area, but not necessarily so in the former. Thus although every city is mapped by use of the same categories, these categories have to be interpreted in terms of the city itself, its region, and the state or province or country it belongs to. A very important feature of cities is that, although they share much in common, they are essentially unique entities, reflecting unique factors in geography and history.

Boundaries

Black

International

State or Province

County

Highways

Red

Limited access and rapid transit

Other main highways

Tunnels

Red

Railroads and transportation yards

Airports and airfields

L o n g   I s l a n d   S o u n d

CONNECTICUT
NEW YORK

SUFFOLK COUNTY
NASSAU COUNTY

Huntington

Quinnipiac State Park

Port Chester
Mamaroneck

WESTCHESTER COUNTY

Hicksville

Westbury

New Rochelle

MOUNT VERNON

YONKERS

Glen Cove

Port Washington

Great Neck

City Island

Bethpage

Levittown

Hempstead

Adelphi Univ.

Hofstra Univ.

C.W. Post College (Long Is.)

State Univ. of N.Y.

New Hyde Park

Garden City

Freeport

Long Beach

Rockville Centre

Valley Stream

BRONX COUNTY
QUEENS COUNTY

THE BRONX

Fordham Univ.

Lehman College

Pelham Bay Park

FLUSHING

Queens College

St. John's Univ.

Long   Island

MANHATTAN

QUEENS

BROOKLYN

JOHN F. KENNEDY INTERNATIONAL

Jamaica Bay

Rockaway Beach

Rockaway Inlet

Coney Island

HACKENSACK

PATERSON

Hawthorne

Ridgewood

Paramus

Fair Lawn

Wayne

Pompton Lakes

BERGEN COUNTY

Clifton

Passaic

Garfield

Montclair

Orange

Glen Ridge

Irvington

Seton Hall Univ.

ESSEX COUNTY
PASSAIC COUNTY

Hudson River

NEW JERSEY
NEW YORK

Edgewater

Hoboken

N. Bergen

JERSEY CITY

Upper New York Bay

KINGS COUNTY
RICHMOND COUNTY

Bayonne

Newark Bay

NEWARK

ELIZABETH

Great Kills Park

RICHMOND

Staten Island

Lower New York Bay

Perth Amboy

NEW YORK
NEW JERSEY

Raritan Bay

Sandy Hook

MONMOUTH

New Brunswick

Plainfield

Summit

UNION COUNTY
MIDDLESEX COUNTY

SOMERSET CO.

Morristown

MORRIS COUNTY

NEW YORK

A T L A N T I C   O C E A N

John F. Kennedy International Airport

	J	F	M	A	M	J	J	A	S	O	N	D	Year
Temp.°F	31	33	40	50	60	70	75	74	68	58	47	36	53
Rain inches	2.4	3.4	3.9	3.7	3.2	2.5	3.7	4.3	3.2	2.9	3.9	3.5	40.6

Height 13 feet (4 metres)

SCALE 6 MILES TO 1": SEE LEGEND FACING PAGE 1

© Oxford University Press

Page 1

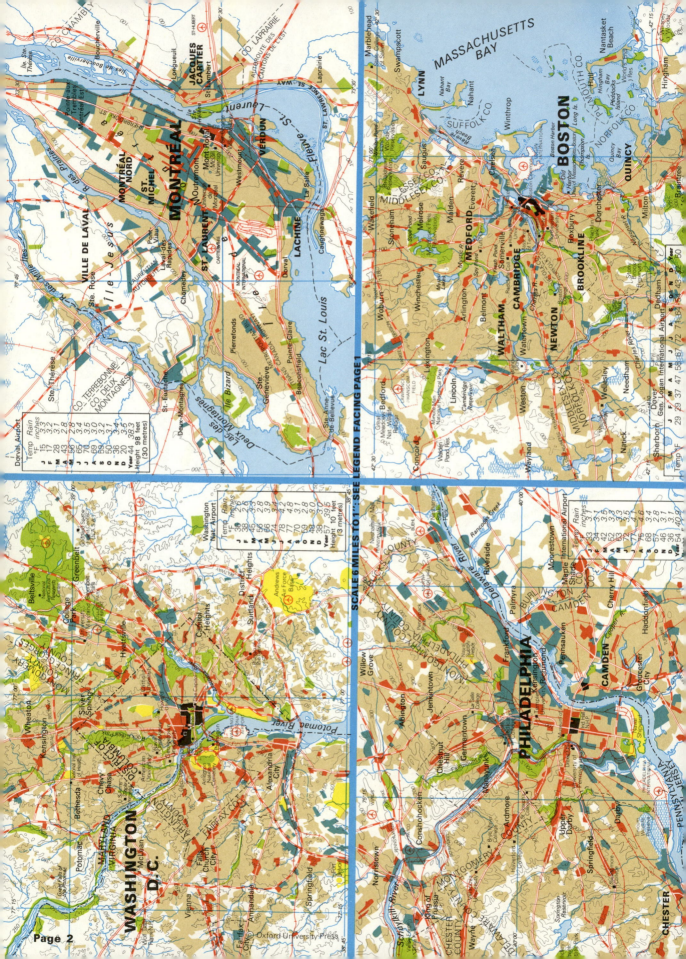

© Oxford University Press

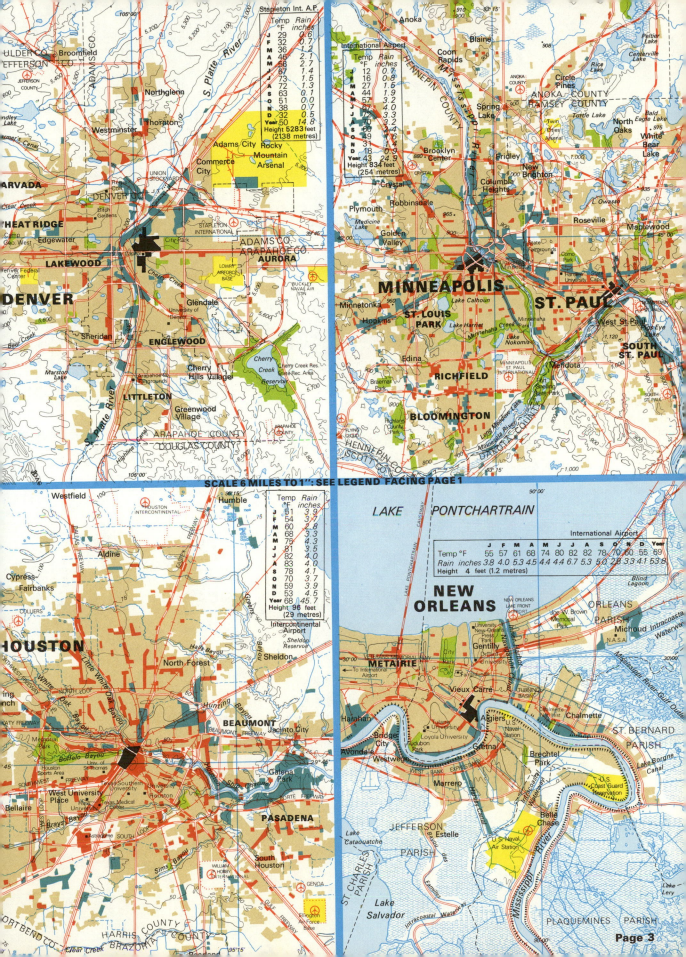

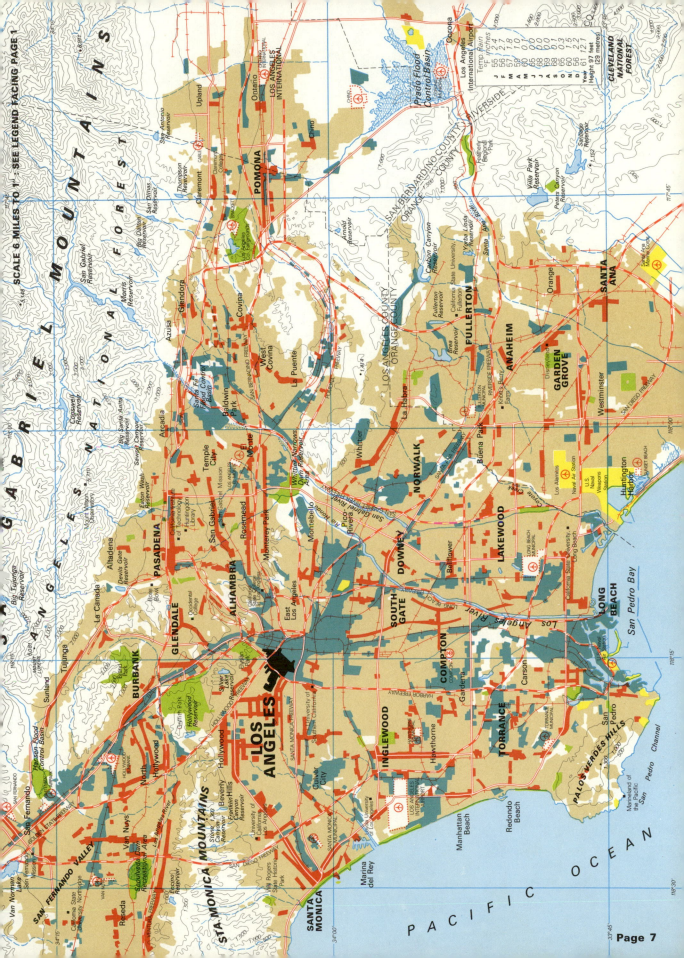

MARITIME CANADA

Boundaries   Capital cities underlined
International
State   National, State or Provincial Parks
Canals   Railroads   Tunnel
Roads
   Limited access   Other main
   divided highways   highways
Airports   ⊕ International   ○ Domestic

Scale 1:6·3M approx.
1cm to 63km : 1 in. to 100 miles

© Oxford University Press

Spot Heights in Metres

Feet
3,000
1,500
1,000
600
300
Sea Level

Boundaries · Capital cities underlined
International
State · National, State or Provincial Parks
Canals · Railroads · Tunnel
Roads
Limited access divided highways · Other main highways
Airports · ⊕ International · ○ Domestic

QUÉBEC

MAINE

NEW HAMPSHIRE

VERMONT

LAKE ONTARIO

NEW YORK

LAKE ERIE

PENNSYLVANIA

WEST VIRGINIA

VIRGINIA

MARYLAND

NEW JERSEY

ATLANTIC OCEAN

Montréal

Ottawa

Québec

Toronto

Hamilton

Buffalo

Rochester

Syracuse

Albany

Boston

Cleveland

Pittsburgh

New York

Philadelphia

Baltimore

Washington D.C.

Richmond

Norfolk

Feet
3,000
1,500
1,000
600
300
Sea Level

Spot Heights in Metres

Scale 1:6·3M approx.
1cm to 63km : 1 in. to 100 miles

© Oxford University Press

Page 11

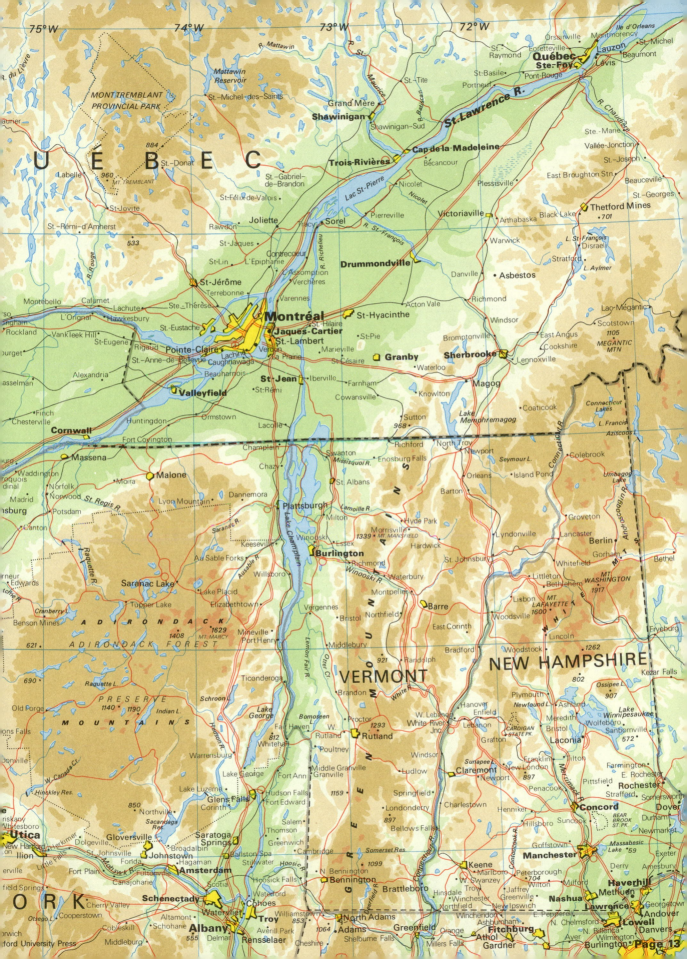

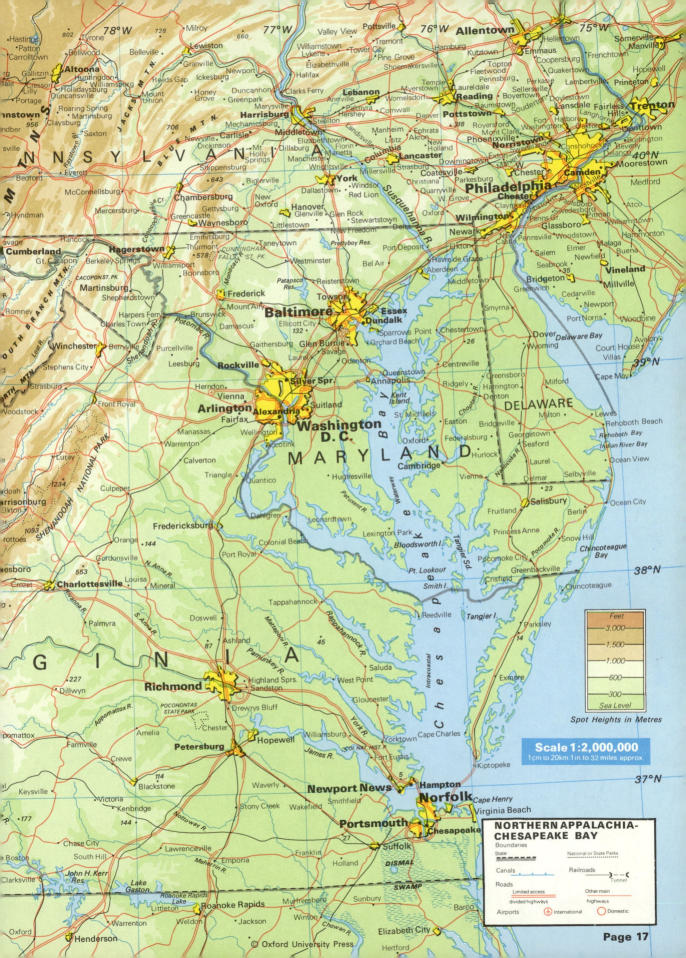

NORTHERN APPALACHIA-
CHESAPEAKE BAY

Boundaries
State
National or State Parks

Canals
Railroads
Tunnel

Roads
Limited access
divided highways
Other main
highways

Airports
International
Domestic

Scale 1:2,000,000
1cm to 20km 1in to 32 miles approx

Feet
3,000
1,500
1,000
600
300
Sea Level

Spot Heights in Metres

© Oxford University Press

Page 17

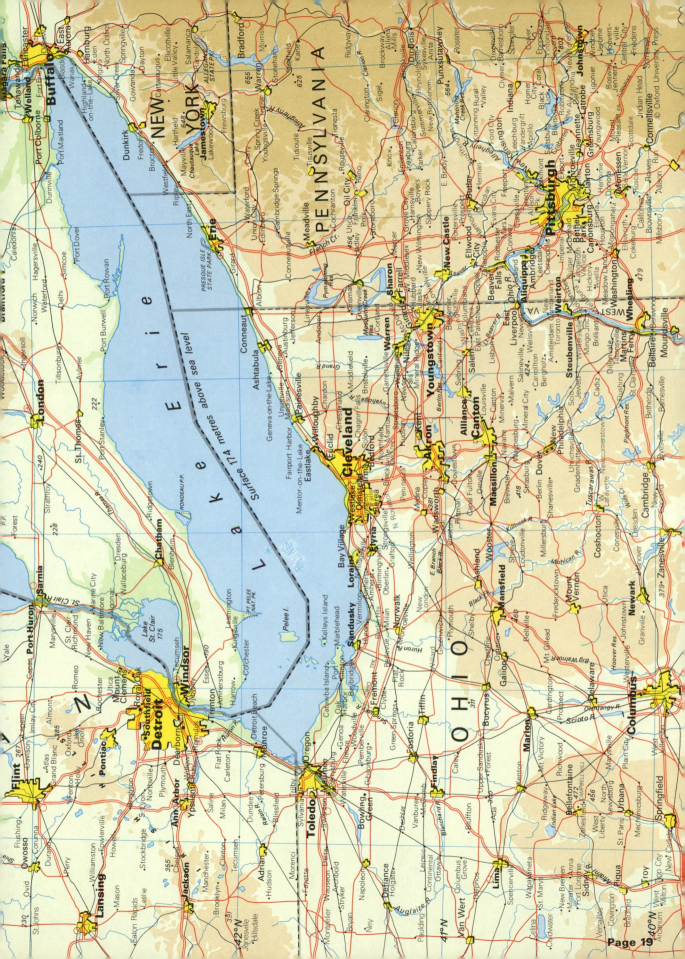

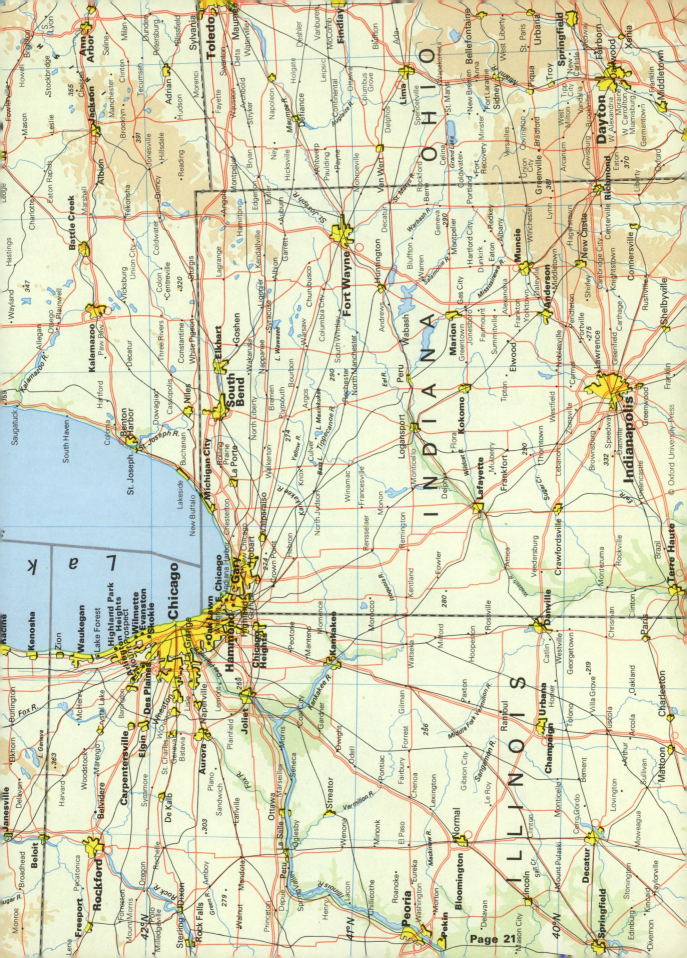

© Oxford University Press

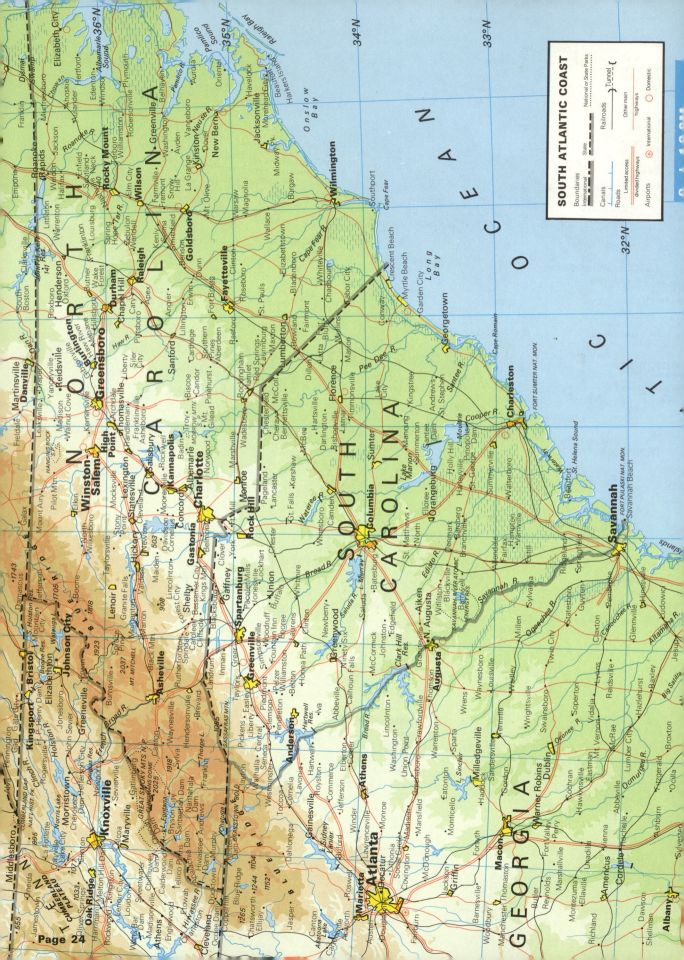

Puerto Rico

19°N · 18°N

Cabezas de San Juan
Isla de Culebra
San Juan · Fajardo
Manati · Bayamón · 1074 · Humacao
Arecibo · Utuado · **Caguas** · Cayey
Aguadilla · 1338 · Coamo · Guayama
Bahía Mayagüez · **Ponce**
Mayagüez · Cabo Rojo
Punta Aguirreada
Punta Brea
Isla Mona

To New York 1,610 miles
To Miami 1,050 miles

66°W · 67°W · 68°W

27°N · 26°N · 25°N

Lake Pk. **Palm Beach**
West Lake Worth · Boynton Beach
Palm · Delray Beach
Beach · Boca Raton
Belle · Pompano Beach
Glade · Port Everglades
Hollywood
Miami Beach
Clewiston · **Miami**
Lake · Coral · Biscayne Bay
Okeechobee · Gables · Homestead
4 metres · Key Largo
Miami Canal
The Everglades
EVERGLADES
NATIONAL
PARK
La Belle · Cape Sable
Immokalee · Florida Bay
Big Cypress Swamp
Punta Gorda · Ten Thousand Islands
Fort Myers · Cape Romano
Charlotte Harbor · Naples · **Key West**
Pine I. Sd.
Sanibel I.

82°W · 81°W · 80°W

Florida to Straits · Florida Keys

To Puerto Rico 1,050 miles

30°N · 29°N · 28°N · 27°N · 26°N

A T L A N T I C

CASTILLO DE SAN MARCO NAT. MON.
FORT MATANZAS NAT. MON.

Jacksonville
Jacksonville Beach
Green Cove Springs
St. Augustine
Ormond Beach
Daytona Beach
New Smyrna Beach
Edgewater
Bunnell
Crescent City
Palatka
Titusville
Orange City
De Land
Sanford
Orlando
Cocoa
Ft. Pierce
Vero Beach
Stuart
Lake Pk. **Palm Beach**
West Lake Worth
Palm Boynton Beach
Beach Delray Beach
Boca Raton
Pompano Beach
Ft. Lauderdale
J.F. KENNEDY SPACE CENTER
Cape Canaveral
Melbourne

St. Johns R.
Bellevue
Gainesville
Ocala
L. George
Oklawaha R.
Eustis
Mt. Dora
Longwood
Oviedo
Kissimmee
St. Cloud
PARKWAY
Kissimmee R.

FLORIDA

Belle
Glade
Clewiston
Lake
Okeechobee
4 metres
Okeechobee
Miami Canal

Gainesville
Alachua
Tsala
Apopka L.
Apopka
Winter
Garden
Davenport
Haines City
Lake Wales
Babson Park
Frostproof
Avon Park
Sebring
La Belle
Immokalee
Big Cypress Swamp

High Springs
Lake City
Fort White
Starke
Keystone
Inverness
Wildwood
Coleman
Clermont
Zephyrhills
Nichols
Mulberry
Bartow
Ft.
Meade
Bowling Green
Wauchula
Arcadia
Peace R.
Punta Gorda
Fort Myers
Naples
Charlotte Harbor
Pine I. Sd.
Sanibel I.

Brooksville
Dade City
New Port
Richey
Tarpon
Springs
Lakeland
Plant City
Tampa
Clearwater
St. Petersburg
Tampa Bay
Palmetto
Bradenton
Sarasota
Venice
MYAKKA RIVER
S.P.

G U L F   O F   M E X I C O

Intracoastal

Homerville
Folkston
Okefenokee
Swamp
Live Oak
Jasper
Madison
High Springs
Valdosta
Quitman
Monticello
Tallahassee
Boston
Greenville
Perry
Mayo
Cross City
Suwannee R.
Steinhatchee R.
Waccasassa B.
Dunnellon
Apalachee
Bay
St. George Sound
Carrabelle
Lake Talquin
Havana
Quincy
Thomasville
Bainbridge
Cairo
St. Marys R.
Satilla R.
Baldwin
Middleburg

84°W · 83°W · 82°W · 81°W · 80°W

© Oxford University Press

Feet	
3,000	Spot Heights in Metres
1,500	
1,000	
600	
300	
Sea Level	

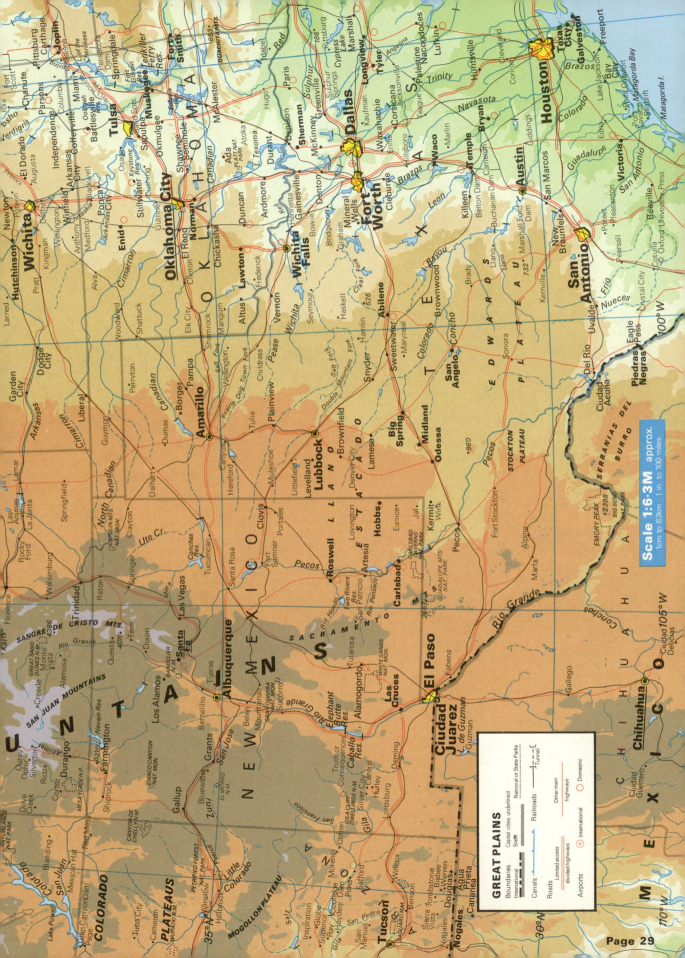

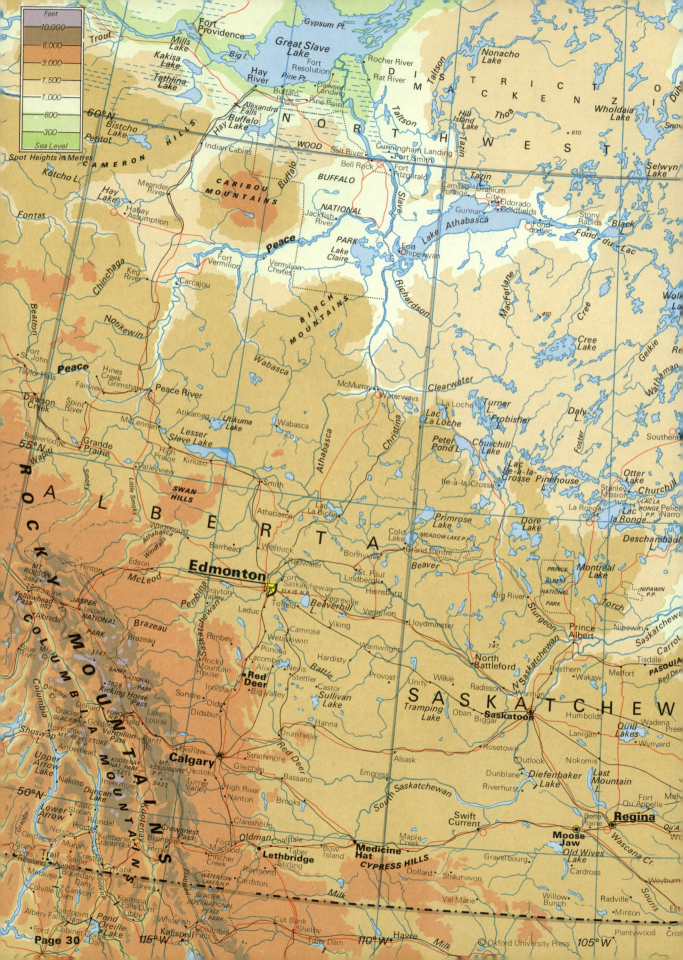

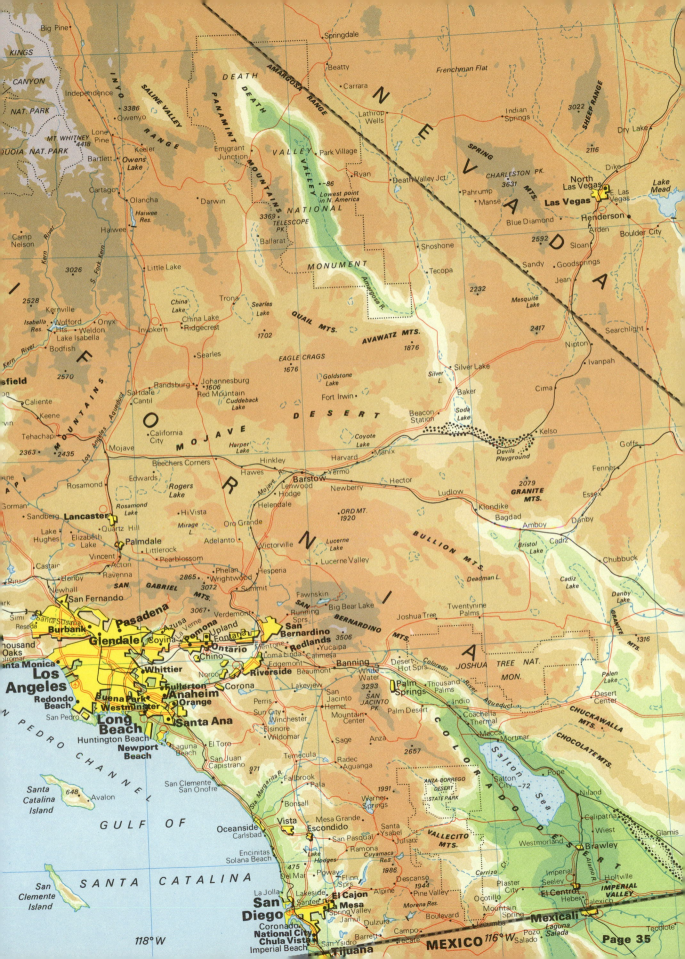

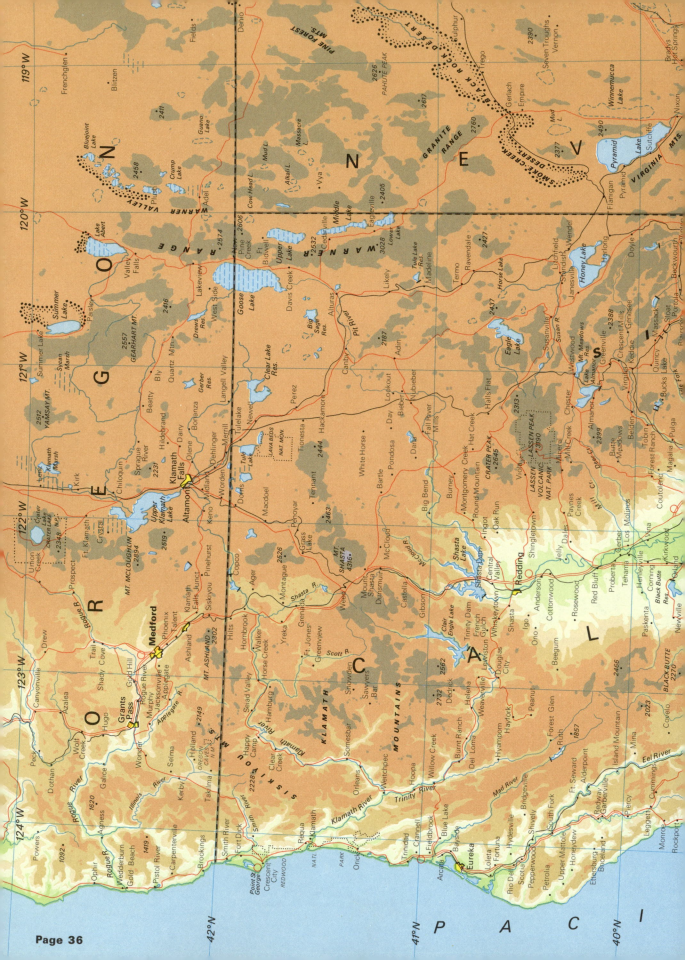

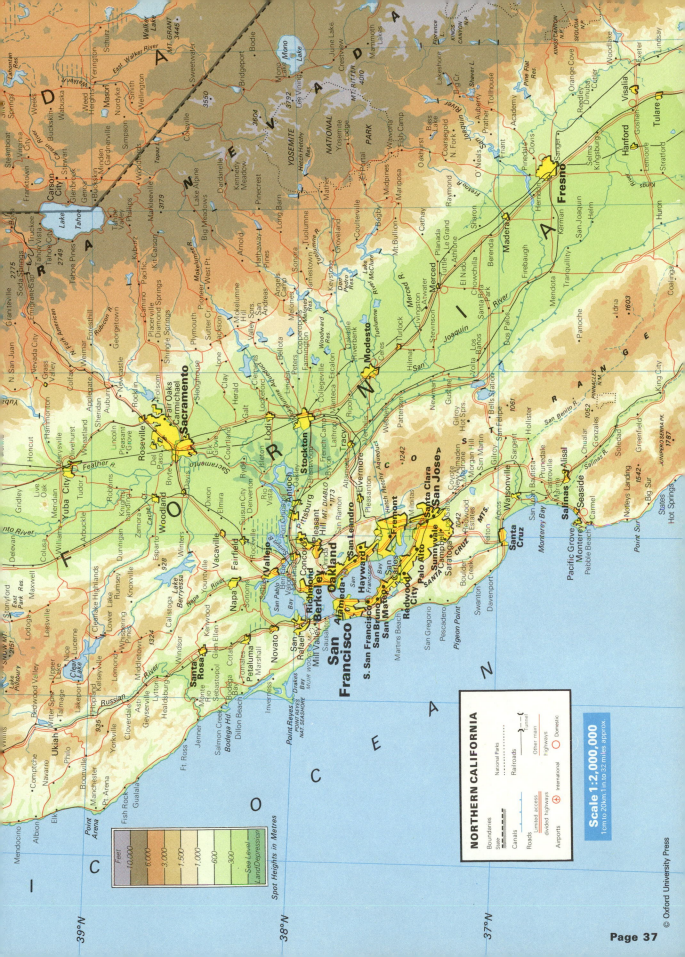

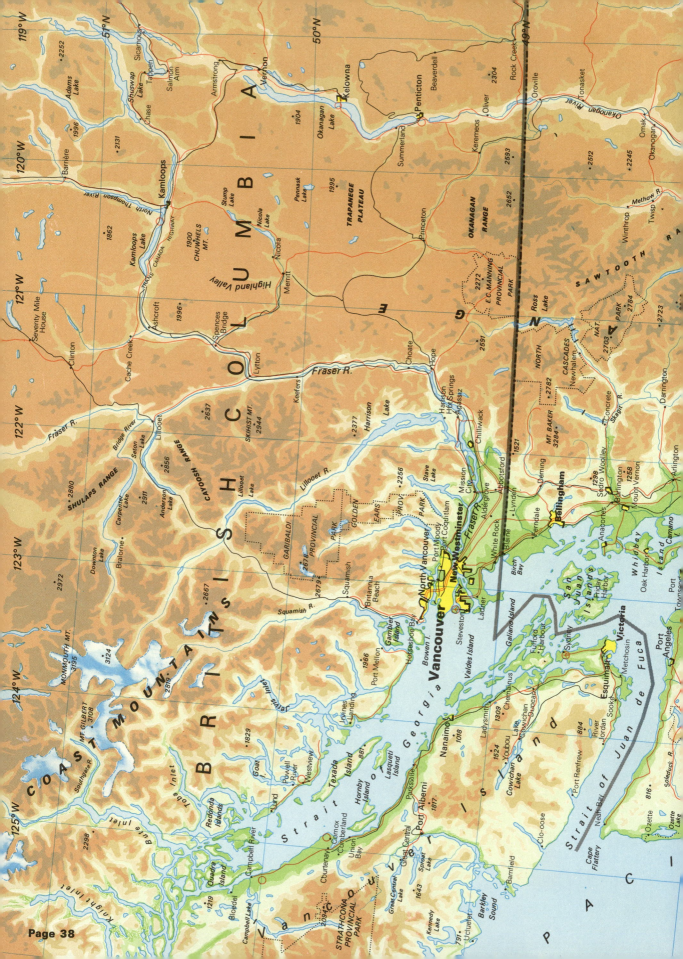

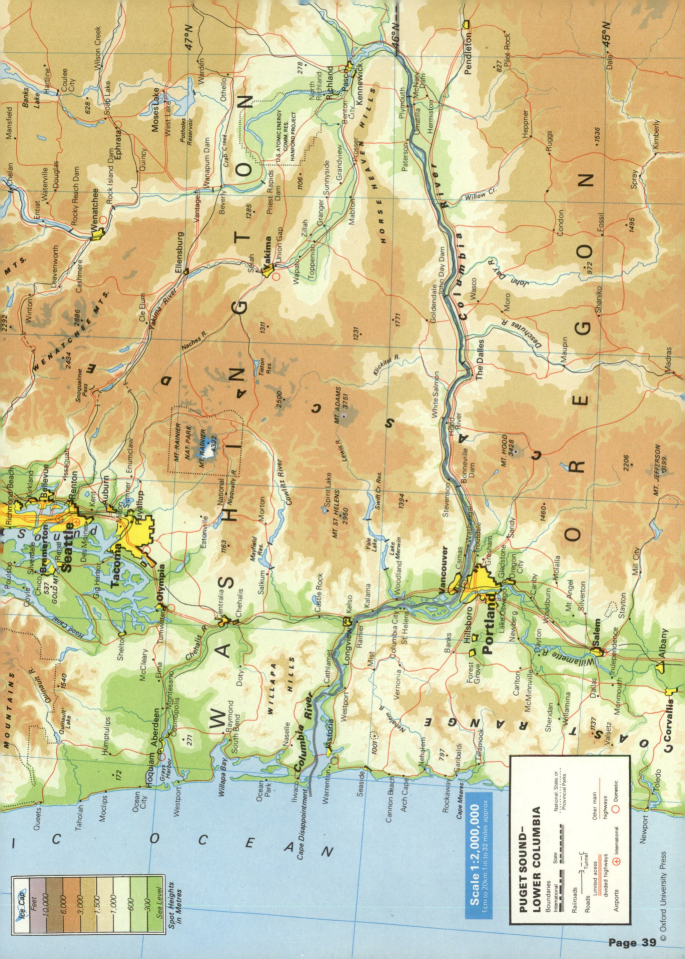

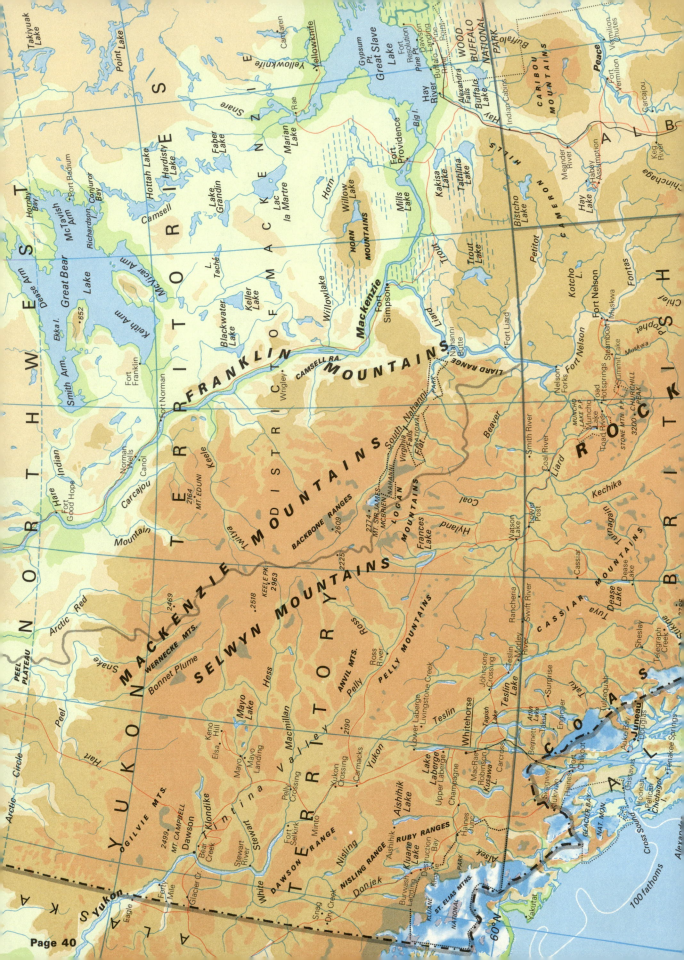

NORTH PACIFIC COAST-ALASKA PANHANDLE

Scale 1:6.3M approx.
1cm to 63km; 1 in. to 100 miles

Boundaries
International
State

Capital cities underlined
National, State or
Provincial Park

Railroads ━━━━
Roads ┤─┤ Tunnel
Limited access
divided highways
Airports ⊕ International
Other main
highways
◯ Domestic

© Oxford University Press

Spot Heights in Metres

Ice Cap
Feet
10,000
6,000
3,000
1,500
1,000
600
300
Sea Level

NORTHWEST TERRITORIES

Boundaries   Capital Cities underlined
International   Provincial   District   National State or
                                            Provincial Parks
Railroads   Tunnel
Roads
Main Highways
Airports   International ⊕   Domestic ○

90° 85° 80° Cape Sherard 75° 70° 65° 60° 55°

Devon Island

Wellington
Strait
Garnier
Bay
Maxwell
Prince Leopold I.
Clarence Cape
York
Somerset

Lancaster Sound

Coker
Bay
C. Hay
Crauford

Baffin Bay

Cape Liverpool
Bylot C. Walter Bathurst
Island 2134
C. Graham Moore
Pond Inlet
Eclipse Sd. Pond Inlet

Skal I.

Cape
Cranstown Kartats I.
Umanak Fiord Umanak

Hare I.
Outqlegset 4,213 70°
Disko I.
Dawn

BRODEUR
PENINSULA
Adams Sd.
Milne 762
Inlet
Nova
Zembla I.
Buchan Gulf

Cape Adair

Greenland
Canada

Davis Strait

Prince Regent Inlet
Fitzgerald
Bay
Cape Scoresby
Port Logan

Berlinguet Inlet
Bernier Bay

Gifford
Gifford Fd.

Steensby Inlet

Cape Eglinton

Clyde
Cape Hewett

Kekertaluk
Kivitoo

Broughton I.
Padloping

FRANKLIN Baffin

Gulf
of
Boothia

Mary Jones
Bay
Cape Margaret
KIMAKTO
PEN.
Agu Bay
Crown Prince
Frederik I.
Fury and Hecla Str.
Igloolik

Murray
Maxwell
Bay
Jens
Munk
I.
Koch I.
Bray I.

Gibbs Fd.
Scott Fd.
Inugsuin Fd.
McBeth Fd.
C. Henry
Kater

Isabella
C. Bay
Home

1250 Sam Ford Fd.

BAFFIN
ISLAND
NATIONAL
PARK
PENNY HIGHLAND

Merchants Bay

Cape Dyer
Cape Dyer
Exeter Bay
Exeter Sound
Cape Walsingham

Lord Mayor
Bay
Cape
Chapman
Franklin Bay
Garry Bay
Hall Lake
Hall Lake
564
Foley I.
Flint L.

Spicer
Islands

Cockburn Strait

Air
Force I.

Arctic Circle

Angliak I.
Hoare
Bay
Leopold I.

65°

Simpson
Lake
Pelly
Bay
SIMPSON
PENIN.
Committee
Bay
Colville
Bay
Wales I.

PRINCE ALBERT HILLS

MELVILLE
PEN.
AMITOKE
PEN.

Prince
Charles
Island

Foxe

Taverner Bay

Koukdjuak

Nettilling
Lake
Nettilling
Fiord

Cumberland Sound

Pangnirtung

HALL
PENINSULA

Brevoort Harbour
Lemieux
Islands
Cornelius Grinnell
Bay

Haye
240
RAE
ISTHMUS

TERRITORIES Basin

Repulse
Bay

Winter I.

C. Robert
Brown
Gravell Pt.
C. Wilson

Arctic Circle

Cape Dominion
Bowman Bay

Amadjuak
Lake

Frobisher
Bay
EVERET MTS.

Loks
Land

Brown
Lake
Wager Bay
Wager Bay

Lyon Inlet
Vansittart I.

Cape
Dorchester
Finnie Bay
FOXE
PENINSULA

Garnet Bay
Tessik
Lake
Andrew
Gordon Bay

Markham Bay
Fair Ness

Frobisher
Bay
Lake
Harbour

Grinnell
Ice Cap

Gabriel Str.
Edgell

Resolution

Resolution
Island

Chesterfield Inlet
Daly
Bay
Cape
Fullerton
Cape
Kendall
Bay of
Gods Mercy
Cape
Low

Duke of York
Bay
Frozen Str.
White I.

Harkin Bay
Cape Comfort

Southampton

Coral
Harbour

Terror Pt.
Mill I.

Salisbury
I.
Big I.

Hudson Strait

Chesterfield
Inlet
Rankin
Inlet
Rankin Inlet
Marble I.

Ell
Bay
South Bay
Native
Bay

BELL
PENIN.
Seahorse Pt.
Leyson Pt.
Nottingham I.
Nottingham
Island

Evans

Fisher Strait Str.
Cape Pembroke

Digges Is. C. Wolstenholme
(C. St. Louis)
Charles I.

Cape Weggs
(C. de la Nouvelle
France)

Wakeham Bay
(Maricourt)
Cape Prince
of Wales

Koattak
(Kaktak)

Akpatok

Port
Burwell

Whale Cove
Tavani
Dawson Inlet

Cape
Southampton

Coats
Island

Mansel
I.

Kovik Bay
Kettlestone
Bay

UNGAVA

Saglouc
(Sugluk)
Putunia

UNGAVA

Cape Hopes
Advance

Ablqviak
Fiord

Maguse River
Eskimo Point

100 fathoms

Cape Smith

PENINSULA UNGAVA
BAY

Lepellie
(Payne)
Payne Bay
(Bellin)

Hopes Advance
Bay

Kikkertsoak I.

Port-Nouveau
Quebec

HUDSON

Povungnituk

Kogaluk

Lac
Payne

Armanda
(Payne)

Lac
Faribault

L. aux
Feuilles
(Leaf Inlet)

Gyrfalcon
Is.

Koksoak
Fort
Chimo

George River

Erlandson
Lake

BAY

Kogaluk
Bay

Tassialuk

Lac
Potherie
(Leaf)

aux Feuilles (Leaf)

Lake
Minto

Larch
du Guè

Fort
McKenzie

Churchill
Cape Churchill

Ottawa Islands

Hopewell Islands
Port Harrison
(Inoucdjouac)

Richmond
Gulf

Nastapoka

Nastapoka

QUEBEC

316

Whale
Wheeler

Port
Nelson
York
Factory
Cape
Tatnam

Sleeper
Is.

King George
Is.
Bakers
Dozen
Is.

Nastapoka Islands

Little Whale

Clearwater
Lake

Lac d'Iberville

55°

Serigny
Kaniapiskau

Black Duck
Nelson
Hayes
Fort
Severn
Wabuk Pt.

Belcher
Islands

Great
Whale
River
Great Whale
(Poste-de-
la-Baleine)

Lac
Bienville

Lac Delorme

Kaniapiskau
Lake

L. Bermen

Ice Cap
Feet
6,000
3,000
1,500
1,000
600
300
Sea Level
Spot Heights in Metres

Shamattawa
© Oxford University Press
Kiniss
Cape
Henrietta Maria
Long I.
168

ARCTIC OCEAN

BERING Strait

BEAUFORT SEA

Unnavigable polar ice

North Magnetic Pole

Innutian Region

Viscount Melville Sound

Amundsen Gulf

Lancaster Sound

Gulf of Boothia

BERING SEA

Arctic Mountain System

Rocky

MT. MICHELSON 8239 (2886)

MT. McKINLEY 20320 (7074)

Pacific

ALEUTIAN TRENCH

•3.505

GULF OF ALASKA

•426

MT. ST. ELIAS 18008 (5488)

Mountain

Interior

Canadian

HUDSON

BAY

Hudson

Lowla

PACIFIC

MENDOCINO SEASCARP

•3.440

Gorda Escarpment

MURRAY FRACTURE ZONE

OCEAN

BAJA

CALIFORNIA

SEAMOUNT

PROVINCE

System

MT. ROBSON 12972 (3954)

MT. WADDINGTON 13260 (4042)

MT. ASSINIBOINE 11870 (3429)

MT. RAINIER 14410 (4392)

MT. HOOD 11245 (3428)

MT. SHASTA 14166 (4316)

LASSEN PEAK 10466 (3190)

MT. WHITNEY 14495 (4418)

Inter-

montane

Basins

DEATH VALLEY 282 (-86)

Mountain

Plains

GANNETT PEAK 13785 (4201)

LONGS PEAK 14255 (4345)

PIKES PEAK 14100 (4201)

BALDY PEAK 11590 (3532)

System

MT. CURWOOD 1980 (603)

Interior

Highlands

Atlanti

Gulf of California

GULF OF MEXI

Feet **Metres** **Fathoms**

Feet	Metres	Fathoms
		Sea level
16000	5000	200 — 100
10000	3000	2000 — 1000
6000	2000	3658 — 2000
3000 / 1000	900 / 500	
		9144 — 3000
0	Sea level	
	Below sea level	

Spot heights in feet (metres)

Soundings in fathoms

Continental Divide

Physical Regions

50°W 40°W 30°W

Davis Strait

Denmark Strait

NORTH SEA

Faeroe Iceland Rise

REYKJANES RIDGE
•4641

Rockall Bank

WEST EUROPEAN BASIN
•3,292

FFIN BAY

Hudson Strait

Shield

Ungava Bay

LABRADOR SEA

GIBBS FRACTURE ZONE
•530 Faraday Seamount Group

•487

M I D - A T L A N T I C   R I D G E

•28

AZORES PLATEAU
•10

•269

•173

Limit of pack ice average min. (fall)

Limit of pack ice average max. (spring)

Flemish Cap

Gulf of St Lawrence

Grand Banks
25• 35 •20

NEWFOUNDLAND BASIN

Southeast Newfoundland Ridge

OCEANOGRAPHER FRACTURE ZONE

chian Highlands

Banquereau Bank

Sable Is. Bank 27

MT. KATAHDIN 5267 (1605)

MT. WASHINGTON 6288 (1917)

Browns Bank

Georges Bank

A T L A N T I C

•604

•628

ATLANTIS FRACTURE ZONE

MT. MARCY 5344 (1629)

NORTH AMERICAN

•3.572

•3.718 •1.017

O C E A N
•3.503

•781

RUCE KNOB 4860 (1481)

OGERS (1743)

CHELL

lain

•30

Bermuda Rise
•951

BASIN

•3.825 •3.581

•3.554

Tropic of Cancer

•22 Blake Terrace

Charleston Rise

Sargasso Sea

•2.987

•3.450

Relief

Scale : 1 inch to 400 miles 1:25·43 M

Page 47

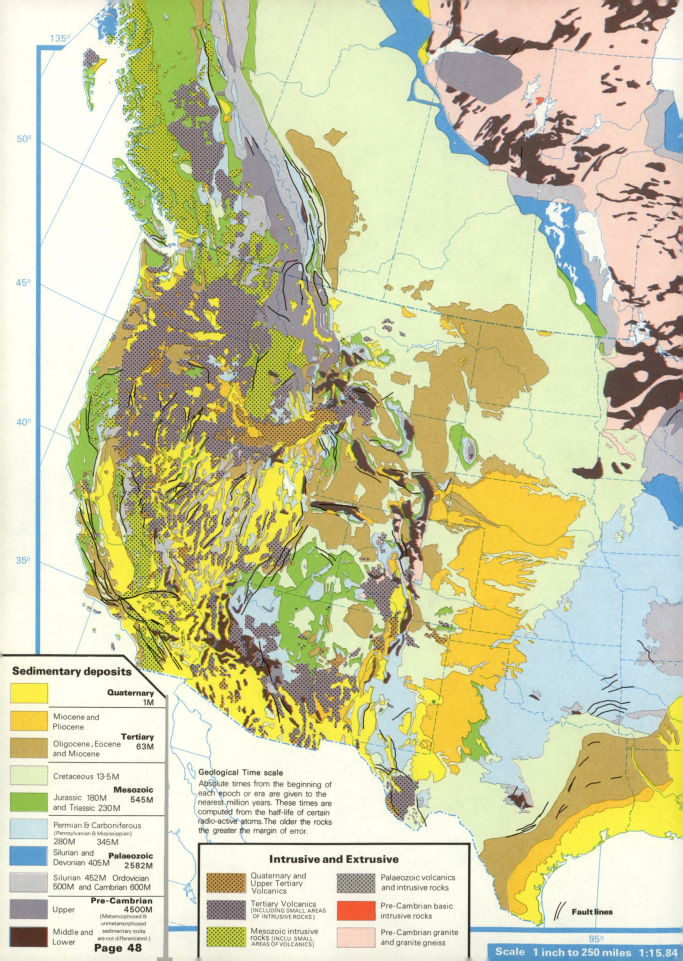

Sedimentary deposits

	Quaternary 1M
	Miocene and Pliocene
	Oligocene, Eocene and Miocene — **Tertiary** 63M
	Cretaceous 13·5M
	Jurassic 180M and Triassic 230M — **Mesozoic** 545M
	Permian & Carboniferous (Pennsylvanian & Mississippian) 280M 345M
	Silurian and Devonian 405M — **Palaeozoic** 2582M
	Silurian 452M Ordovician 500M and Cambrian 600M
	Upper — **Pre-Cambrian** 4500M (Metamorphosed & unmetamorphosed sedimentary rocks are not differentiated.)
	Middle and Lower

Page 48

Geological Time scale
Absolute times from the beginning of each epoch or era are given to the nearest million years. These times are computed from the half-life of certain radio-active atoms. The older the rocks the greater the margin of error.

Intrusive and Extrusive

	Quaternary and Upper Tertiary Volcanics		Palaeozoic volcanics and intrusive rocks
	Tertiary Volcanics [INCLUDING SMALL AREAS OF INTRUSIVE ROCKS]		Pre-Cambrian basic intrusive rocks
	Mesozoic intrusive rocks (INCLU. SMALL AREAS OF VOLCANICS]		Pre-Cambrian granite and granite gneiss

Fault lines

Scale 1 inch to 250 miles 1:15.84

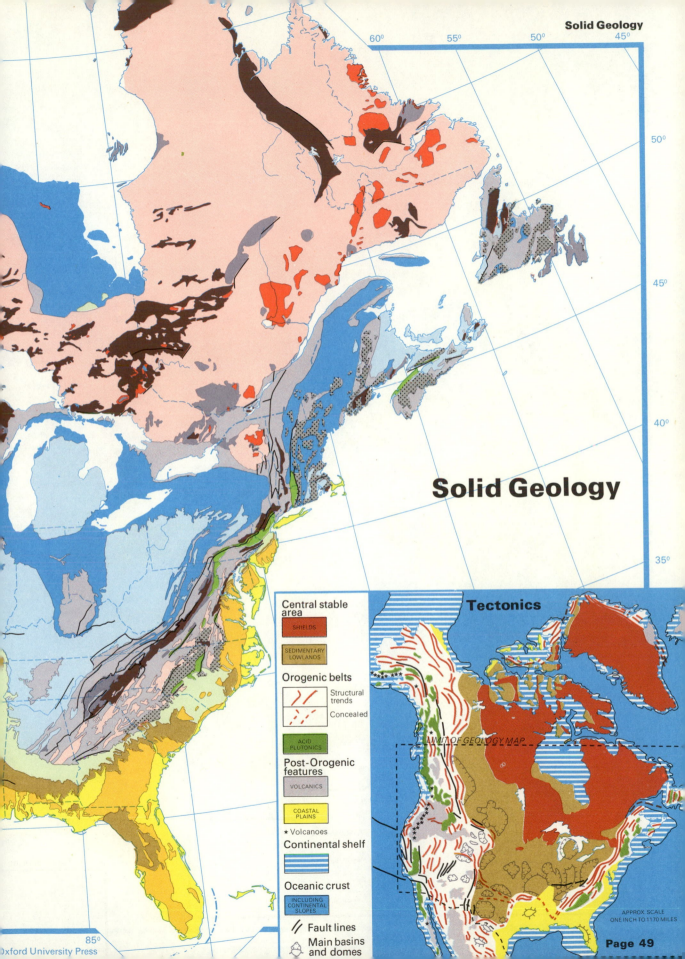

60° 55° 50° 45°

50°

45°

40°

35°

Solid Geology

Tectonics

Central stable area
- SHIELDS
- SEDIMENTARY LOWLANDS

Orogenic belts
- Structural trends
- Concealed
- ACID PLUTONICS

Post-Orogenic features
- VOLCANICS
- COASTAL PLAINS
- ★ Volcanoes

Continental shelf

Oceanic crust
- INCLUDING CONTINENTAL SLOPES

// Fault lines

Main basins and domes

LIMIT OF GEOLOGY MAP

APPROX SCALE
ONE INCH TO 1170 MILES

85°

Oxford University Press

Page 49

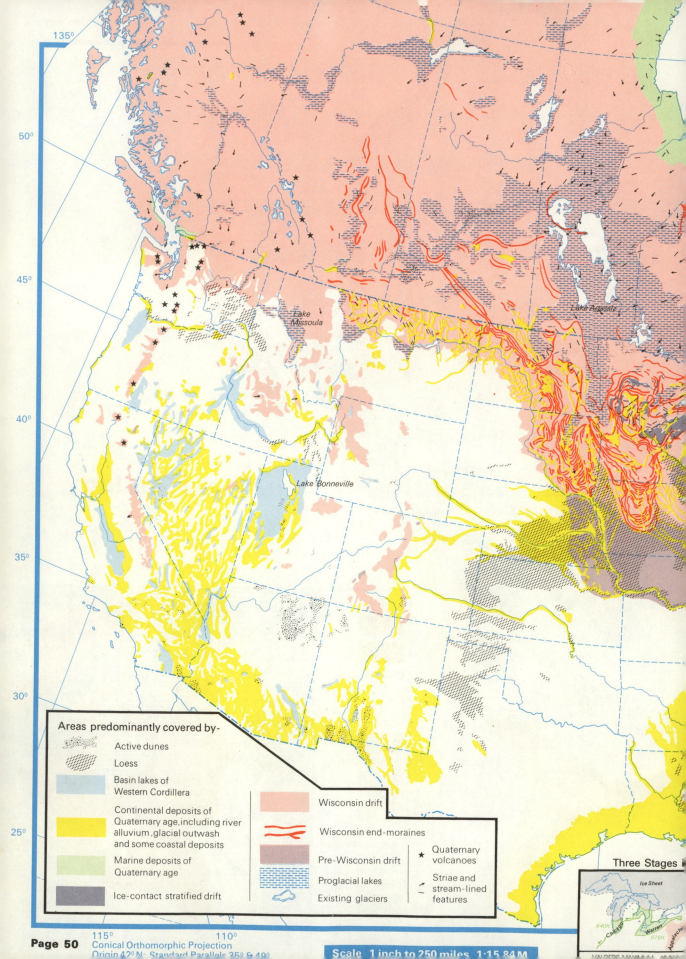

Areas predominantly covered by-

- ·.:.:. Active dunes
- ⬡ Loess
- ▨ Basin lakes of Western Cordillera
- ▨ Continental deposits of Quaternary age, including river alluvium, glacial outwash and some coastal deposits
- ▨ Marine deposits of Quaternary age
- ▨ Ice-contact stratified drift
- ▨ Wisconsin drift
- ∿ Wisconsin end-moraines
- ▨ Pre-Wisconsin drift
- ≋ Proglacial lakes
- ∿ Existing glaciers
- ★ Quaternary volcanoes
- ⌇ Striae and stream-lined features

Lake Missoula

Lake Bonneville

Lake Agassiz

Three Stages

Ice Sheet

Conical Orthomorphic Projection
Origin 42° N. Standard Parallels 35° & 49°

Scale 1 inch to 250 miles 1:15 84M

60° 55° 50° 45°
50°
45°
40°

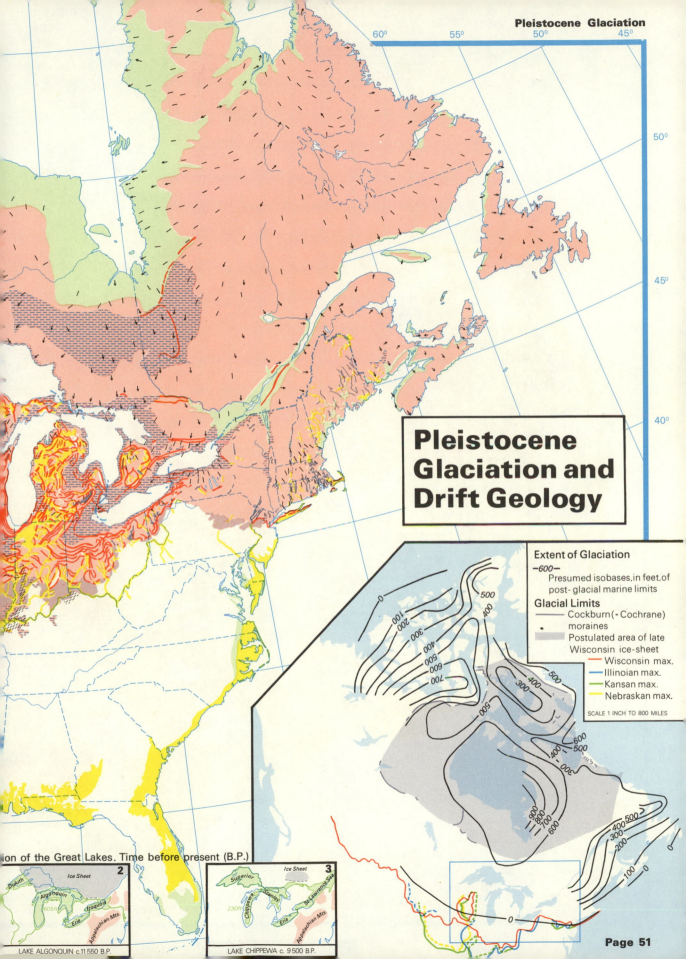

Pleistocene Glaciation and Drift Geology

Extent of Glaciation

—600— Presumed isobases, in feet, of post-glacial marine limits

Glacial Limits

⸺ Cockburn (-Cochrane) moraines

⸱⸱⸱ Postulated area of late Wisconsin ice-sheet

⸺ Wisconsin max.
⸺ Illinoian max.
⸺ Kansan max.
⸺ Nebraskan max.

SCALE 1 INCH TO 800 MILES

...on of the Great Lakes. Time before present (B.P.)

2
Ice Sheet
Duluth
Algonquin
605ft.
Erie
Iroquois
Appalachian Mts.
LAKE ALGONQUIN c.11.550 B.P.

3
Ice Sheet
Superior
Stanley
Chippewa
230ft.
Erie
St.Lawrence Sea
Appalachian Mts.
LAKE CHIPPEWA c. 9.500 B.P.

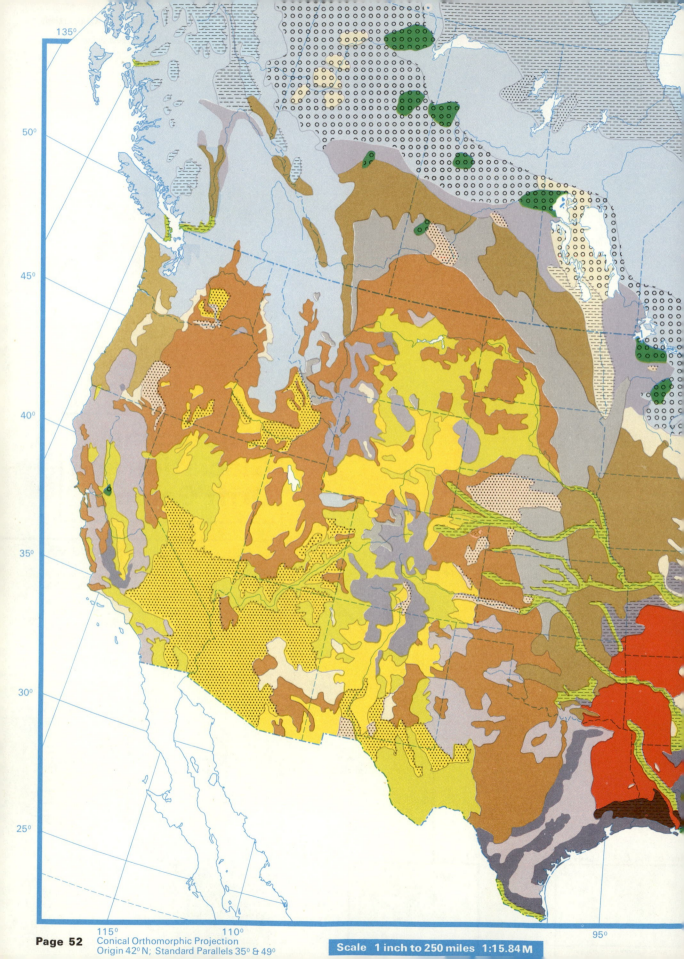

Conical Orthomorphic Projection
Origin 42° N; Standard Parallels 35° & 49°

Scale 1 inch to 250 miles 1:15.84 M

135°

50°

45°

40°

35°

30°

25°

115°

110°

95°

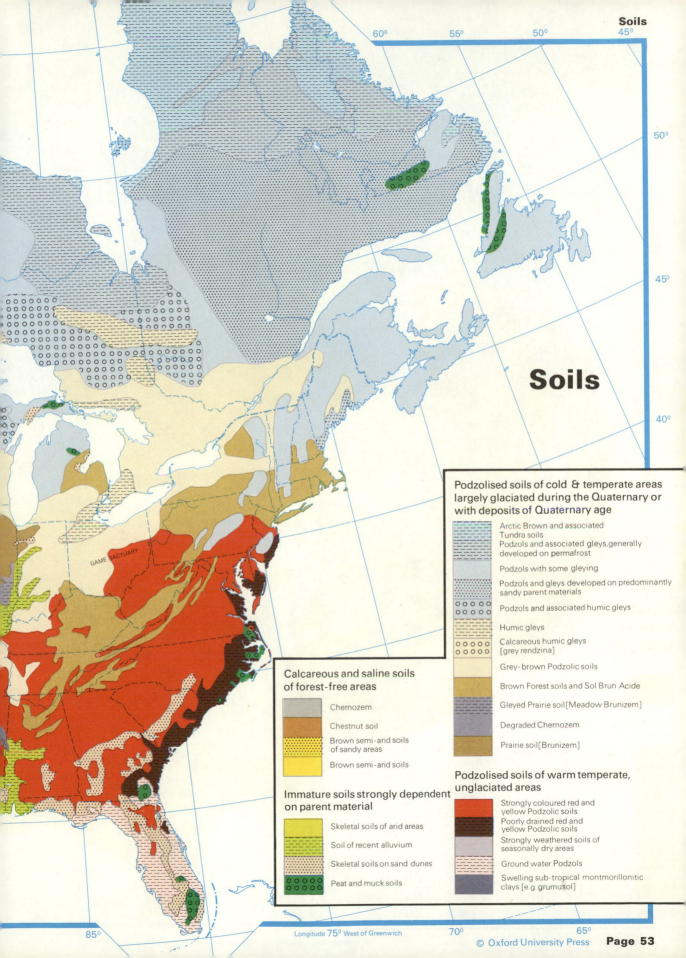

Soils

GAME SANCTUARY

Podzolised soils of cold & temperate areas largely glaciated during the Quaternary or with deposits of Quaternary age

Arctic Brown and associated Tundra soils

Podzols and associated gleys, generally developed on permafrost

Podzols with some gleying

Podzols and gleys developed on predominantly sandy parent materials

Podzols and associated humic gleys

Humic gleys

Calcareous humic gleys [grey rendzina]

Grey-brown Podzolic soils

Brown Forest soils and Sol Brun Acide

Gleyed Prairie soil [Meadow Brunizem]

Degraded Chernozem

Prairie soil [Brunizem]

Calcareous and saline soils of forest-free areas

Chernozem

Chestnut soil

Brown semi-arid soils of sandy areas

Brown semi-arid soils

Immature soils strongly dependent on parent material

Skeletal soils of arid areas

Soil of recent alluvium

Skeletal soils on sand dunes

Peat and muck soils

Podzolised soils of warm temperate, unglaciated areas

Strongly coloured red and yellow Podzolic soils

Poorly drained red and yellow Podzolic soils

Strongly weathered soils of seasonally dry areas

Ground water Podzols

Swelling sub-tropical montmorillonitic clays [e.g. grumusol]

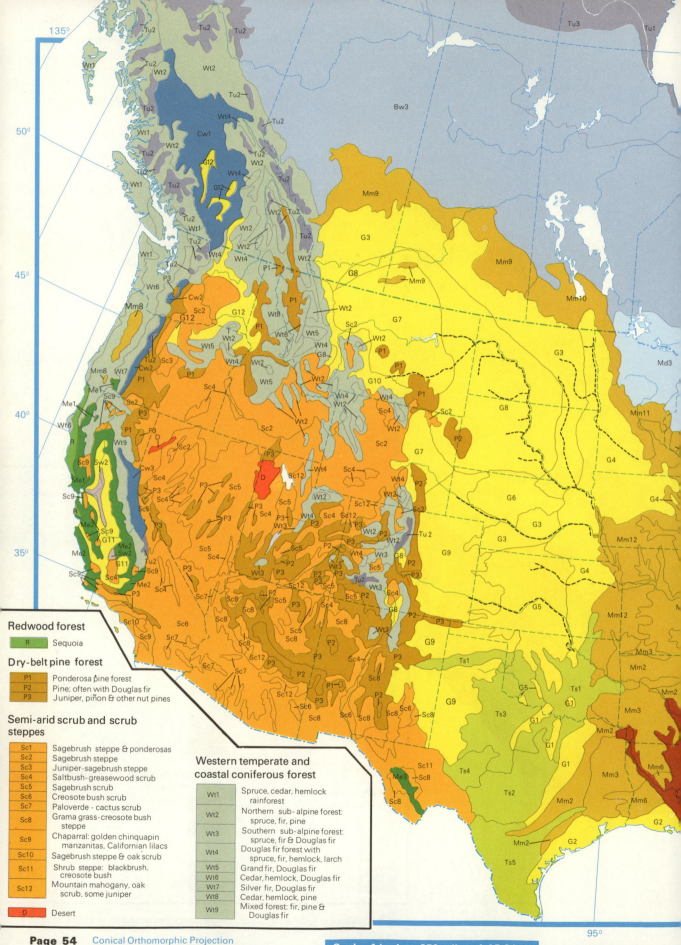

Redwood forest

R	Sequoia

Dry-belt pine forest

P1	Ponderosa pine forest
P2	Pine; often with Douglas fir
P3	Juniper, piñon & other nut pines

Semi-arid scrub and scrub steppes

Sc1	Sagebrush steppe & ponderosas
Sc2	Sagebrush steppe
Sc3	Juniper-sagebrush steppe
Sc4	Saltbush-greasewood scrub
Sc5	Sagebrush scrub
Sc6	Creosote bush scrub
Sc7	Paloverde - cactus scrub
Sc8	Grama grass-creosote bush steppe
Sc9	Chaparral: golden chinquapin manzanitas, Californian lilacs
Sc10	Sagebrush steppe & oak scrub
Sc11	Shrub steppe: blackbrush, creosote bush
Sc12	Mountain mahogany, oak scrub, some juniper

D	Desert

Western temperate and coastal coniferous forest

Wt1	Spruce, cedar, hemlock rainforest
Wt2	Northern sub-alpine forest: spruce, fir, pine
Wt3	Southern sub-alpine forest: spruce, fir & Douglas fir
Wt4	Douglas fir forest with spruce, fir, hemlock, larch
Wt5	Grand fir, Douglas fir
Wt6	Cedar, hemlock, Douglas fir
Wt7	Silver fir, Douglas fir
Wt8	Cedar, hemlock, pine
Wt9	Mixed forest: fir, pine & Douglas fir

Conical Orthomorphic Projection
Origin 42° N; Standard Parallels 35° & 49°

Scale 1 inch to 250 miles 1:15·84 M

Potential Vegetation

Tundra

Tu1	Sedges, lichens, grasses & dwarf shrubs
Tu2	Alpine meadows, scrub, bare rock & ice
Tu3	Tundra with woodland patches

Boreal woodland and coniferous forest

Bw1	Spruce larch, much bog & lichen floor
Bw2	Spruce & larch muskeg
Bw3	Spruce & fir forest; shaded floor
Bw4	Extensive bog & moss barrens; spruce & fir patches

Coniferous forest: montane and sub-alpine

Cw1	Montane forest: pine, spruce Douglas fir
Cw2	Fir, hemlock forest
Cw3	Sierran sub-alpine forest: fir, hemlock, pine

Mixed deciduous and coniferous forest

Md1	Spruce, pine, hemlock, maple, beech & other Northern hardwoods
Md2	Northern hardwoods
Md3	Rainy lake forest: intermingled Bw3 & Md1

Mixed evergreen and deciduous forest

Me1	Mixed evergreen forest: oak, Douglas fir
Me2	Oak; incl. evergreen species
Me3	Oak, juniper woodland

Mixed mesophytic and deciduous forest

Mm1	Rich forest: many hardwood species
Mm2	Oak, hickory
Mm3	Oak, hickory, pine
Mm4	Maple, beech & other hardwoods
Mm5	Mixed oak
Mm6	Southern mixed forest: sweet gum, beech, magnolia, pine, oak
Mm7	Elm, ash & other hardwoods
Mm8	Mixed oak-conifer forest: oak, cedar, hemlock, Douglas fir
Mm9	Aspen groves: scattered spruce, grassy openings
Mm10	Aspen-oak groves; grassy openings
Mm11	Maple, basswood
Mm12	Prairie, oak, hickory

Swamp

| Sw1 | Sub-tropical swamp (everglades): grass, sedge, bald cypress, palmetto |
| Sw2 | Tule marshes: bulrushes, reeds |

Swamp forest

| Sf | Southern floodplain forest: oak, tupelos, bald cypress |

Tree and shrub savanna

Ts1	Oak, bluestem savanna
Ts2	Savanna with mesquite-oak scrub & juniper
Ts3	Mesquite scrub, some openings with oak, juniper & buffalo grass
Ts4	Mesquite savanna
Ts5	Mesquite-acacia scrub

Grassland: prairie and steppe

G1	Blackland prairie
G2	Coastal prairie
G3	Wheatgrass prairie
G4	Bluestem prairie
G5	Bluestem-grama grass prairie
G6	Nebraska sandhills prairie
G7	Drybelt prairies & steppe
G8	Wheatgrass-needlegrass prairie
G9	Grama-buffalo grass prairie
G10	Foothills prairie
G11	Great Valley steppe
G12	Plateau prairies; including meadow & fescue grasses

Galeria forests: willows, cottonwood

© Oxford University Press **Page 55**

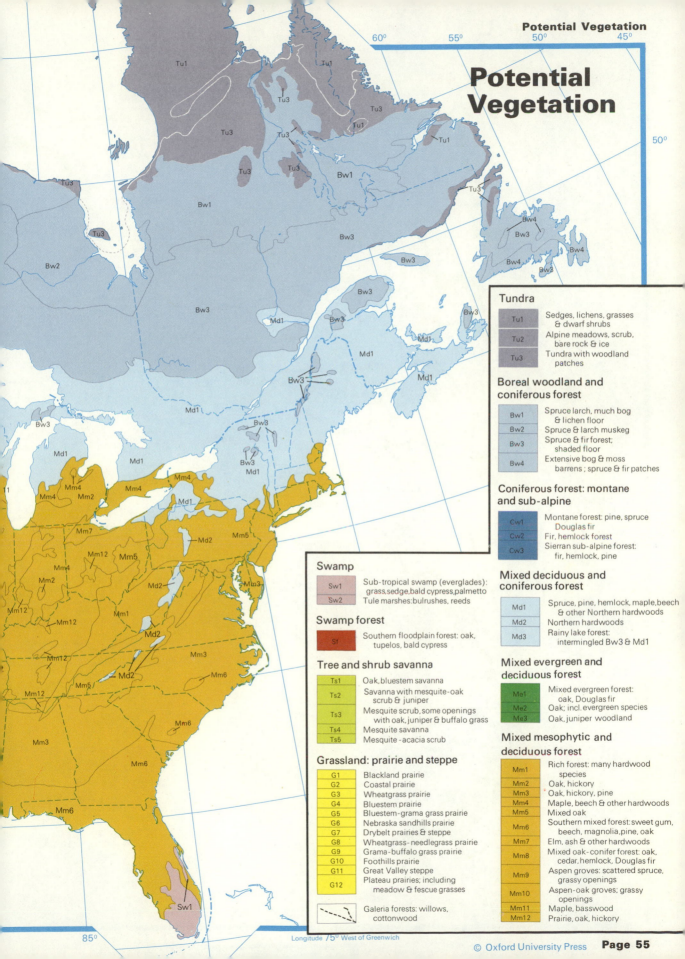

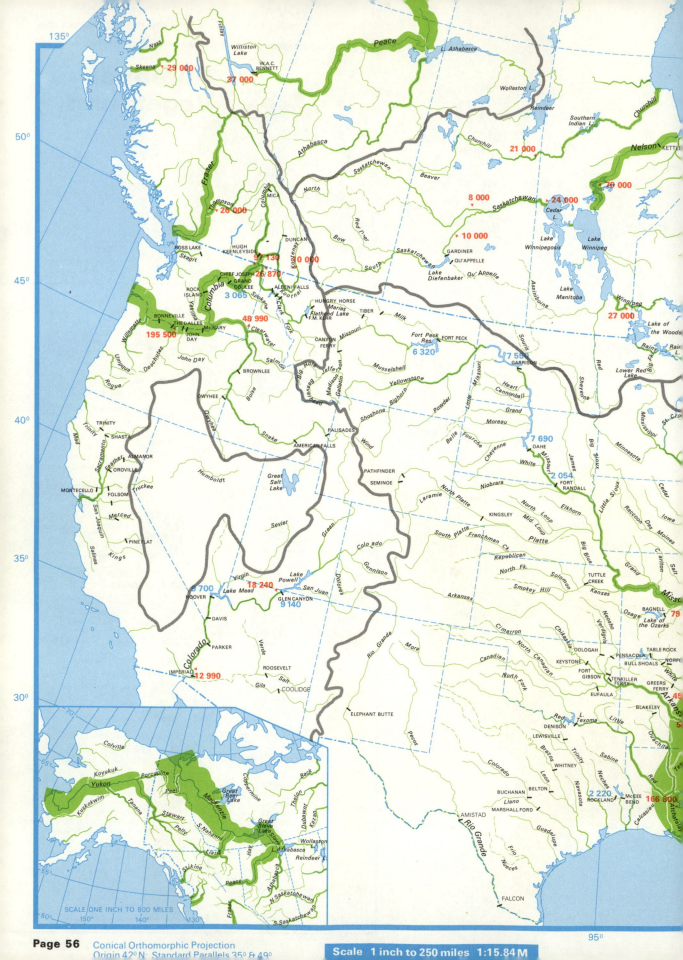

Scale 1 inch to 250 miles 1:15.84 M

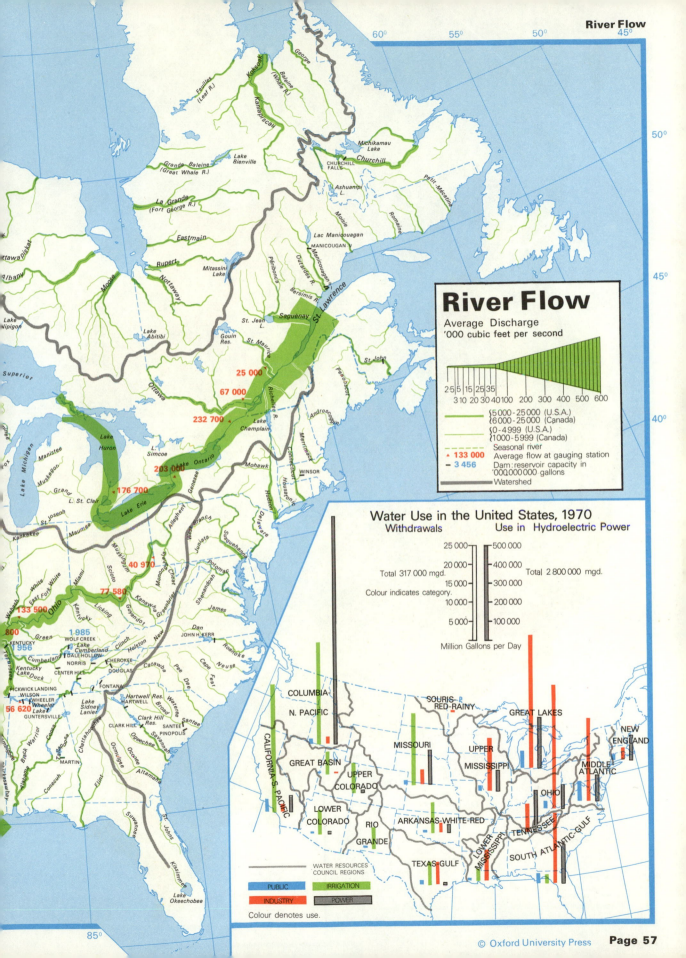

River Flow

Average Discharge
'000 cubic feet per second

2·5 5 15 25 35
3 10 20 30 40 100 200 300 400 500 600

5000–25000 (U.S.A.)
6000–25000 (Canada)
0–4999 (U.S.A.)
1000–5999 (Canada)
Seasonal river
▲ **133 000** Average flow at gauging station
— **3 456** Dam: reservoir capacity in '000 000 000 gallons
Watershed

Water Use in the United States, 1970
Withdrawals   **Use in Hydroelectric Power**

25 000   500 000
20 000   400 000
15 000   300 000
10 000   200 000
5 000   100 000

Total 317 000 mgd.   Total 2 800 000 mgd.
Colour indicates category.

Million Gallons per Day

COLUMBIA–
N. PACIFIC

CALIFORNIA–S. PACIFIC

GREAT BASIN

UPPER
COLORADO

LOWER
COLORADO

RIO
GRANDE

MISSOURI

ARKANSAS-WHITE-RED

TEXAS-GULF

SOURIS–
RED-RAINY

UPPER
MISSISSIPPI

LOWER
MISSISSIPPI

GREAT LAKES

OHIO

TENNESSEE

SOUTH ATLANTIC-GULF

MIDDLE
ATLANTIC

NEW
ENGLAND

WATER RESOURCES
COUNCIL REGIONS

PUBLIC   IRRIGATION
INDUSTRY   POWER

Colour denotes use.

25 000
67 000
232 700
203 000
176 700
40 970
77 580
133 500
800
1 985
WOLF CREEK
956
56 620

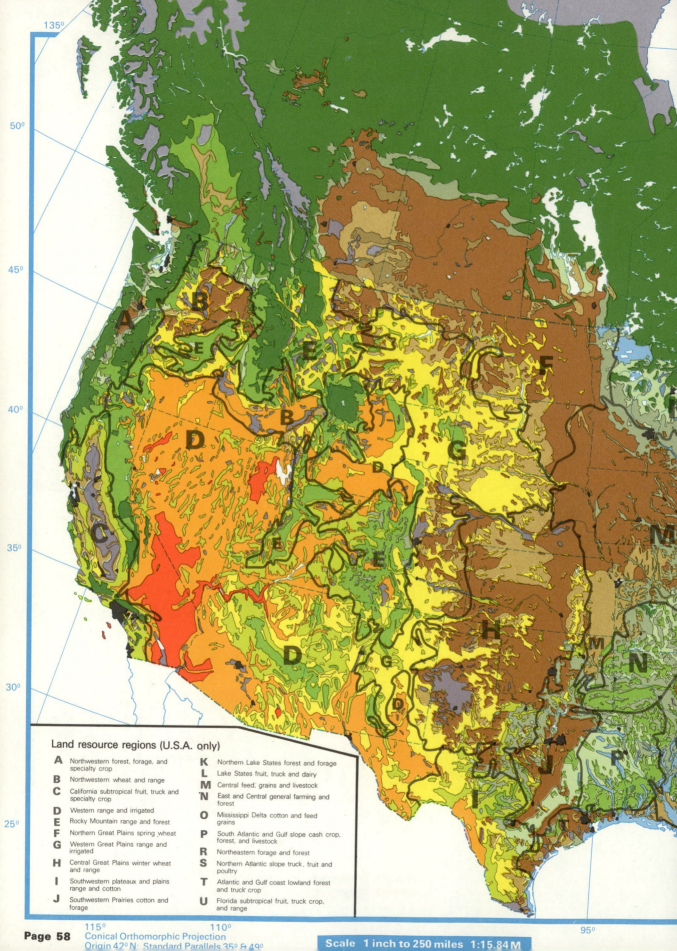

Land resource regions (U.S.A. only)

A Northwestern forest, forage, and specialty crop

B Northwestern wheat and range

C California subtropical fruit, truck and specialty crop

D Western range and irrigated

E Rocky Mountain range and forest

F Northern Great Plains spring wheat

G Western Great Plains range and irrigated

H Central Great Plains winter wheat and range

I Southwestern plateaux and plains range and cotton

J Southwestern Prairies cotton and forage

K Northern Lake States forest and forage

L Lake States fruit, truck and dairy

M Central feed; grains and livestock

N East and Central general farming and forest

O Mississippi Delta cotton and feed grains

P South Atlantic and Gulf slope cash crop, forest, and livestock

R Northeastern forage and forest

S Northern Atlantic slope truck, fruit and poultry

T Atlantic and Gulf coast lowland forest and truck crop

U Florida subtropical fruit, truck crop, and range

Conical Orthomorphic Projection
Origin 42° N. Standard Parallels 35° & 49°

Scale 1 inch to 250 miles 1:15.84 M

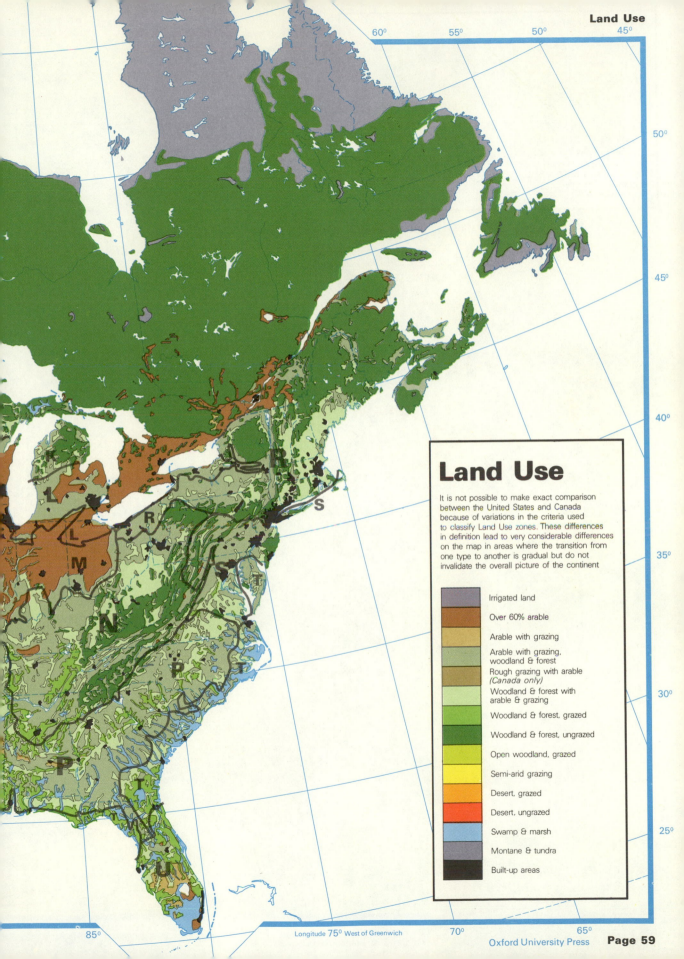

Land Use

It is not possible to make exact comparison
between the United States and Canada
because of variations in the criteria used
to classify Land Use zones. These differences
in definition lead to very considerable differences
on the map in areas where the transition from
one type to another is gradual but do not
invalidate the overall picture of the continent

- Irrigated land
- Over 60% arable
- Arable with grazing
- Arable with grazing,
  woodland & forest
- Rough grazing with arable
  (Canada only)
- Woodland & forest with
  arable & grazing
- Woodland & forest, grazed
- Woodland & forest, ungrazed
- Open woodland, grazed
- Semi-arid grazing
- Desert, grazed
- Desert, ungrazed
- Swamp & marsh
- Montane & tundra
- Built-up areas

60° 55° 50° 45° 50° 45° 40° 35° 30° 25°

Longitude 75° West of Greenwich   70°   65°

85°   70°   65°

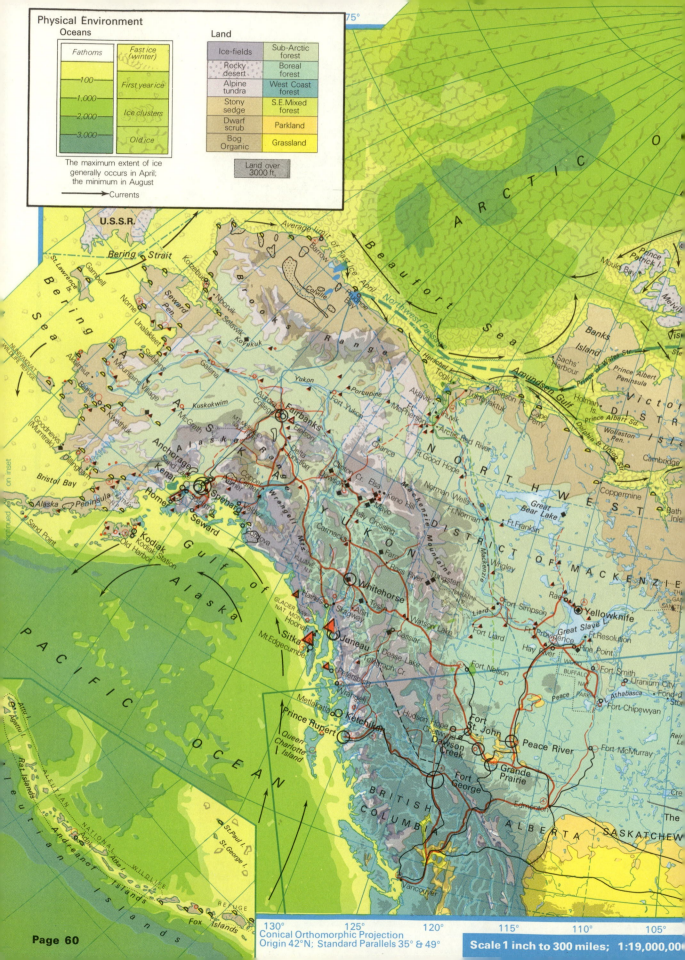

Physical Environment

Oceans

Fathoms		Fast ice (winter)
	—100—	
	—1,000—	First year ice
	—2,000—	Ice clusters
	—3,000—	Old ice

The maximum extent of ice generally occurs in April; the minimum in August

→ Currents

Land

Ice-fields	Sub-Arctic forest
Rocky desert	Boreal forest
Alpine tundra	West Coast forest
Stony sedge	S.E.Mixed forest
Dwarf scrub	Parkland
Bog Organic	Grassland

Land over 3000 ft.

U.S.S.R.

Bering Strait

Beaufort Sea

ARCTIC O

Barrow

Average limit of fast ice. April

Northwest Passage

Banks Island

Sachs' Harbour

Prince Patrick I.

Mould Bay

Melville

Vis

Prince of Wales St.

Amundsen Gulf

Prince Albert Peninsula

Holman

Cape Perry

Dolphin & Union Str.

Victoria

Prince Albert

Wollaston Pen.

Cambridge

BERING SEA

St. Lawrence I.

Gambell

Kotzebue

Nome

Unalakleet

Seward Pen.

Brooks Range

Colville

Prudhoe Bay

Herschel I.

Togli

Aklavik

Inuvik

Tuktoyaktuk

Atkinson Pt.

NORTHWEST

DISTRICT OF MACKENZIE

Coppermine

Bath Inlet

INNOKO NAT WILDLIFE REFUGE

Akiachak

Bethel

Mountains Village

Stebbins

Galena

Koyukuk

Yukon

Porcupine

Fort Yukon

Chance

McPherson

Arctic Red River

Ft Good Hope

Norman Wells

Ft.Norman

Great Bear Lake

Ft.Franklin

Whigley

Rae

Yellowknife

McGrath

Kuskokwim

Kwethluk

Alaska College

Fairbanks

Eielson

Mt. McKINLEY NAT PK

Delta Junction

Clinton Cr.

Dawson

Elsa

Keno Hill

Mayo

Mackenzie Mountains

Ft.Simpson

Great Slave Lake

Goodnews (Mumtrak)

Dillingham

Bristol Bay

Anchorage

Kenai

Homer

Spenard

Sand Lake

Palmer

Copper Center

Glennallen

Wrangell Mts.

Valdez

Cordova

Carmacks

YUKON

Pelly Crossing

Faro

Ross River

Tungsten

Liard

Fort Liard

Fort Providence

Hay River

Pine Point

Fort Resolution

Ft.Smith

Uranium City

Fond-d

Alaska

Peninsula

Sand Point

Kodiak

Kodiak Station

Old Harbor

Seward

Tok

Burwash

KLUANE N.P.

Whitehorse

Teslin

Watson Lake

Cassiar

NAHANNI N.P.

Fort Nelson

Fort Simpson

BUFFALO NAT PARK

L.Athabasca

Fort Chipewyan

GULF OF ALASKA

PACIFIC OCEAN

GLACIER BAY NAT MON

Hoonah

Sitka

Mt.Edgecumbe

Haines

Skagway

Atlin

Juneau

Dease Lake

Telegraph Cr.

Peace

Wood Buffalo

Fort Smith

Fort McMurray

Reir La

Cre

Petersburg

Wrangell

Metlakatla

Prince Rupert

Ketchikan

Queen Charlotte Island

Hudson Hope

Chetwynd

Fort St.John

Dawson Creek

Peace River

The

Fort George

Grande Prairie

BRITISH COLUMBIA

ALBERTA

SASKATCHEW

Edmonton

Vancouver

Attu I.

Agattu I.

Rat Islands

St.Paul I.

St.George I.

Adak

Atka I.

N A T I O N A L

W.I.L.D.L.I.F.E

REFUGE

Andreanof Islands

Fox Islands

ALEUTIAN ISLANDS

A L E U T I A N   R a.

130° 125° 120° 115° 110° 105°

The North

Communications
- Railroads
- Under construction
- Main road
- All-weather road --- U/C
- Winter roads

Airports: passengers embarked 1971/72

over 10 000	5 000- 9 999	1 000- 4 999	500- 999

Mineral Resources
- Coalfields
- Oilfields
- Natural Gas fields
- Petroleum pipeline U/C
- proposed
- Natural Gas pipeline, proposed

Only those fields shown on the maps pp.90-95 are productive

- Mining centres, see pp.98-105

Other Resources

National Parks and Wildlife Refuges

For fishing ground see pp.88-89
Detail is taken south of the standard map area only when sense demands it.

Population   USA 1970 : Canada 1971
Settlements including Eskimo & Indian population

- over 25 000 inhabitants
- 10 000 - 25 000
- 5 000 - 9 999
- 2 500 - 4 999
- 1 000 - 2 499
- 500 - 999
- under 500
- Weather stations

Eskimos:	Total Alaska c. 25 000
	Canada c. 12 000
Indians:	Total Alaska c. 29 000
	Canada c. 20 000

A substantial number of Eskimo and Indian inhabitants are widely scattered so the symbols indicate areas of occupation as well as settlements

- Eskimo — approx. 300 persons
- Indian — approx. 300 persons
- 600 - 1 999 persons
- over 2 000 persons

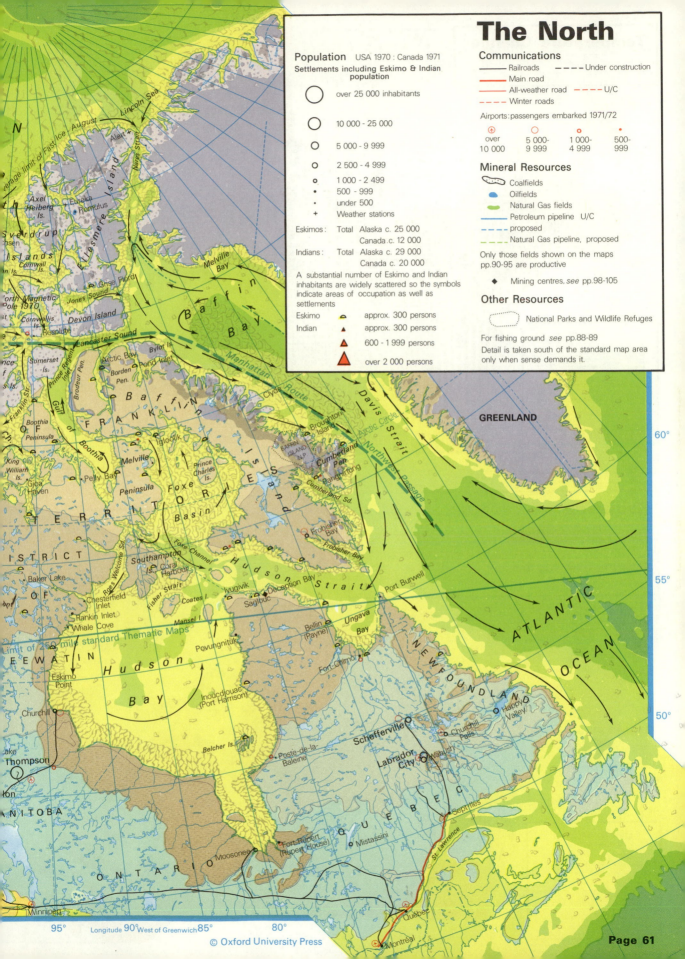

Lincoln Sea
Average limit of Fast Ice August
Alert
Axel Heiberg Is.
Eureka
Romulus
Ellesmere Island
Nares Strait
North Magnetic Pole 1970
Grise Fiord
Jones Sound
Devon Island
Cornwallis Is.
Resolute
Melville Bay
Baffin Bay
Sverdrup Islands
Cornwall
Lancaster Sound
Somerset Is.
Boothia Peninsula
Prince Regent Inlet
Arctic Bay
Borden Pen.
Pond Inlet
Bylot Is.
Brodeur Pen.
Gulf of Boothia
Igloolik
Franklin Str.
King William Is.
Gjoa Haven
Pelly Bay
Melville Peninsula
Prince Charles Is.
BAFFIN ISLAND N.P.
Broughton Island
Clyde River
Manhattan Route
FRANKLIN
Baffin Island
Foxe Basin
Pangnirtung
Cumberland Pen.
Cumberland Sd.
Davis Strait
Arctic Circle
Northwest Passage
GREENLAND
Baker Lake
DISTRICT OF
Southampton Is.
Foxe Channel
Coral Harbour
Frobisher Bay
Frobisher Bay
Chesterfield Inlet
Roes Welcome Sd.
Fisher Strait
Coates I.
Hudson Strait
Port Burwell
Rankin Inlet
Whale Cove
Mansel I.
Ivujivik
Deception Bay
Saglouc
ATLANTIC
KEEWATIN
Limit of 250 mile standard Thematic Maps
Eskimo Point
Povungnituk
Bellin (Payne)
Ungava Bay
Hudson Bay
Inoucdjouac (Port Harrison)
Fort Chimo
NEWFOUNDLAND
OCEAN
Churchill
Belcher Is.
Happy Valley
Lake Thompson
Thompson
Poste-de-la-Baleine
Schefferville
Churchill Falls
Labrador City
Wabush
MANITOBA
Fort Rupert (Rupert House)
Mistassini
Septiles
ONTARIO
Moosonee
QUEBEC
St. Lawrence
Winnipeg
Québec
Montreal

60°
55°
50°

95° Longitude 90° West of Greenwich 85° 80°

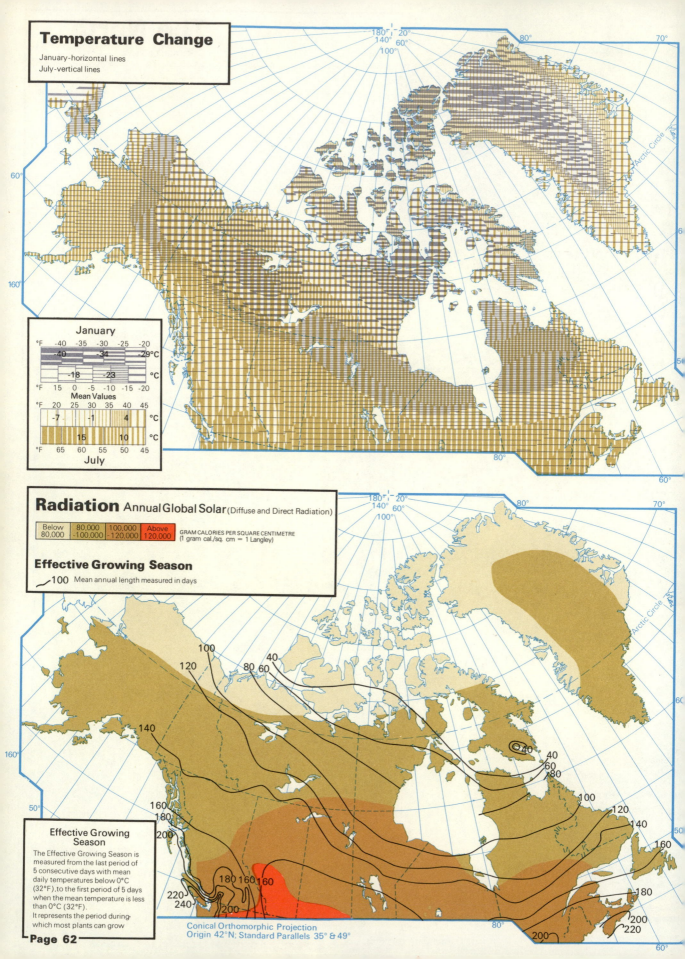

Temperature Change

January-horizontal lines
July-vertical lines

January

°F	-40	-35	-30	-25	-20
	-40		-34		-29°C
		-18		-23	°C

°F	15	0	-5	-10	-15	-20

Mean Values

°F	20	25	30	35	40	45
	-7		-1		4	°C
		15		10		°C

°F	65	60	55	50	45

July

Radiation Annual Global Solar (Diffuse and Direct Radiation)

Below 80,000	80,000 -100,000	100,000 -120,000	Above 120,000

GRAM CALORIES PER SQUARE CENTIMETRE
(1 gram cal./sq. cm = 1 Langley)

Effective Growing Season

——100 Mean annual length measured in days

Effective Growing Season

The Effective Growing Season is measured from the last period of 5 consecutive days with mean daily temperatures below 0°C (32°F), to the first period of 5 days when the mean temperature is less than 0°C (32°F).
It represents the period during which most plants can grow

Conical Orthomorphic Projection
Origin 42°N; Standard Parallels 35° & 49°

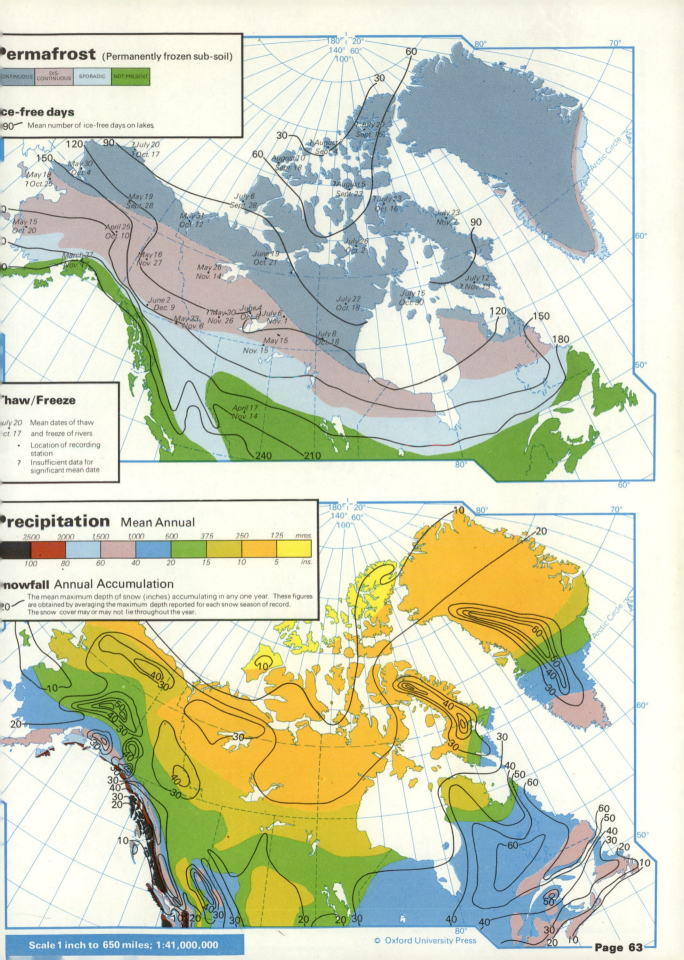

Permafrost (Permanently frozen sub-soil)

CONTINUOUS | DIS-CONTINUOUS | SPORADIC | NOT PRESENT

ice-free days

—90— Mean number of ice-free days on lakes.

120 90 ?July 20
150 Oct. 17
May 30
Oct. 4
May 19
? Oct. 25
May 19
Sept. 28
May 15
Oct. 20
April 25
Oct. 10
March 27
Nov. 17
May 16
Nov. 27
May 26
Nov. 14
June 2
Dec. 9
?May 30
May 23
Nov. 8
Nov. 26
June 4
Oct. 8
July 6
Nov. 1
May 15
Nov. 15
July 8
Oct. 18
April 17
Nov. 14

30 60
60 August 10
Sept. 18
? August
30 ? Sept.
August 5
Sept. 23
May 31
Oct. 12
June 19
Oct. 21
July 6
Sept. 28
July 26
Oct. 2
July 22
Oct. 18
July 20
Sept. 15
?July 23
Oct. 16
July 23
Nov. 7
90
July 15
Oct. 30
July 12
? Nov. 13
120 150
180

240 210

Thaw/Freeze

July 20 / Oct. 17   Mean dates of thaw and freeze of rivers

• Location of recording station

? Insufficient data for significant mean date

Precipitation   Mean Annual

2500 | 2000 | 1,500 | 1,000 | 500 | 375 | 250 | 125 | mms.
100 | 80 | 60 | 40 | 20 | 15 | 10 | 5 | ins.

Snowfall   Annual Accumulation

The mean maximum depth of snow (inches) accumulating in any one year. These figures are obtained by averaging the maximum depth reported for each snow season of record. The snow cover may or may not lie throughout the year.

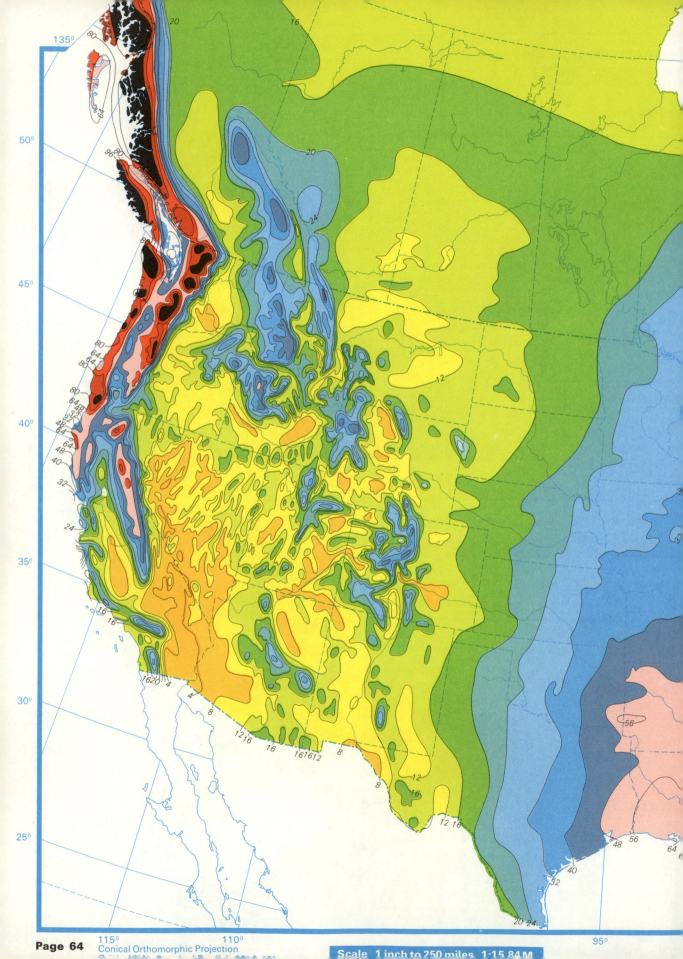

Conical Orthomorphic Projection

Scale 1 inch to 250 miles 1:15.84M

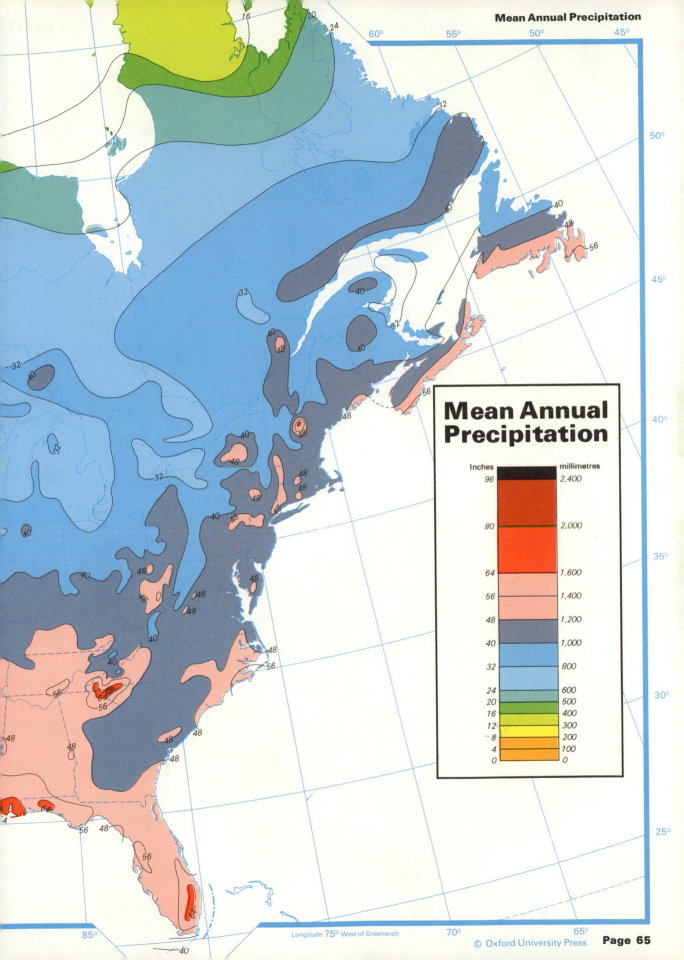

Mean Annual Precipitation

Inches		millimetres
96		2,400
80		2,000
64		1,600
56		1,400
48		1,200
40		1,000
32		800
24		600
20		500
16		400
12		300
8		200
4		100
0		0

Longitude 75° West of Greenwich

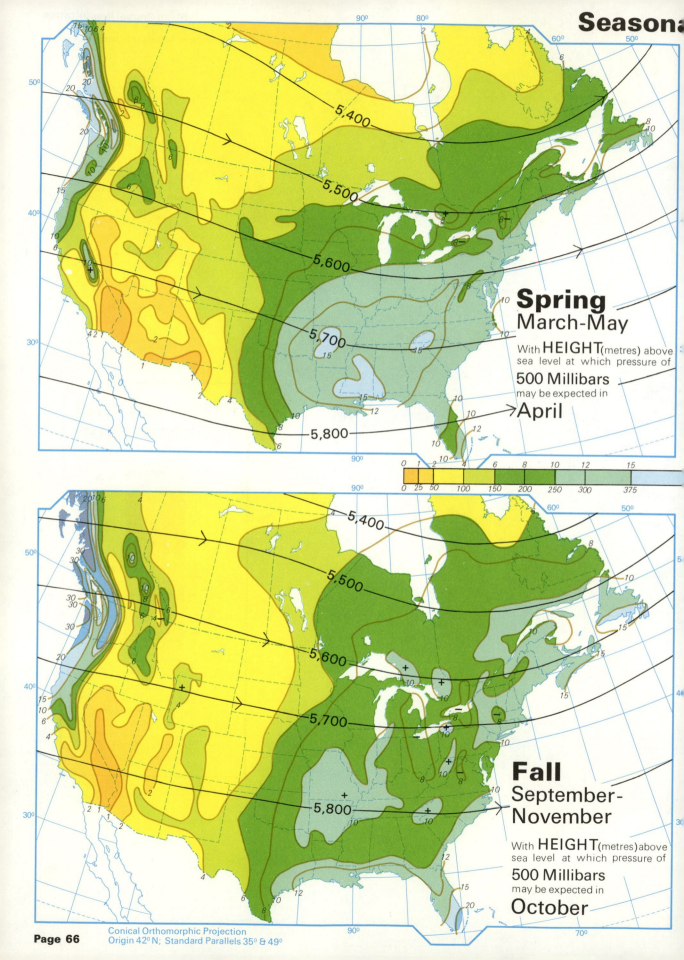

Spring
March-May

With HEIGHT(metres) above
sea level at which pressure of

500 Millibars
may be expected in
April

Fall
September-
November

With HEIGHT(metres)above
sea level at which pressure of

500 Millibars
may be expected in
October

Conical Orthomorphic Projection
Origin 42° N; Standard Parallels 35° & 49°

recipitation

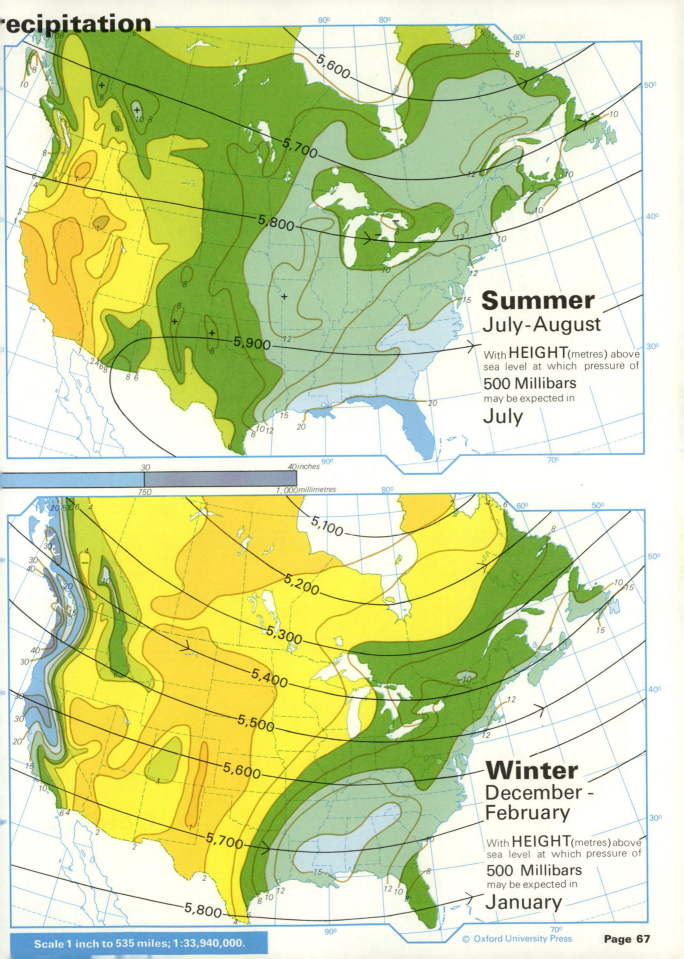

Summer
July-August

With HEIGHT (metres) above sea level at which pressure of **500 Millibars** may be expected in **July**

Winter
December - February

With HEIGHT (metres) above sea level at which pressure of **500 Millibars** may be expected in **January**

30   40 inches
750   1,000 millimetres

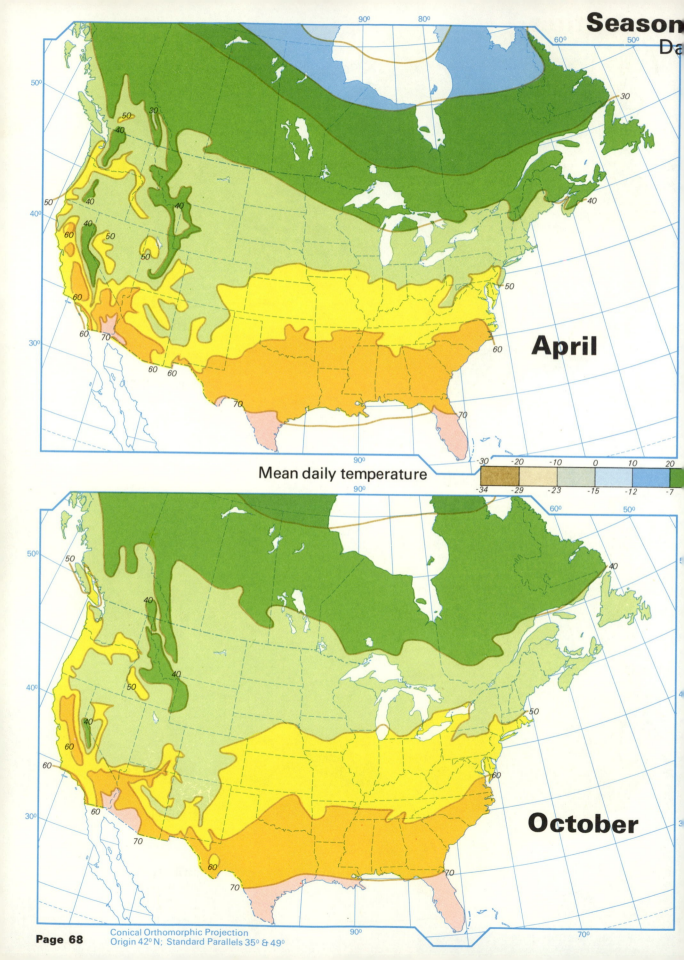

April

Mean daily temperature

	-30	-20	-10	0	10	20
	-34	-29	-23	-15	-12	-7

October

Conical Orthomorphic Projection
Origin 42° N; Standard Parallels 35° & 49°

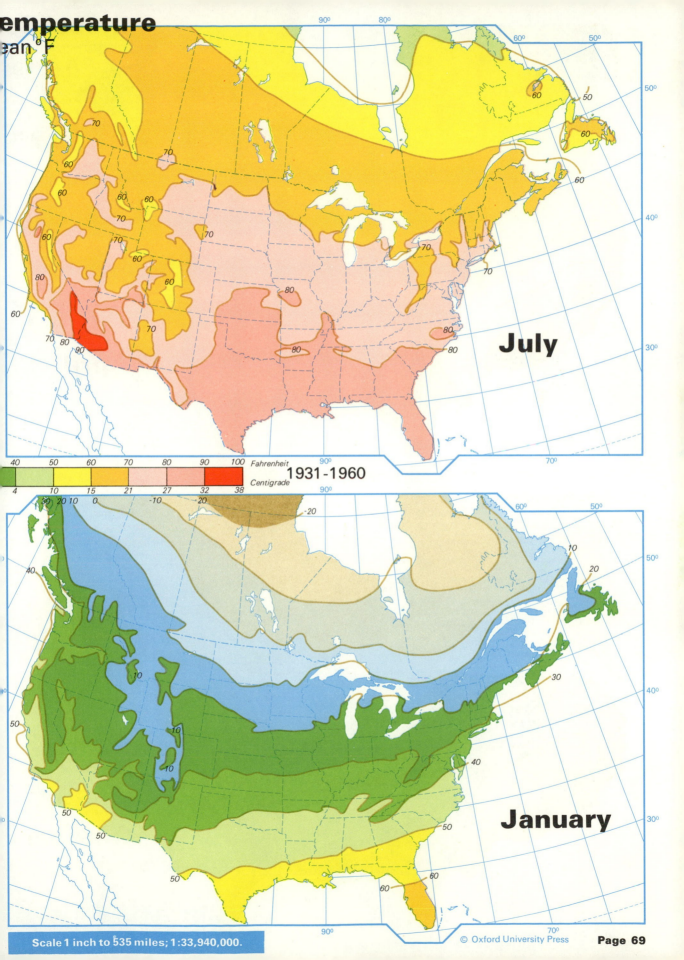

Temperature
Mean °F

July

40 50 60 70 80 90 100 *Fahrenheit*
4 10 15 21 27 32 38 *Centigrade*

1931-1960

January

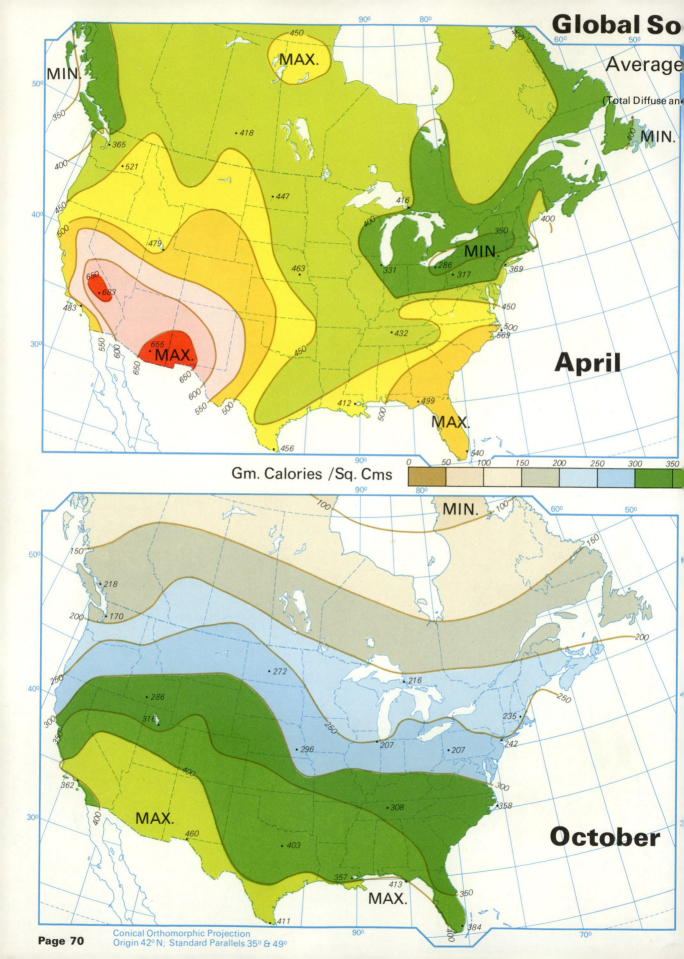

Global So

Average

(Total Diffuse an

Gm. Calories /Sq. Cms

0 50 100 150 200 250 300 350

April

October

MIN.

MIN.

MIN.

MIN.

MAX.

MAX.

MAX.

MAX.

MAX.

MAX.

Conical Orthomorphic Projection
Origin 42°N; Standard Parallels 35° & 49°

diation

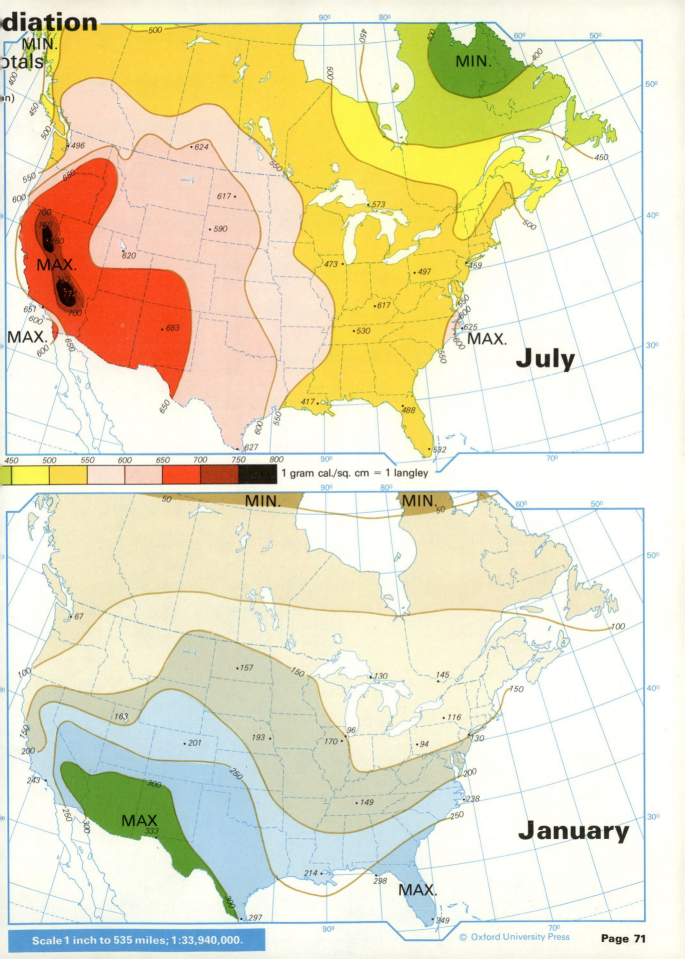

July

MIN.

otals

MIN.

MIN.

MAX.

496 · 624

617

590

620

700
750
760

MAX.

750

772

651
600

700

· 683

MAX.

660

600

573

473

497 459

617 625 MAX.

530

417 488

627 582

| 450 | 500 | 550 | 600 | 650 | 700 | 750 | 800 |

1 gram cal./sq. cm = 1 langley

January

MIN.

MIN.

50

50

67

100

157

150

130

145

150

100

163

201

193

170

96

116

150

200

149

94

130

243

250

300

MAX.
333

250

214

298

238

250

200

MAX.

300 · 297

349

Scale 1 inch to 535 miles; 1:33,940,000.

© Oxford University Press   **Page 71**

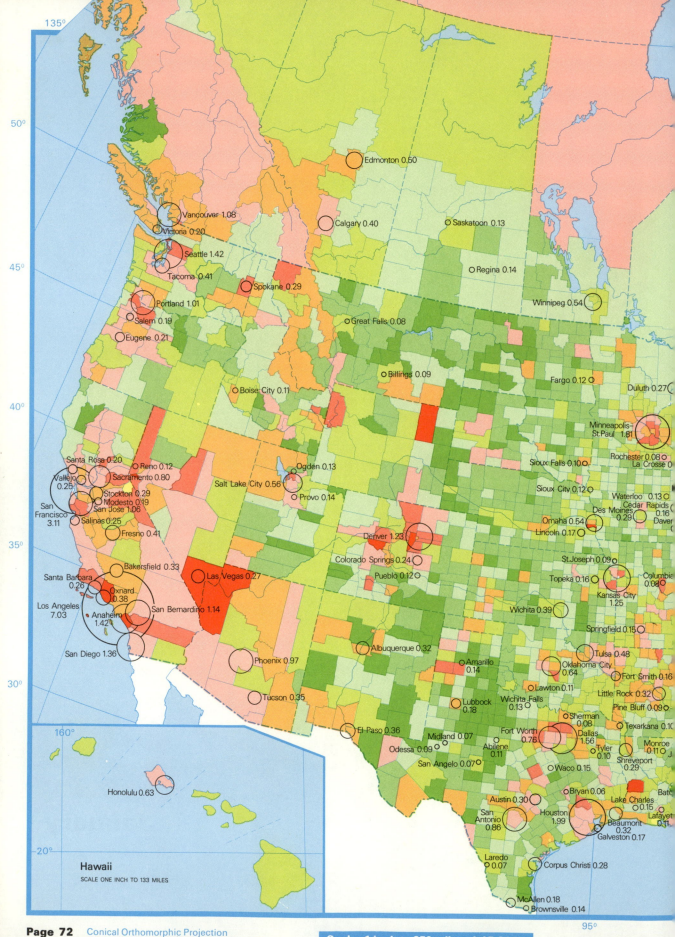

135°
50°
45°
40°
35°
30°

Edmonton 0.50

Vancouver 1.08
Victoria 0.20
Seattle 1.42
Tacoma 0.41
Spokane 0.29

Calgary 0.40

Saskatoon 0.13

Regina 0.14

Winnipeg 0.54

Portland 1.01
Salem 0.19
Eugene 0.21

Great Falls 0.08

Boise City 0.11

Billings 0.09

Fargo 0.12

Duluth 0.27

Minneapolis-
St. Paul 1.81

Santa Rosa 0.20
Vallejo 0.25
Sacramento 0.80
Stockton 0.29
Modesto 0.19
San Jose 1.06
San Francisco 3.11
Salinas 0.25
Fresno 0.41

Reno 0.12

Ogden 0.13
Salt Lake City 0.56
Provo 0.14

Denver 1.23

Colorado Springs 0.24
Pueblo 0.12

Rochester 0.08
La Crosse 0
Sioux Falls 0.10
Sioux City 0.12
Waterloo 0.13
Cedar Rapids 0.16
Daver
Des Moines 0.29
Omaha 0.54
Lincoln 0.17
St. Joseph 0.09
Columbie 0.08
Topeka 0.16
Kansas City 1.25

Santa Barbara 0.26
Bakersfield 0.33
Oxnard 0.38
Los Angeles 7.03
Anaheim 1.42
San Bernardino 1.14
San Diego 1.36

Las Vegas 0.27

Albuquerque 0.32

Amarillo 0.14

Phoenix 0.97
Tucson 0.35

El Paso 0.36

Midland 0.07
Odessa 0.09
San Angelo 0.07

Lubbock 0.18
Wichita Falls 0.13
Lawton 0.11
Sherman 0.08
Abilene 0.11
Fort Worth 0.76
Waco 0.15

Wichita 0.39
Springfield 0.15
Tulsa 0.48
Oklahoma City 0.64
Fort Smith 0.16
Little Rock 0.32
Pine Bluff 0.09
Texarkana 0.11
Dallas 1.56
Tyler 0.10
Monroe 0.11
Shreveport 0.29

160°
Honolulu 0.63

Austin 0.30
San Antonio 0.86
Houston 1.99
Bryan 0.06
Beaumont 0.32
Galveston 0.17
Lake Charles 0.15
Bate
Lafayet
0.11

20°

Hawaii
SCALE ONE INCH TO 133 MILES

Laredo 0.07
Corpus Christi 0.28

McAllen 0.18
Brownsville 0.14

Page 72 Conical Orthomorphic Projection
Origin 42° N; Standard Parallels 35° & 49°

Scale 1 inch to 250 miles 1:15·84 M

95°

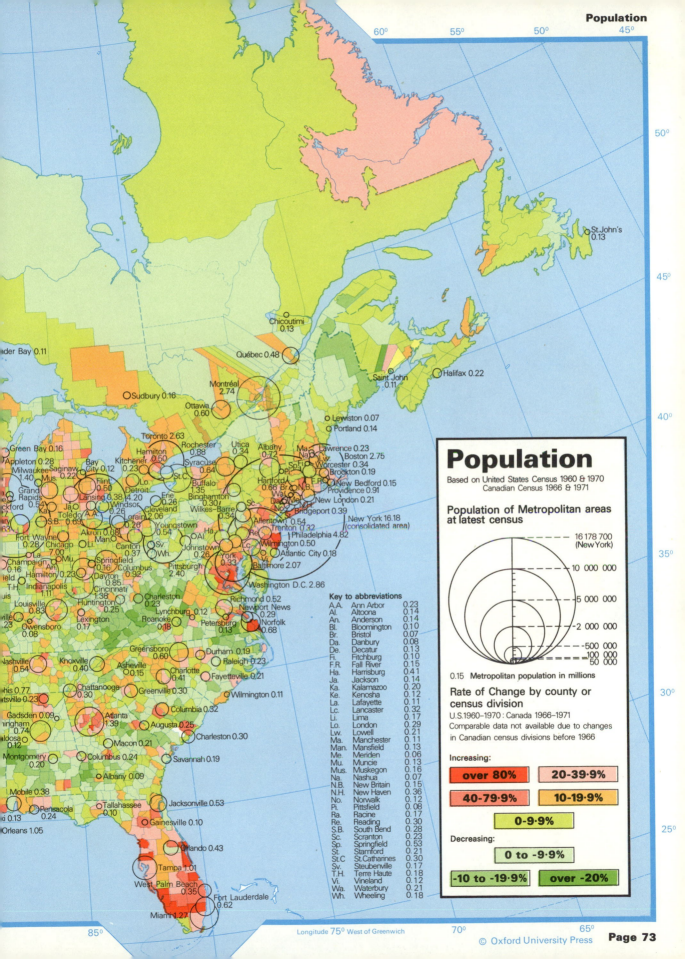

St.John's 0.13

Chicoutimi 0.13

Québec 0.48

Sudbury 0.16

Montréal 2.74

Saint John 0.11

Halifax 0.22

Ottawa 0.60

Lewiston 0.07

Portland 0.14

Toronto 2.63

Rochester 0.88

Utica 0.34

Albany 0.72

Lawrence 0.23

Boston 2.75

Hamilton 0.50

Kitchener 0.23

Syracuse 0.34

Worcester 0.34

Brockton 0.19

Green Bay 0.16

Bay City 0.12

Flint 0.50

Lo. Detroit 4.20

Buffalo .35

Binghamton 0.30

Hartford 0.66

Providence 0.91

New Bedford 0.15

Appleton 0.28

Milwaukee 1.40

Saginaw 0.22

Lansing 0.38

Erie 0.26

Cleveland 2.06

Wilkes-Barre 0.34

New London 0.21

Grand Rapids 0.54

Windsor 0.26

Lorain 0.26

Bridgeport 0.39

Toledo 0.69

Akron 0.68

Youngstown 0.54

Allentown 0.54

New York 16.18 (consolidated area)

Fort Wayne 0.28

Man.

Canton 0.37

Johnstown 0.26

Trenton 0.32

Philadelphia 4.82

Chicago 7.00

Springfield 0.16

Columbus 0.92

York 0.33

Wilmington 0.50

Atlantic City 0.18

Champaign 0.16

Dayton 0.85

Pittsburgh 2.40

Baltimore 2.07

Hamilton 0.23

Indianapolis 1.11

Cincinnati 1.38

Washington D.C. 2.86

Huntington 0.25

Charleston 0.23

Richmond 0.52

Louisville 0.83

Lexington 0.17

Lynchburg 0.12

Roanoke 0.18

Newport News 0.29

Norfolk 0.68

Owensboro 0.08

Petersburg 0.13

Nashville 0.54

Knoxville 0.40

Greensboro 0.60

Durham 0.19

Raleigh 0.23

Asheville 0.15

Charlotte 0.41

Fayetteville 0.21

Chattanooga 0.30

Greenville 0.30

Wilmington 0.11

Gadsden 0.09

Atlanta 1.39

Columbia 0.32

Charleston 0.30

Macon 0.21

Augusta 0.25

Montgomery 0.20

Columbus 0.24

Savannah 0.19

Mobile 0.38

Albany 0.09

Jacksonville 0.53

Pensacola 0.24

Tallahassee 0.10

Orleans 1.05

Gainesville 0.10

Orlando 0.43

Tampa 1.01

West Palm Beach 0.35

Fort Lauderdale 0.62

Miami 1.27

der Bay 0.11

Key to abbreviations

A.A.	Ann Arbor	0.23
Al.	Altoona	0.14
An.	Anderson	0.14
Bl.	Bloomington	0.10
Br.	Bristol	0.07
Da.	Danbury	0.08
De.	Decatur	0.13
Fi.	Fitchburg	0.10
F.R.	Fall River	0.15
Ha.	Harrisburg	0.41
Ja.	Jackson	0.14
Ka.	Kalamazoo	0.20
Ke.	Kenosha	0.12
La.	Lafayette	0.11
Lc.	Lancaster	0.32
Li.	Lima	0.17
Lo.	London	0.29
Lw.	Lowell	0.21
Ma.	Manchester	0.11
Man.	Mansfield	0.13
Me.	Meriden	0.06
Mu.	Muncie	0.13
Mus.	Muskegon	0.16
Na.	Nashua	0.07
N.B.	New Britain	0.15
N.H.	New Haven	0.36
No.	Norwalk	0.12
Pi.	Pittsfield	0.08
Ra.	Racine	0.17
Re.	Reading	0.30
S.B.	South Bend	0.28
Sc.	Scranton	0.23
Sp.	Springfield	0.53
St.	Stamford	0.21
St.C	St.Catharines	0.30
Sv.	Steubenville	0.17
T.H.	Terre Haute	0.18
Vi.	Vineland	0.12
Wa.	Waterbury	0.21
Wh.	Wheeling	0.18

Population

Based on United States Census 1960 & 1970
Canadian Census 1966 & 1971

Population of Metropolitan areas at latest census

— 16 178 700 (New York)
— 10 000 000
— 5 000 000
— 2 000 000
— 500 000
— 100 000
— 50 000

0.15   Metropolitan population in millions

Rate of Change by county or census division

U.S.1960–1970 : Canada 1966–1971
Comparable data not available due to changes in Canadian census divisions before 1966

Increasing:

over 80%	20-39·9%
40-79·9%	10-19·9%
0-9·9%	

Decreasing:

	0 to -9·9%
-10 to -19·9%	over -20%

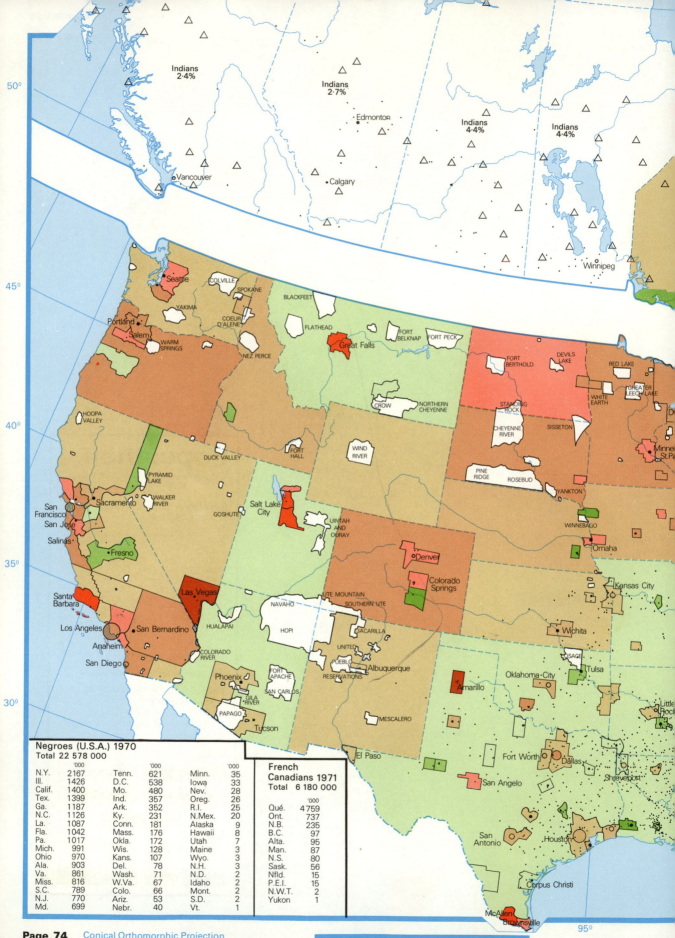

Negroes (U.S.A.) 1970
Total 22 578 000

	'000		'000		'000
N.Y.	2167	Tenn.	621	Minn.	35
Ill.	1426	D.C.	538	Iowa	33
Calif.	1400	Mo.	480	Nev.	28
Tex.	1399	Ind.	357	Oreg.	26
Ga.	1187	Ark.	352	R.I.	25
N.C.	1126	Ky.	231	N.Mex.	20
La.	1087	Conn.	181	Alaska	9
Fla.	1042	Mass.	176	Hawaii	8
Pa.	1017	Okla.	172	Utah	7
Mich.	991	Wis.	128	Maine	3
Ohio	970	Kans.	107	Wyo.	3
Ala.	903	Del.	78	N.H.	3
Va.	861	Wash.	71	N.D.	2
Miss.	816	W.Va.	67	Idaho	2
S.C.	789	Colo.	66	Mont.	2
N.J.	770	Ariz.	53	S.D.	2
Md.	699	Nebr.	40	Vt.	1

French Canadians 1971
Total 6 180 000

	'000
Qué.	4759
Ont.	737
N.B.	235
B.C.	97
Alta.	95
Man.	87
N.S.	80
Sask.	56
Nfld.	15
P.E.I.	15
N.W.T.	2
Yukon	1

Conical Orthomorphic Projection
Origin 42° N; Standard Parallels 35° & 49°

Scale 1 inch to 250 miles 1:15.84 M

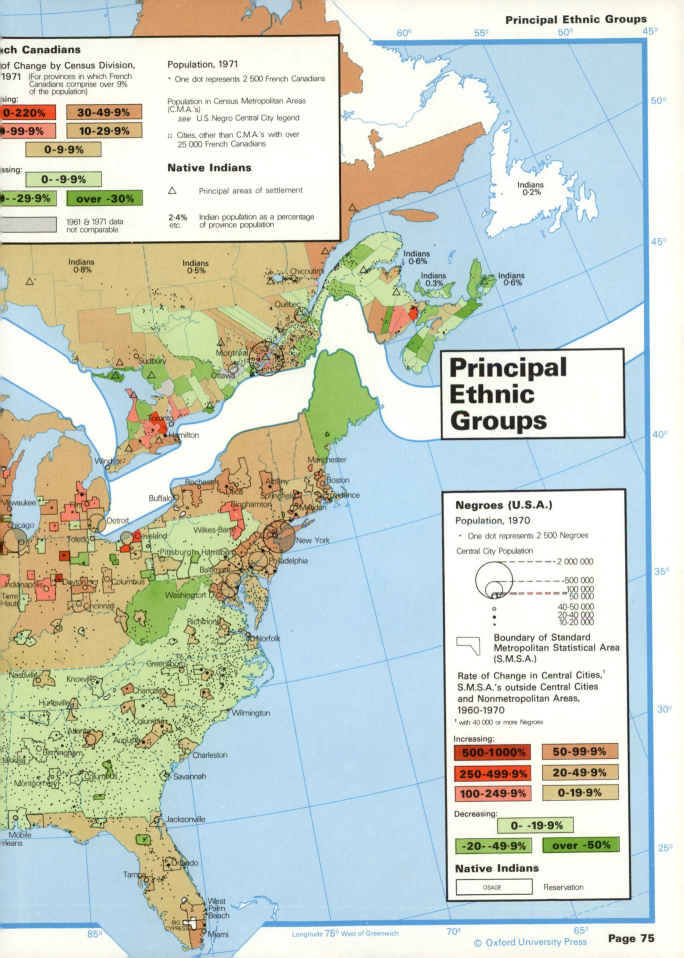

ch Canadians

of Change by Census Division,
1971 (For provinces in which French
Canadians comprise over 9%
of the population)

Population, 1971

- One dot represents 2 500 French Canadians

Population in Census Metropolitan Areas
(C.M.A.'s)
  see U.S. Negro Central City legend

□ Cities, other than C.M.A.'s with over
25 000 French Canadians

sing:

0-220%	30-49·9%
0-99·9%	10-29·9%
0-9·9%	

asing:

0- -9·9%	
0- -29·9%	**over -30%**

1961 & 1971 data
not comparable

Native Indians

△   Principal areas of settlement

2·4%   Indian population as a percentage
etc.   of province population

**Principal
Ethnic
Groups**

Negroes (U.S.A.)

Population, 1970

- One dot represents 2 500 Negroes

Central City Population

─ 2 000 000
─ ─500 000
─ ─100 000
─ ─50 000

○   40-50 000
·   20-40 000
·   10-20 000

Boundary of Standard
Metropolitan Statistical Area
(S.M.S.A.)

**Rate of Change in Central Cities,[1]
S.M.S.A.'s outside Central Cities
and Nonmetropolitan Areas,
1960-1970**

[1] with 40 000 or more Negroes

Increasing:

500-1000%	50-99·9%
250-499·9%	20-49·9%
100-249·9%	0-19·9%

Decreasing:

0- -19·9%	
-20- -49·9%	**over -50%**

Native Indians

OSAGE	Reservation

Indians
0·2%

Indians
0·8%

Indians
0·5%

Indians
0·6%

Indians
0.3%

Indians
0·6%

Chicoutimi

Québec

Montréal

Ottawa

Sudbury

Toronto

Hamilton

Windsor

Manchester

Rochester

Albany

Boston

Providence

Buffalo

Utica

Springfield

Meriden

Binghamton

Detroit

Wilkes-Barre

Milwaukee

Flint

New York

Chicago

Cleveland

Toledo

Pittsburgh

Harrisburg

Philadelphia

Indianapolis

Dayton

Columbus

Baltimore

Terre
Haute

Cincinnati

Washington D.C.

Richmond

Norfolk

Nashville

Knoxville

Greensboro

Charlotte

Wilmington

Huntsville

Columbia

Atlanta

Augusta

Birmingham

Charleston

Montgomery

Columbus

Savannah

aloosa

Mobile
rleans

Jacksonville

Orlando

Tampa

West
Palm
Beach

BIG
CYPRESS

Miami

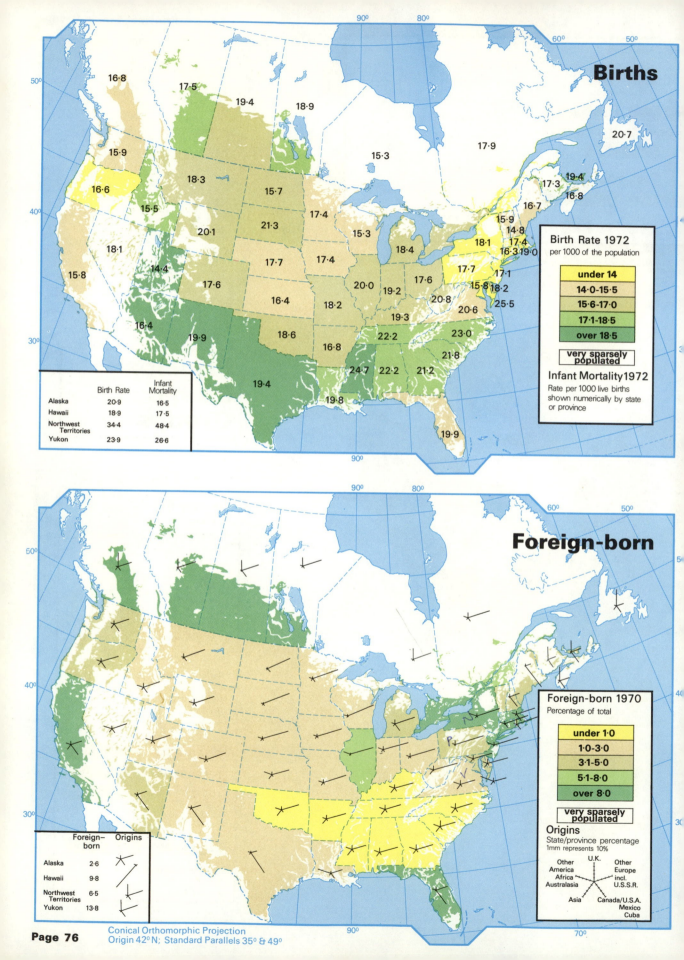

Births

Birth Rate 1972
per 1000 of the population

- under 14
- 14·0–15·5
- 15·6–17·0
- 17·1–18·5
- over 18·5
- very sparsely populated

Infant Mortality 1972
Rate per 1000 live births shown numerically by state or province

	Birth Rate	Infant Mortality
Alaska	20·9	16·5
Hawaii	18·9	17·5
Northwest Territories	34·4	48·4
Yukon	23·9	26·6

Foreign-born

Foreign-born 1970
Percentage of total

- under 1·0
- 1·0–3·0
- 3·1–5·0
- 5·1–8·0
- over 8·0
- very sparsely populated

Origins
State/province percentage
1mm represents 10%

Other America Africa Australasia / U.K. / Other Europe incl. U.S.S.R. / Asia / Canada/U.S.A. Mexico Cuba

	Foreign-born	Origins
Alaska	2·6	
Hawaii	9·8	
Northwest Territories	6·5	
Yukon	13·8	

Conical Orthomorphic Projection
Origin 42°N; Standard Parallels 35° & 49°

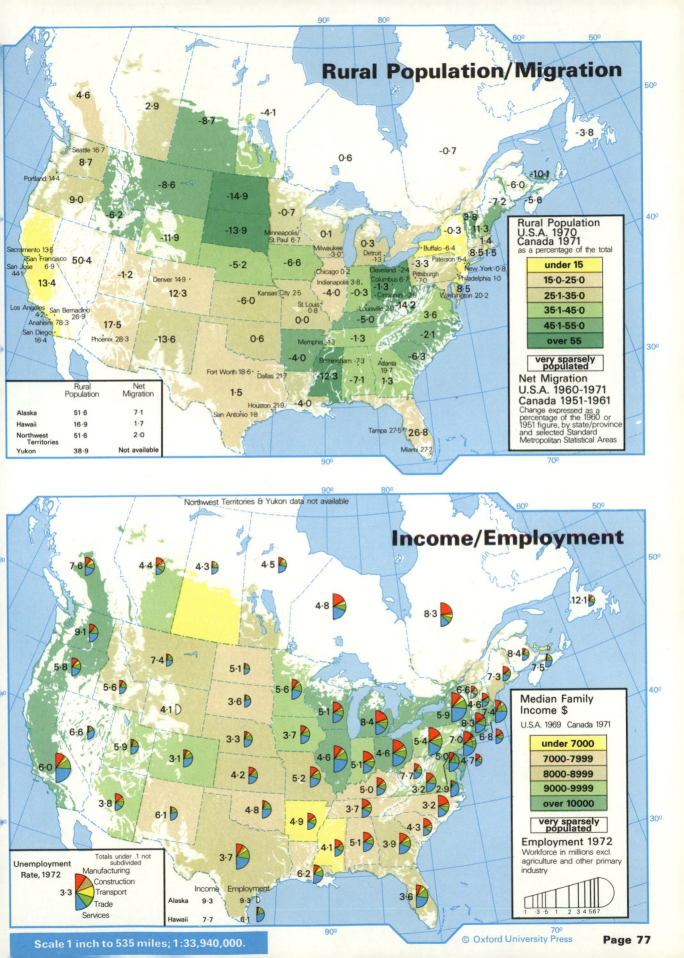

Rural Population/Migration

Income/Employment

Scale 1 inch to 535 miles; 1:33,940,000.

© Oxford University Press   **Page 77**

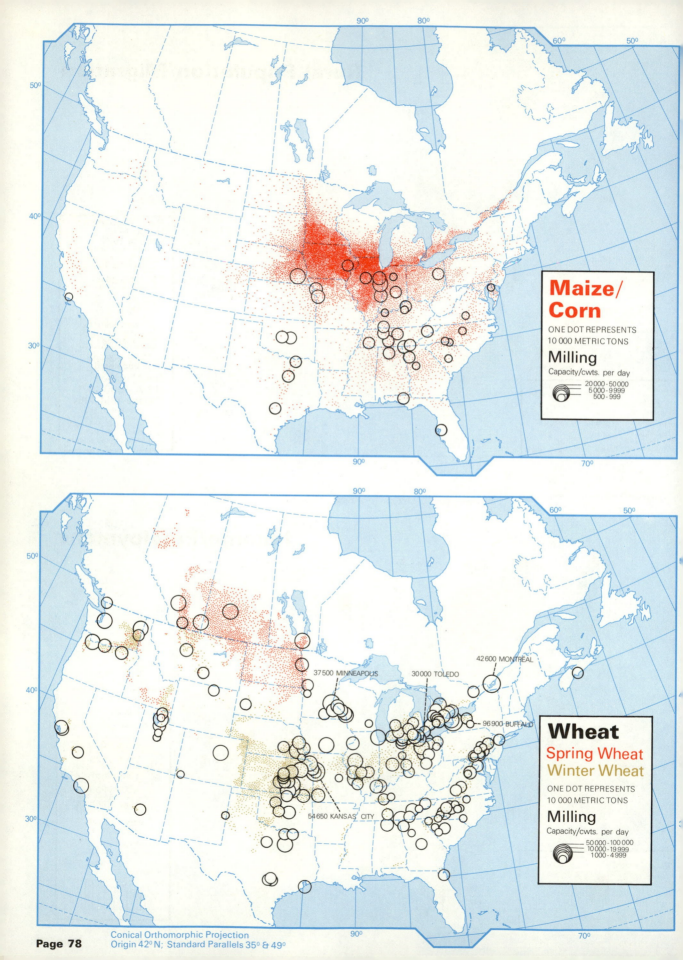

Maize/Corn

ONE DOT REPRESENTS
10 000 METRIC TONS

Milling
Capacity/cwts. per day

20 000 - 50 000
5 000 - 9 999
500 - 999

Wheat

Spring Wheat
Winter Wheat

ONE DOT REPRESENTS
10 000 METRIC TONS

Milling
Capacity/cwts. per day

50 000 - 100 000
10 000 - 19 999
1 000 - 4 999

37 500 MINNEAPOLIS

54 650 KANSAS CITY

30 000 TOLEDO

96 900 BUFFALO

42 600 MONTREAL

Conical Orthomorphic Projection
Origin 42° N; Standard Parallels 35° & 49°

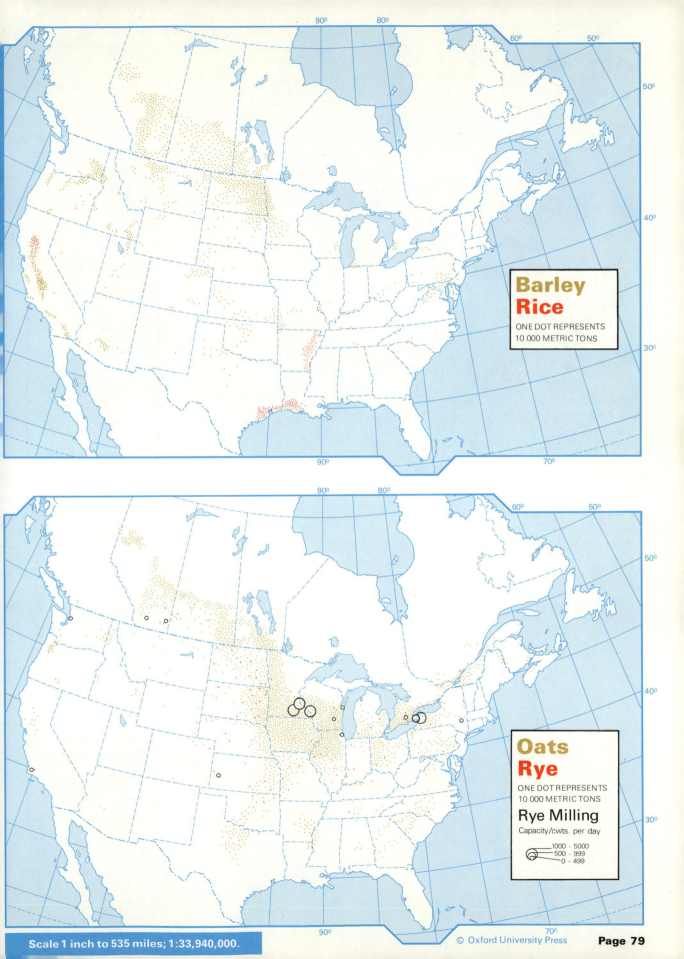

Barley
Rice

ONE DOT REPRESENTS
10 000 METRIC TONS

Oats
Rye

ONE DOT REPRESENTS
10 000 METRIC TONS

Rye Milling

Capacity/cwts. per day

1000 - 5000
500 - 999
0 - 499

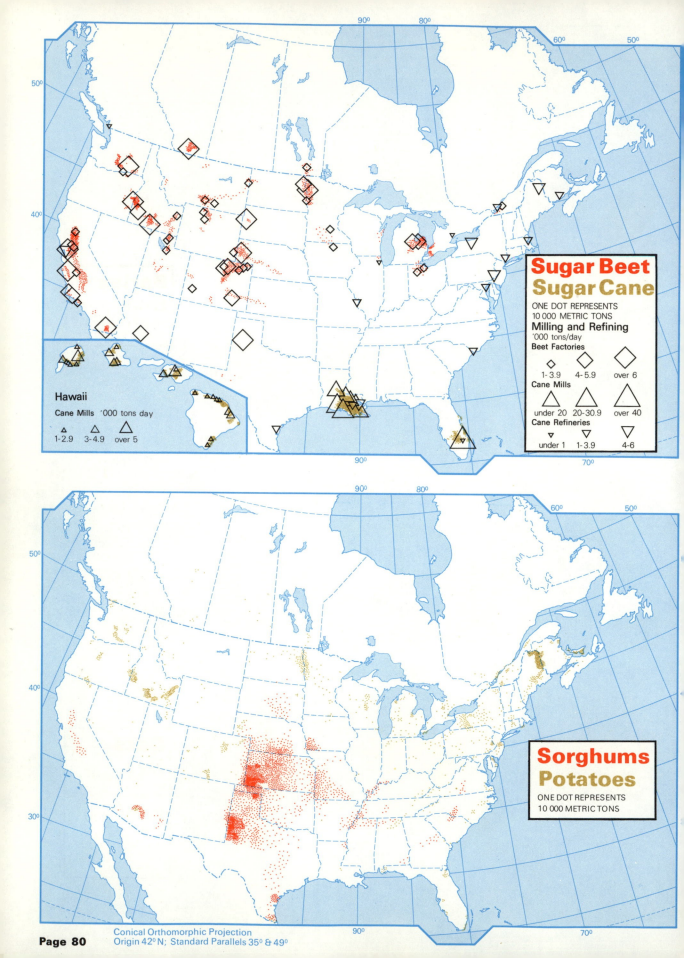

Sugar Beet
Sugar Cane

ONE DOT REPRESENTS
10 000 METRIC TONS
Milling and Refining
'000 tons/day
Beet Factories

◇ ◈ ◆
1- 3.9   4- 5.9   over 6

Cane Mills

△ △ △
under 20   20-30.9   over 40

Cane Refineries

▽ ▽ ▽
under 1   1- 3.9   4-6

Hawaii

Cane Mills   '000 tons day

△ △ △
1-2.9   3-4.9   over 5

Sorghums
Potatoes

ONE DOT REPRESENTS
10 000 METRIC TONS

Conical Orthomorphic Projection
Origin 42° N; Standard Parallels 35° & 49°

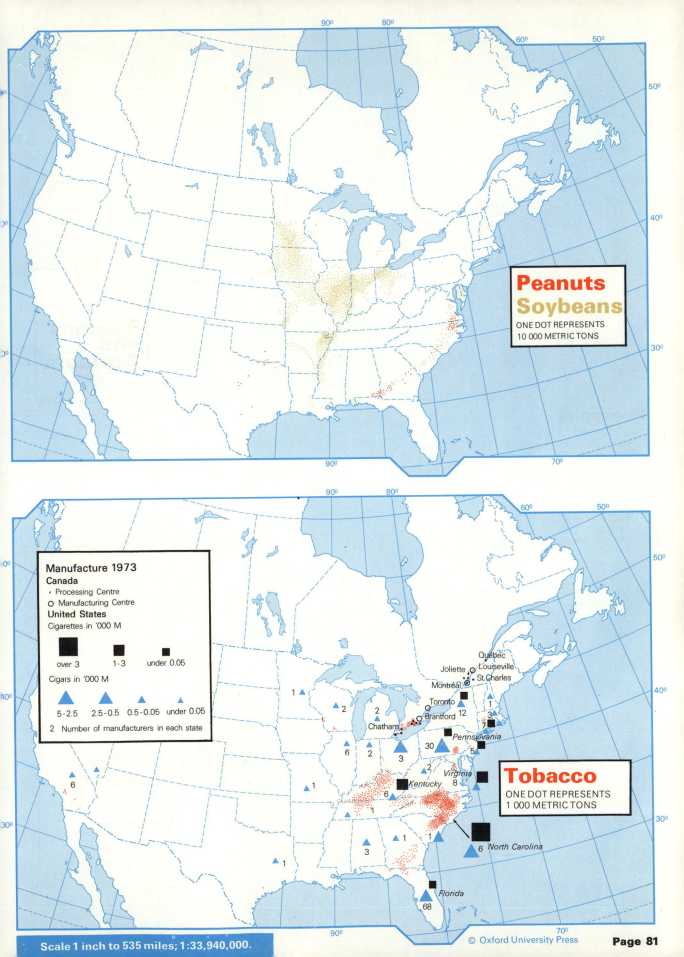

Peanuts
Soybeans

ONE DOT REPRESENTS
10 000 METRIC TONS

Manufacture 1973

Canada
- Processing Centre
○ Manufacturing Centre

United States
Cigarettes in '000 M

over 3　　1-3　　under 0.05

Cigars in '000 M

▲ 5-2.5　▲ 2.5-0.5　▲ 0.5-0.05　▲ under 0.05

2　Number of manufacturers in each state

Québec
Joliette　Louiseville
　　　　St.Charles
Montréal
Toronto
Brantford　12
Chatham
1
2
2
Pennsylvania
6　2
3　30　5
6
2
Kentucky　Virginia
6　8
1
1
1
Tobacco

ONE DOT REPRESENTS
1 000 METRIC TONS

6

3
1

6　North Carolina

Florida
68

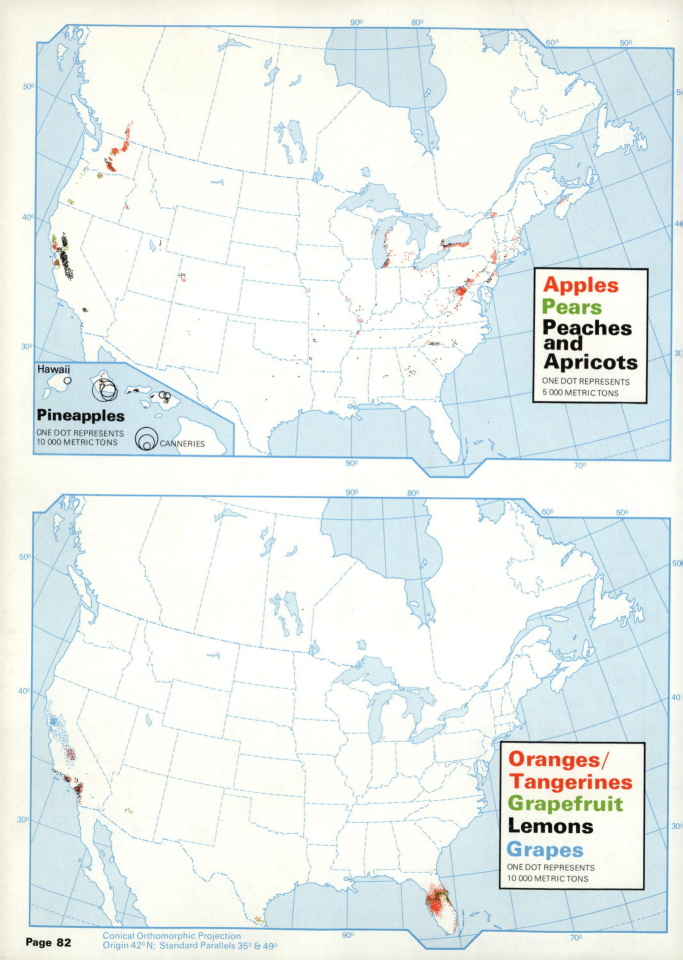

Apples
Pears
Peaches and Apricots

ONE DOT REPRESENTS
5 000 METRIC TONS

Hawaii

Pineapples

ONE DOT REPRESENTS
10 000 METRIC TONS   CANNERIES

Oranges/ Tangerines
Grapefruit
Lemons
Grapes

ONE DOT REPRESENTS
10 000 METRIC TONS

Conical Orthomorphic Projection
Origin 42° N; Standard Parallels 35° & 49°

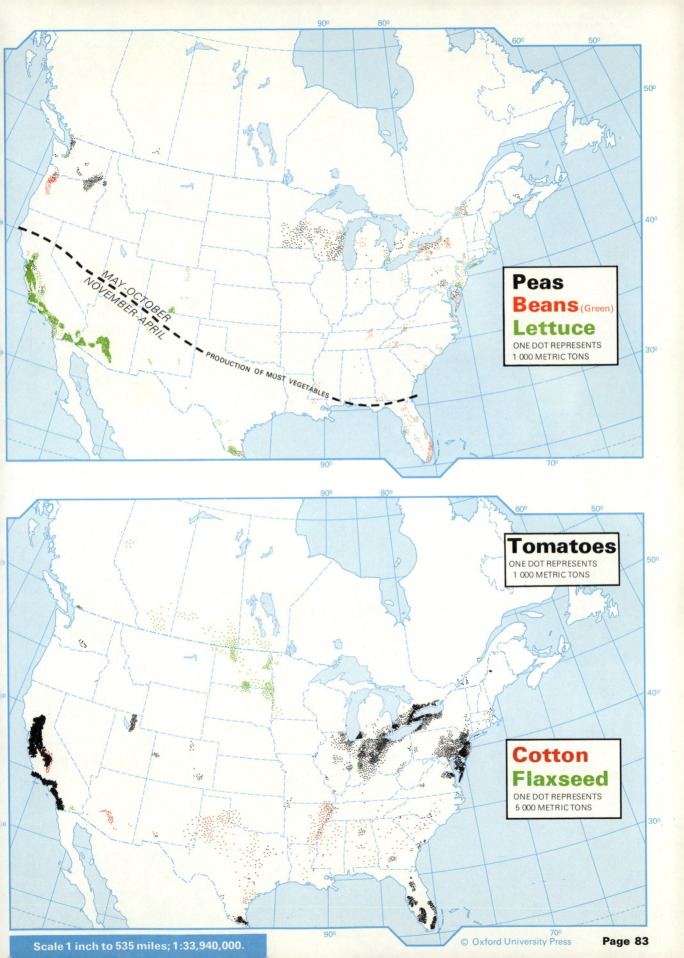

Peas
Beans (Green)
Lettuce

ONE DOT REPRESENTS
1 000 METRIC TONS

MAY-OCTOBER
NOVEMBER-APRIL
PRODUCTION OF MOST VEGETABLES

Tomatoes

ONE DOT REPRESENTS
1 000 METRIC TONS

Cotton
Flaxseed

ONE DOT REPRESENTS
5 000 METRIC TONS

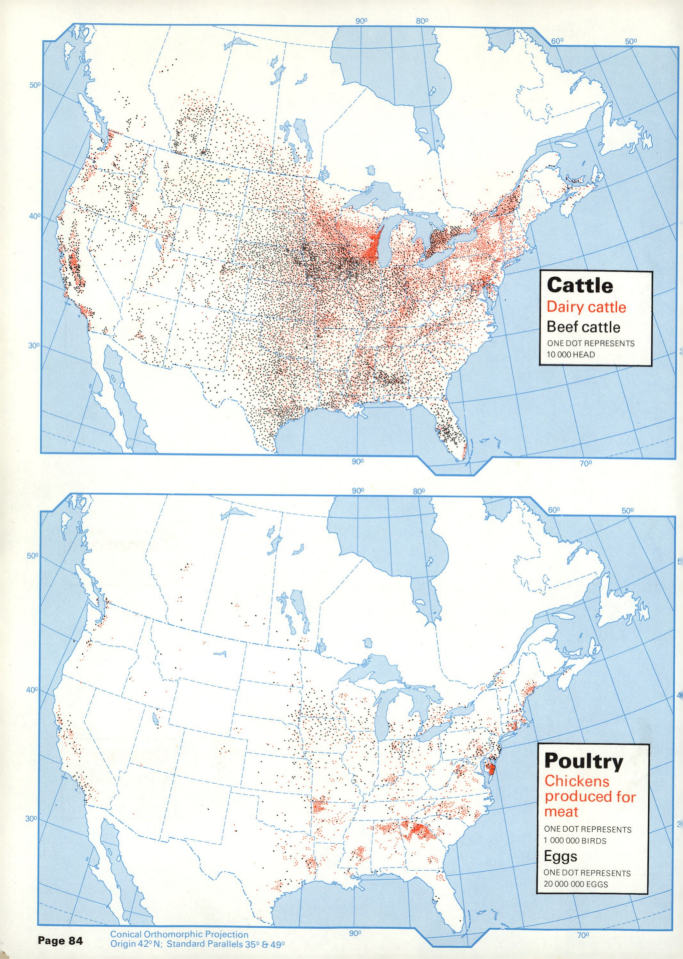

Cattle
Dairy cattle
Beef cattle
ONE DOT REPRESENTS
10 000 HEAD

Poultry
Chickens
produced for
meat
ONE DOT REPRESENTS
1 000 000 BIRDS
Eggs
ONE DOT REPRESENTS
20 000 000 EGGS

Conical Orthomorphic Projection
Origin 42° N; Standard Parallels 35° & 49°

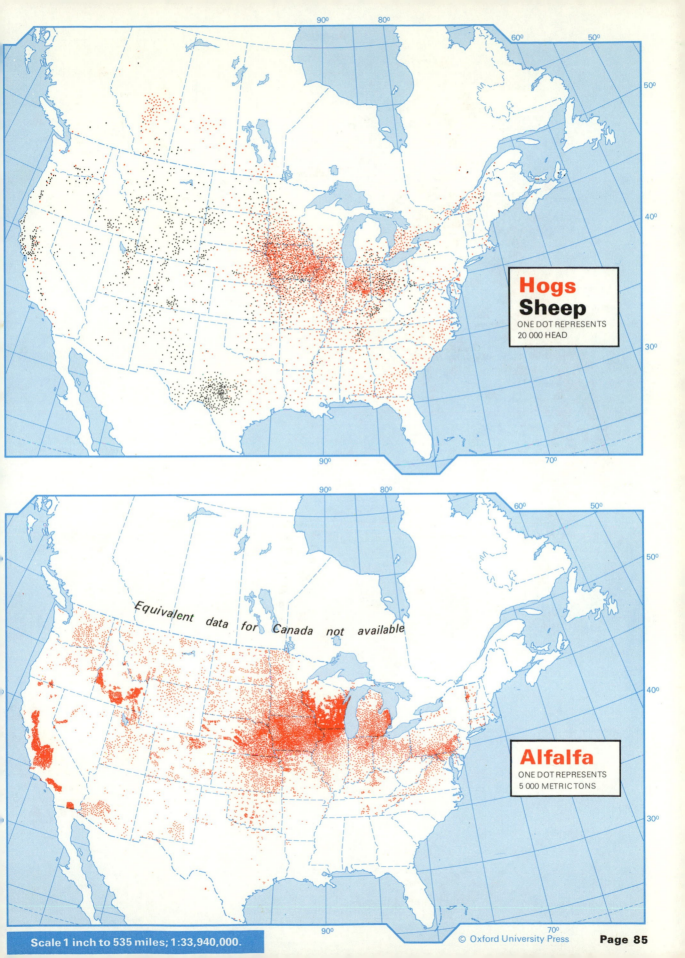

Hogs
Sheep

ONE DOT REPRESENTS
20 000 HEAD

Equivalent data for Canada not available

Alfalfa

ONE DOT REPRESENTS
5 000 METRIC TONS

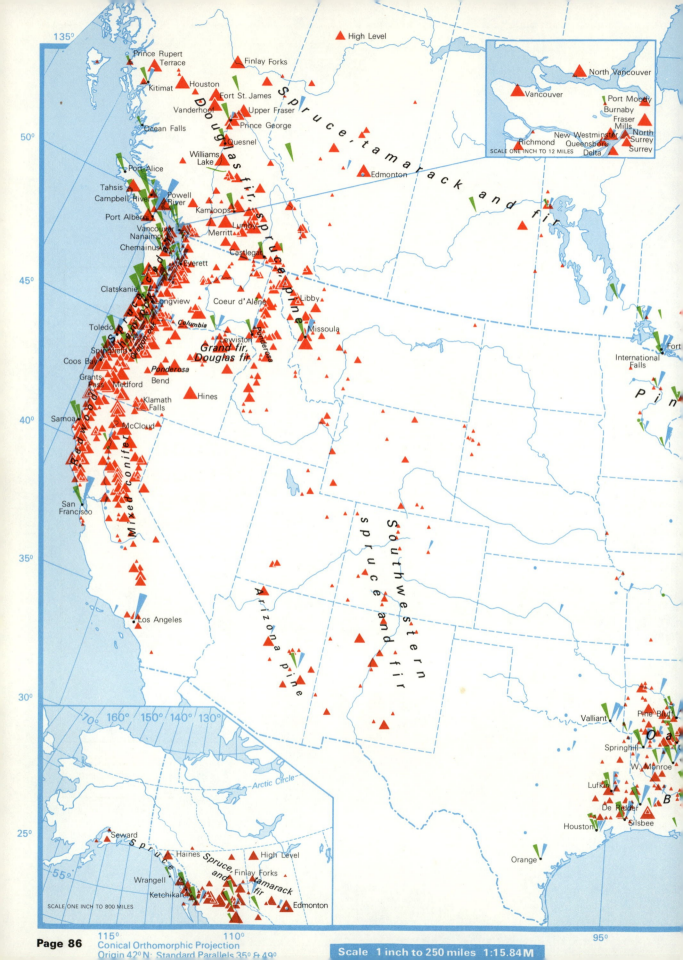

High Level

Prince Rupert
Terrace
Kitimat

Houston

Finlay Forks

Spruce, tamarack and fir

North Vancouver

Vancouver
Port Moody
Burnaby
Fraser
Mills

New Westminster
Richmond
Queensboro
North
Surrey
Delta
Surrey

SCALE ONE INCH TO 12 MILES

Fort St. James
Vanderhoof
Upper Fraser
Prince George
Quesnel

Ocean Falls

Williams
Lake

Edmonton

Port Alice

Tahsis
Campbell River
Powell
River

Port Alberni
Kamloops
Vancouver
Nanaimo
Lumby
Merritt
Chemainus
Castlegar
Everett
Libby

Clatskanie
Coeur d'Alene
Longview
Missoula
Toledo
Lewiston
Springfield
Grand fir,
Douglas fir
Coos Bay
Ponderosa
Grants
Pass
Medford
Bend

Klamath
Falls
Hines

Samoa
McCloud

San
Francisco

Mixed conifer

Redwood

Columbia

Douglas fir, spruce, pine

Spruce and

Ponderosa

Fort
International
Falls

P i n

Los Angeles

Arizona pine

Southwestern
spruce and fir

Valliant
Pine Bluff

O a

Springhill

W. Monroe

Lufkin

B

De Ridder
Silsbee

Seward

Houston

Orange

s p r u c e

Haines

Spruce and tamarack fir

Wrangell
Ketchikan

Finlay Forks

High Level

Edmonton

Arctic Circle

SCALE ONE INCH TO 800 MILES

Conical Orthomorphic Projection
Origin 42° N. Standard Parallels 35° & 49°

Scale 1 inch to 250 miles 1:15.84 M

135°
50°
45°
40°
35°
30°
25°
55°
70° 160° 150° 140° 130°
115°
110°
95°

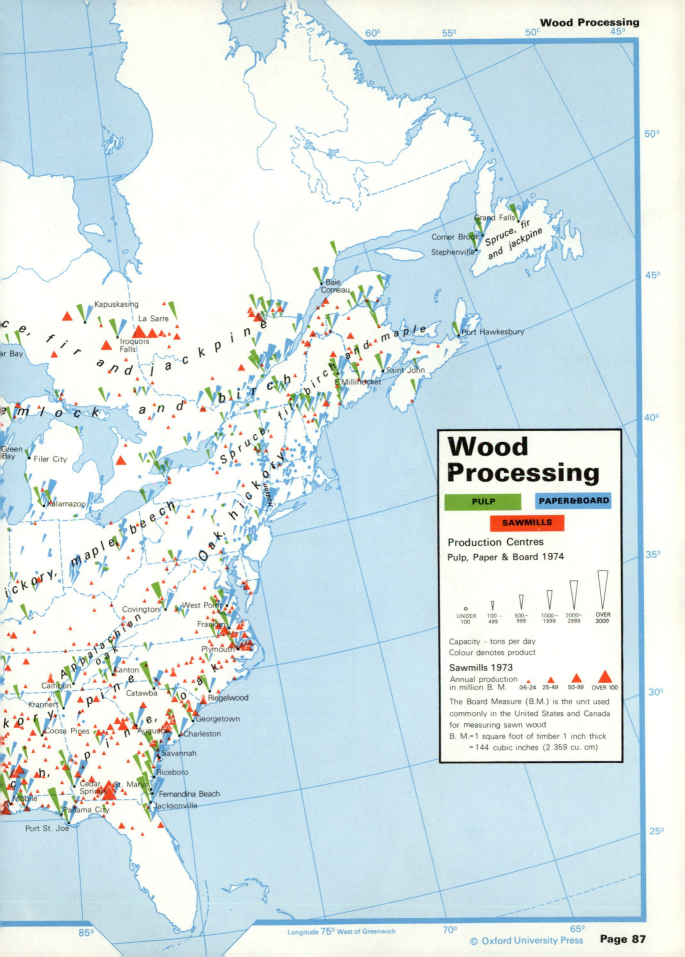

Kapuskasing

La Sarre

Iroquois Falls

Baie Comeau

Grand Falls

Corner Brook

Stephenville

Spruce, fir and jackpine

Port Hawkesbury

ce, fir and jackpine

r Bay

emlock and birch and maple

Saint John

E Millinocket

Spruce, fir, birch and maple

Green Bay

Filer City

Kalamazoo

ickory, maple, beech

Oak, hickory

Hudson

Covington

West Point

Franklin

Plymouth

Appalachian oak

pine

Canton

Catawba

oak

Riegelwood

Calhoun

Krannert

Coosa Pines

Augusta

Georgetown

Charleston

kory

pine,

Savannah

Riceboro

Cedar Springs

St. Marys

Mobile

Fernandina Beach

Panama City

Jacksonville

Port St. Joe

Wood Processing

PULP	PAPER&BOARD

SAWMILLS

Production Centres
Pulp, Paper & Board 1974

UNDER 100	100 – 499	500 – 999	1000 – 1999	2000 – 2999	OVER 3000

Capacity - tons per day
Colour denotes product

Sawmills 1973
Annual production in million B. M.

0·5-24 25-49 50-99 OVER 100

The Board Measure (B.M.) is the unit used commonly in the United States and Canada for measuring sawn wood

B. M.=1 square foot of timber 1 inch thick
= 144 cubic inches (2 359 cu. cm)

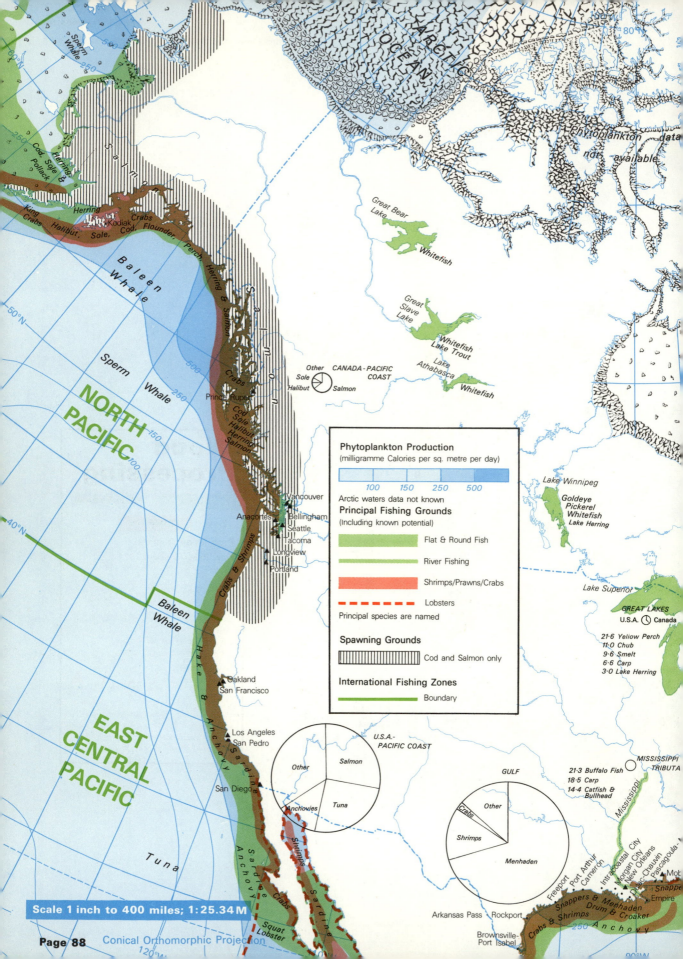

ARCTIC OCEAN

Phytoplankton data not available

Sperm Whale 250

Cod Sole & Pollack 250

King Crabs Halibut Sole, Cod, Flounder, Perch Herring & Salmon

Kodiak Crabs

Herring

Baleen Whale

Great Bear Lake

Whitefish

Salmon

Great Slave Lake

Whitefish Lake Trout

Lake Athabasca

Whitefish

Sperm Whale

NORTH PACIFIC

250 500 150 100

Prince Rupert

Cod Sole Halibut Herring Salmon

Other

Sole Halibut

CANADA - PACIFIC COAST

Salmon

Vancouver
Anacortes   Bellingham
            Seattle
            Tacoma
            Longview
            Portland

Crabs & Shrimps

Baleen Whale

Lake Winnipeg

Goldeye Pickerel Whitefish Lake Herring

Phytoplankton Production
(milligramme Calories per sq. metre per day)

100   150   250   500

Arctic waters data not known

Principal Fishing Grounds
(Including known potential)

	Flat & Round Fish
	River Fishing
	Shrimps/Prawns/Crabs
- - -	Lobsters

Principal species are named

Spawning Grounds

Cod and Salmon only

International Fishing Zones

Boundary

Lake Superior

GREAT LAKES
U.S.A.   Canada

21·6 Yellow Perch
11·0 Chub
9·6 Smelt
6·6 Carp
3·0 Lake Herring

Oakland
San Francisco

EAST CENTRAL PACIFIC

Hake & Anchovy

Los Angeles
San Pedro

Sardine

San Diego

Other   Salmon

U.S.A.- PACIFIC COAST

Anchovies   Tuna

GULF

21·3 Buffalo Fish
18·5 Carp
14·4 Catfish & Bullhead

MISSISSIPPI TRIBUTA

Crabs   Other

Shrimps

Menhaden

Mississippi

Tuna

Sardine Anchovy

Shrimps

Sardine

Crabs

Squat Lobster

Snappers & Menhaden Drum & Croaker

Freeport Port Arthur Cameron
    Intracoastal City
    Morgan City New Orleans
    Delac Pascagoula Mob

Crabs & Shrimps

Snappe

Arkansas Pass   Rockport

Brownsville-
Port Isabel

Anchovy

250

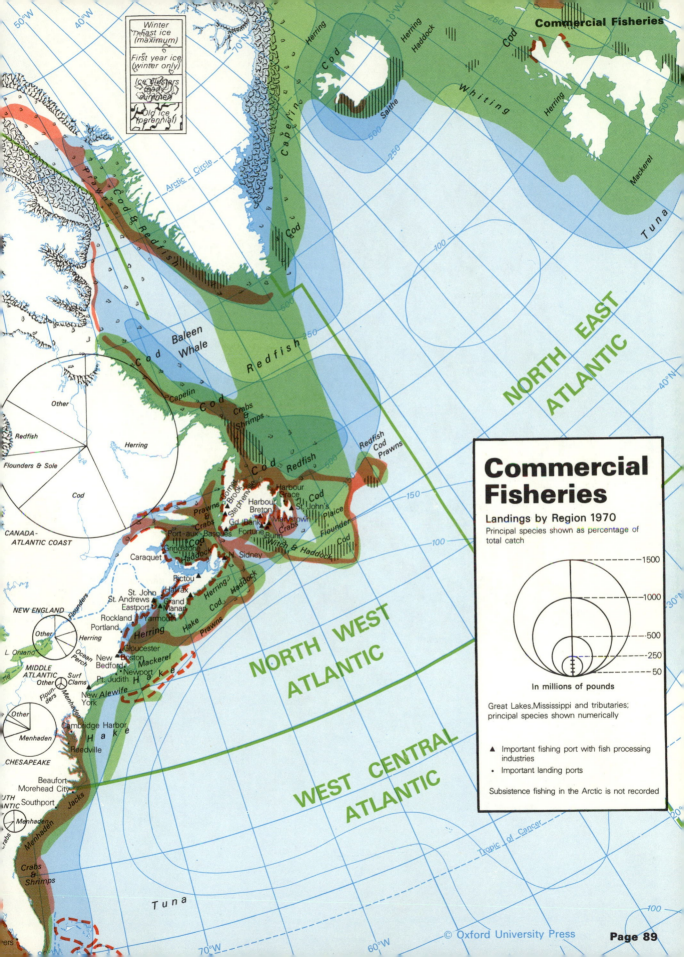

Winter
Fast ice
(maximum)

First year ice
(winter only)

Ice clusters
(early summer)

Old ice
(perennial)

NORTH EAST ATLANTIC

NORTH WEST ATLANTIC

WEST CENTRAL ATLANTIC

Commercial Fisheries

Landings by Region 1970

Principal species shown as percentage of total catch

1500
1000
500
250
50

In millions of pounds

Great Lakes, Mississippi and tributaries; principal species shown numerically

▲ Important fishing port with fish processing industries

• Important landing ports

Subsistence fishing in the Arctic is not recorded

Herring
Haddock
Cod
Whiting
Capelin
Saithe
Herring
Mackerel
Tuna

Cod
Cod & Redfish
Prawns
Baleen Whale
Capelin
Redfish
Crabs & Shrimps
Redfish
Cod
Prawns
Cod
Redfish
Harbour Grace
Corner Brook
Stephenville
Harbour Breton
St. John's
Plaice
Marystown
Burin
Fortune
Crabs
Flounder
Witch & Haddock
Cod
Port-aux-Basques
Grindstone
Haddock
Cod
N. Sidney
Caraquet
Pictou
St. John
Halifax
St. Andrews
Eastport
Grand Manan
Rockland
Yarmouth
Portland
Herring
Hake
Cod
Haddock
Herring
Prawns
Gloucester
New Bedford
Boston
Mackerel
Newport
Pt. Judith
New York
Alewife
Hake
Cambridge Harbor
Reedville
Beaufort
Morehead City
Southport
Jacks
Menhaden
Crabs & Shrimps
Tuna

CANADA-ATLANTIC COAST
Other
Redfish
Flounders & Sole
Herring
Cod

NEW ENGLAND
Other
Herring
Ocean Perch
Flounders
L. Ontario

MIDDLE ATLANTIC
Other
Surf Clams
Flounders
Menhaden
Other

CHESAPEAKE
Other
Menhaden

Menhaden

Arctic Circle

Tropic of Cancer

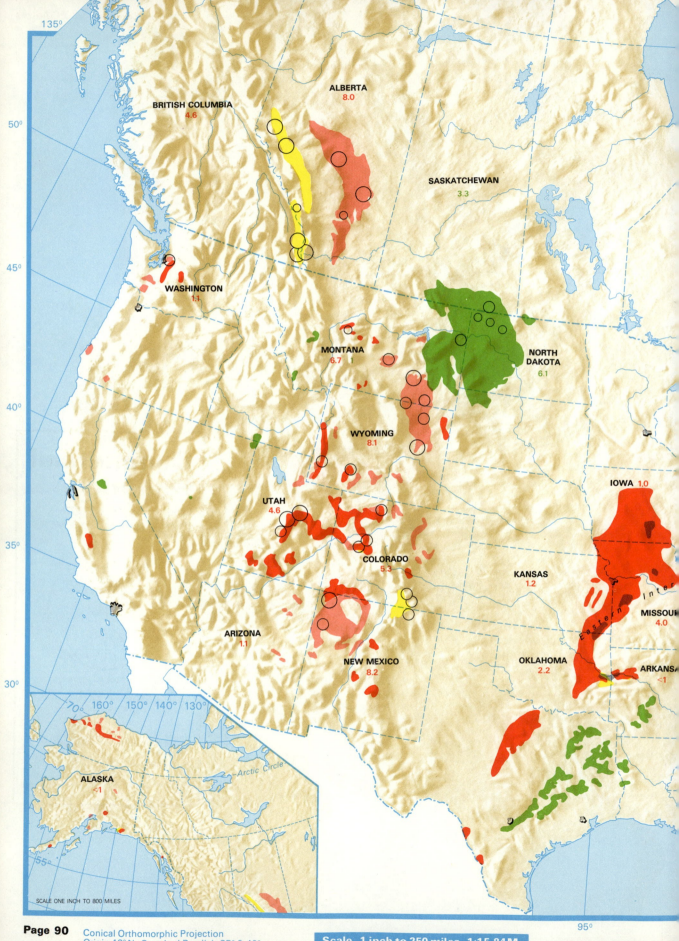

ALBERTA
8.0

BRITISH COLUMBIA
4.6

SASKATCHEWAN
3.3

WASHINGTON
1.1

NORTH DAKOTA
6.1

MONTANA
6.7

WYOMING
8.1

IOWA 1.0

UTAH
4.6

COLORADO
5.3

KANSAS
1.2

Eastern Inter

MISSOURI
4.0

ARIZONA
1.1

NEW MEXICO
8.2

OKLAHOMA
2.2

ARKANSAS
<1

ALASKA
<1

Arctic Circle

SCALE ONE INCH TO 800 MILES

Conical Orthomorphic Projection
Origin 42° N; Standard Parallels 35° & 49°

Scale   1 inch to 250 miles   1:15.84 M

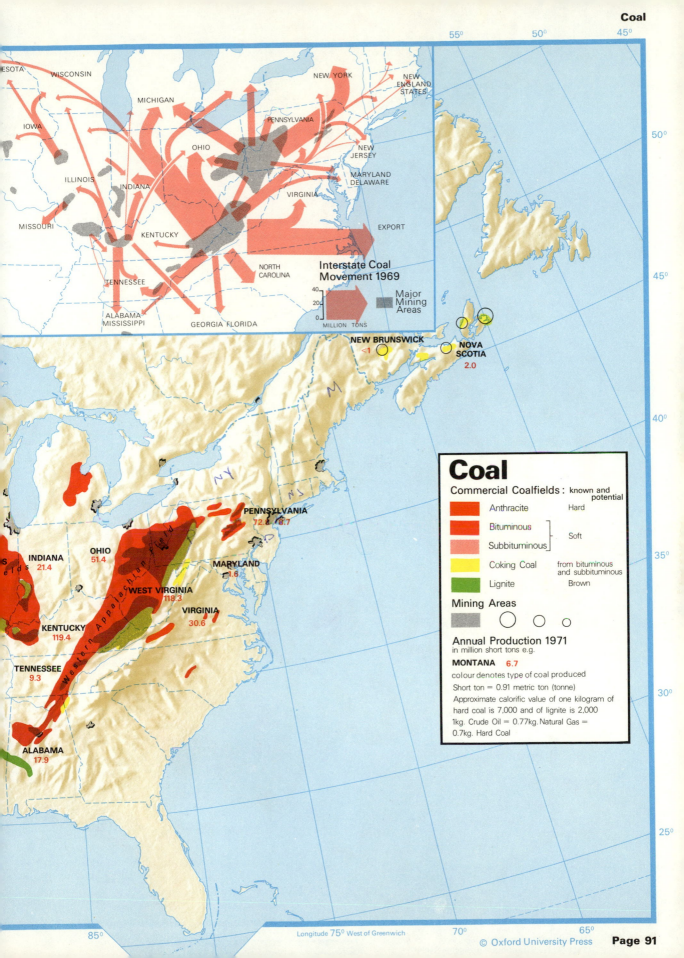

Coal

Commercial Coalfields: known and potential

- Anthracite — Hard
- Bituminous ⎤
- Subbituminous ⎦ Soft
- Coking Coal — from bituminous and subbituminous
- Lignite — Brown

Mining Areas
◯ ◯ ◯

Annual Production 1971
in million short tons e.g.

MONTANA 6.7

colour denotes type of coal produced

Short ton = 0.91 metric ton (tonne)

Approximate calorific value of one kilogram of hard coal is 7,000 and of lignite is 2,000

1kg. Crude Oil = 0.77kg. Natural Gas = 0.7kg. Hard Coal

Interstate Coal Movement 1969

40
20
0
MILLION TONS

◼ Major Mining Areas

NEW BRUNSWICK <1

NOVA SCOTIA 2.0

PENNSYLVANIA 72.0 8.7

OHIO 51.4

INDIANA 21.4

MARYLAND 1.6

WEST VIRGINIA 118.3

VIRGINIA 30.6

KENTUCKY 119.4

TENNESSEE 9.3

ALABAMA 17.9

Western Appalachian field

Conical Orthomorphic Projection
Origin 42°N; Standard Parallels 35° & 49°

Scale 1 inch to 250 miles 1:15.84 M

SCALE ONE INCH TO 800 MILES

BRITISH COLUMBIA
25 447

Taylor Flats

Prince
George

ALBERTA
338 403

ATHABASCA

Fort
McMurray

SASKATCHEWAN
89 486

MANITOBA
5 908

Pembina
Edmonton
Lloydminster

PRAIRIE

Vancouver
Kamloops
Sundre
Big
Valley
Saskatoon

Ferndale
Anacortes
Calgary

Kamsack

Everett
Tacoma

Moose Jaw
Regina

Spokane
Cut Bank
Dollard

Winnipeg

Portland

Great Falls
Chinook

MONTANA
37 879
Poplar

Williston

NORTH DAKOTA
21.998

Mosby

Bismarck

Billings

SOUTH DAKOTA
160

Minneapolis

Cody

WYOMING
160 345
Newcastle

*ROCKY
MOUNTAIN*

Sioux Falls

*GREEN
RIVER
BASIN*

Casper

Salt Lake
City
Sinclair
Fort Laramie

Sacramento
San Francisco

NEVADA
149

Scottsbluff

NEBRASKA
11 451

Des
Moines

Cheyenne

CALIFORNIA
Port San Luis
Obispo
(Marine
Terminal)

CALIFORNIA
372 191

Tonopah

UTAH
23 370

Grand Junction

Denver

COLORADO
24 723

Hanford

KANSAS
84 853

Phillipsburg

MISSOURI
66

Bakersfield

Shallow
Water

Kansas City

E. St

Los
Angeles

Red Mesa
Farmington

Wichita

Coffeyville

ARIZONA
1 784

Gallup

MID-CONTINENT

Ponca City
Enid

Tulsa

San Diego

Phoenix

NEW MEXICO
128 184

Amarillo

Borger

OKLAHOMA
223 574

Duncan

ARKANSAS
18 035

Little Rock

Ardmore

Tucson

Artesia

Dallas

El Paso

Odessa
Wink
Sweetwater
Big Spring
Corsicana

Haynesville
El Dor

Louisiana
906 907

TEXAS
1 249 667

Beaumont

Lake Charles

Prudhoe Bay

San Antonio

Houston

Port Arthur

Arctic Circle

Norman
Wells

Sweeny

Texas City

ALASKA
83 616

NORTHWEST
TERRITORIES
846

GULF COAST

Kenai
Valdez

Corpus
Christi

Prince George

La Blanca

135°

50°

45°

40°

35°

30°

95°

70° 160° 150° 140° 130°

55°

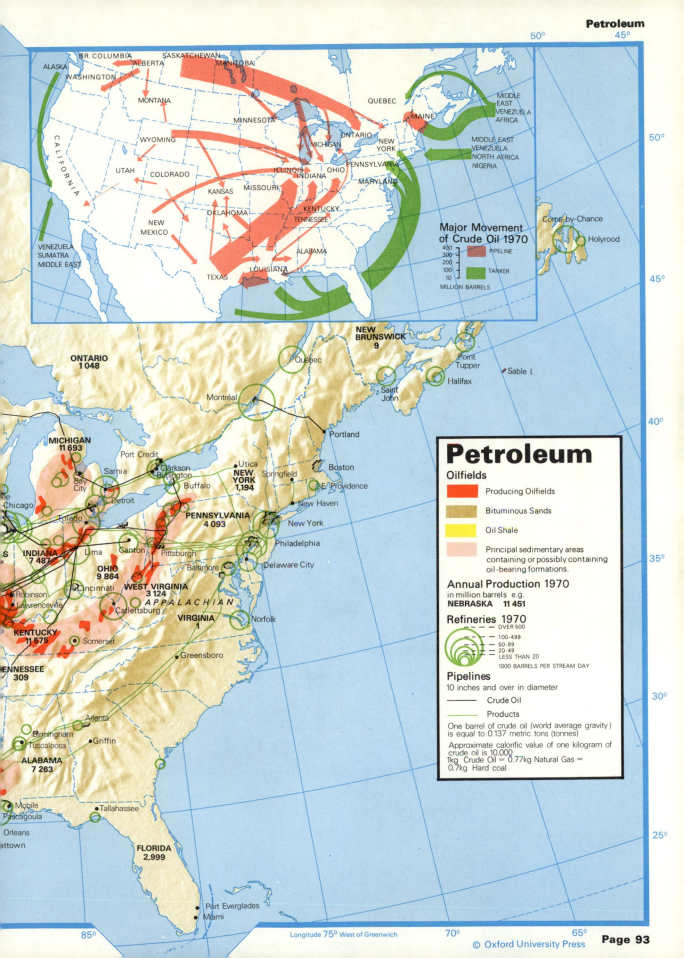

Major Movement of Crude Oil 1970

400
300
200
100
10
MILLION BARRELS

PIPELINE
TANKER

Petroleum

Oilfields

Producing Oilfields

Bituminous Sands

Oil Shale

Principal sedimentary areas containing or possibly containing oil-bearing formations.

Annual Production 1970

in million barrels e.g.
NEBRASKA 11 451

Refineries 1970

OVER 500
100-499
50-99
20-49
LESS THAN 20
1000 BARRELS PER STREAM DAY

Pipelines

10 inches and over in diameter

Crude Oil

Products

One barrel of crude oil (world average gravity) is equal to 0.137 metric tons (tonnes)
Approximate calorific value of one kilogram of crude oil is 10.000
1kg Crude Oil = 0.77kg Natural Gas = 0.7kg Hard coal

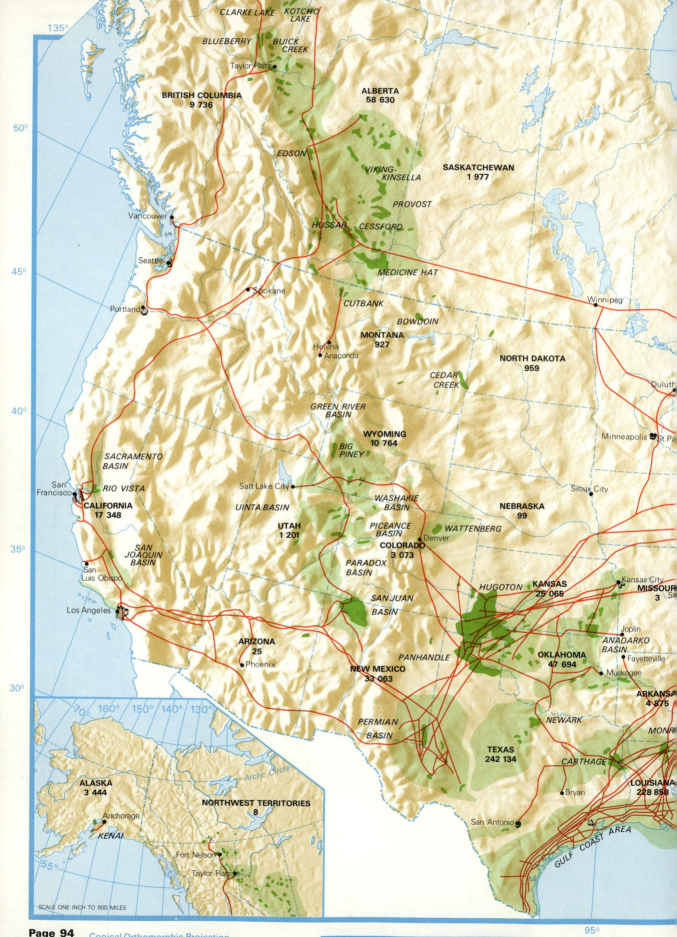

CLARKE LAKE   KOTCHO
                LAKE
BLUEBERRY   BUICK
              CREEK
Taylor Flats

BRITISH COLUMBIA
9 736

ALBERTA
58 630

EDSON

VIKING-
KINSELLA

SASKATCHEWAN
1 977

PROVOST

HUSSAR   CESSFORD

Vancouver

Seattle

MEDICINE HAT

Winnipeg

Spokane

CUTBANK

BOWDOIN

Portland

Helena
Anaconda

MONTANA
927

NORTH DAKOTA
959

Duluth

CEDAR
CREEK

GREEN RIVER
BASIN

Minneapolis St.Pa

SACRAMENTO
BASIN

WYOMING
10 764

BIG
PINEY

San
Francisco   RIO VISTA

Salt Lake City

WASHAKIE
BASIN

Sioux City

CALIFORNIA
17 348

UINTA BASIN

UTAH
1 201

PICEANCE
BASIN

NEBRASKA
99

WATTENBERG

Denver

COLORADO
3 073

San
Luis Obispo

SAN
JOAQUIN
BASIN

PARADOX
BASIN

HUGOTON

KANSAS
25 065

Kansas City

MISSOUR
3

Los Angeles

SAN JUAN
BASIN

Joplin

ANADARKO
BASIN

Fayetteville

ARIZONA
25

OKLAHOMA
47 694

Phoenix

PANHANDLE

Muskogee

ARKANSA
4 875

NEW MEXICO
33 063

NEWARK

MONR

PERMIAN
BASIN

TEXAS
242 134

CARTHAGE

LOUISIANA
228 858

Bryan

ALASKA
3 444

NORTHWEST TERRITORIES
8

Arctic Circle

San Antonio

Anchorage

KENAI

GULF COAST AREA

Fort Nelson

Taylor Flats

SCALE ONE INCH TO 800 MILES

Conical Orthomorphic Projection
Origin 42° N· Standard Parallels 35° & 49°

Scale 1 inch to 250 miles   1:15.84M

50° 45°

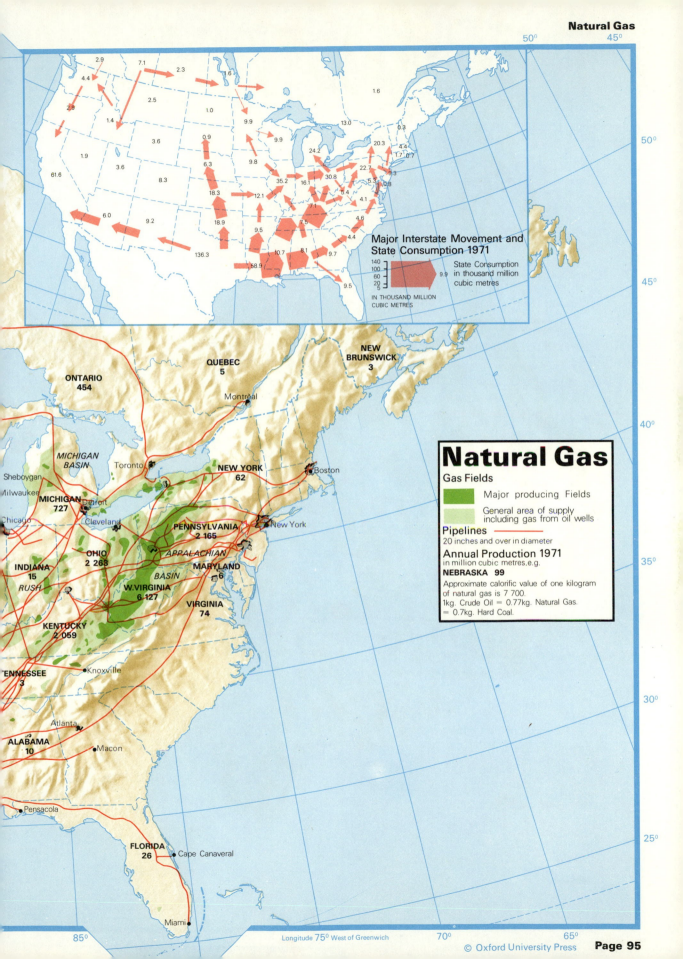

Major Interstate Movement and State Consumption 1971

2.9
7.1
2.3
.6
4.4
2.9
2.5
1.0
1.6
1.4
9.9
13.0
0.3
3.6
9.9
24.2
20.3
4.4
1.9
0.9
9.8
35.2
22.7
1.7 0.7
61.6
3.6
6.3
16.1
30.8
5.3 9.3
8.3
18.3
12.1
5.4 0.8
6.0
9.2
7.1
4.1
18.9
9.5
7.5
4.6
136.3
10.7
8.1
9.7
4.4
58.9
9.5

140
100
60
20
5

IN THOUSAND MILLION
CUBIC METRES

9.9 — State Consumption in thousand million cubic metres

QUEBEC 5

NEW BRUNSWICK 3

ONTARIO 454

Montreal

MICHIGAN BASIN

Toronto

Sheboygan
Milwaukee

MICHIGAN 727 Detroit

NEW YORK 62

Boston

Chicago

Cleveland

PENNSYLVANIA 2 165

New York

OHIO 2 268

APPALACHIAN

INDIANA 15

RUSH

MARYLAND 6

BASIN

W.VIRGINIA 6 127

VIRGINIA 74

KENTUCKY 2 059

Knoxville

ENNESSEE 3

Atlanta

ALABAMA 10

Macon

Pensacola

FLORIDA 26 Cape Canaveral

Miami

Natural Gas

Gas Fields

■ Major producing Fields

■ General area of supply including gas from oil wells

Pipelines

— 20 inches and over in diameter

Annual Production 1971

in million cubic metres, e.g.

NEBRASKA 99

Approximate calorific value of one kilogram of natural gas is 7 700.
1kg. Crude Oil = 0.77kg. Natural Gas.
= 0.7kg. Hard Coal.

85° 40° 50° 35° 30° 25°

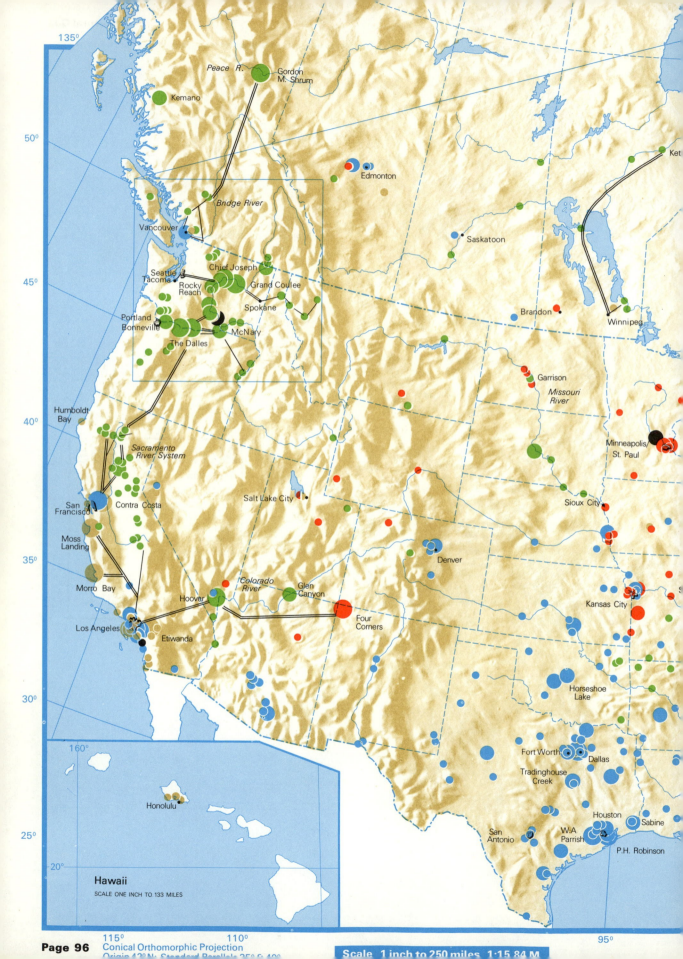

Peace R.
Gordon M. Shrum
Kemano

Edmonton
Ket

Bridge River
Vancouver
Saskatoon

Chief Joseph
Seattle
Tacoma
Rocky Reach
Grand Coulee
Spokane
Brandon
Winnipeg

Portland
Bonneville
McNary
The Dalles

Garrison
Missouri River

Humboldt Bay

Sacramento River System
Minneapolis/ St. Paul

San Francisco
Contra Costa
Salt Lake City
Sioux City

Moss Landing

Denver
Kansas City

Morro Bay
Colorado River
Glen Canyon
Hoover
Four Corners

Los Angeles
Etiwanda

Horseshoe Lake

Fort Worth
Dallas

Tradinghouse Creek

Honolulu

Houston
Sabine
San Antonio
W.A Parrish
P.H. Robinson

Hawaii
SCALE ONE INCH TO 133 MILES

Conical Orthomorphic Projection
Origin 42° N. Standard Parallels 25° & 40°
Scale 1 inch to 250 miles 1:15.84 M

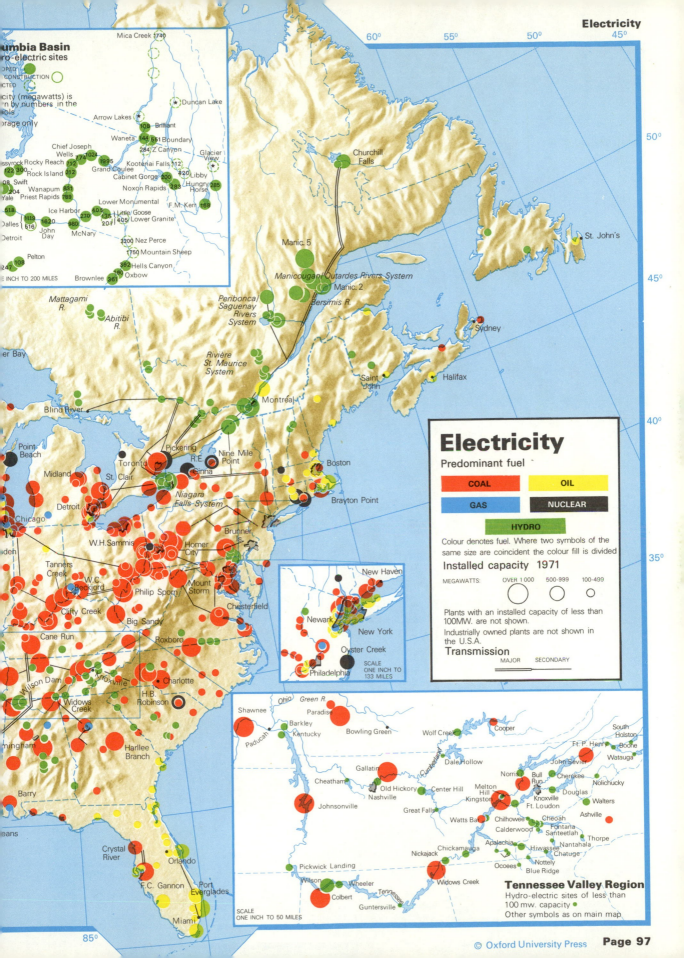

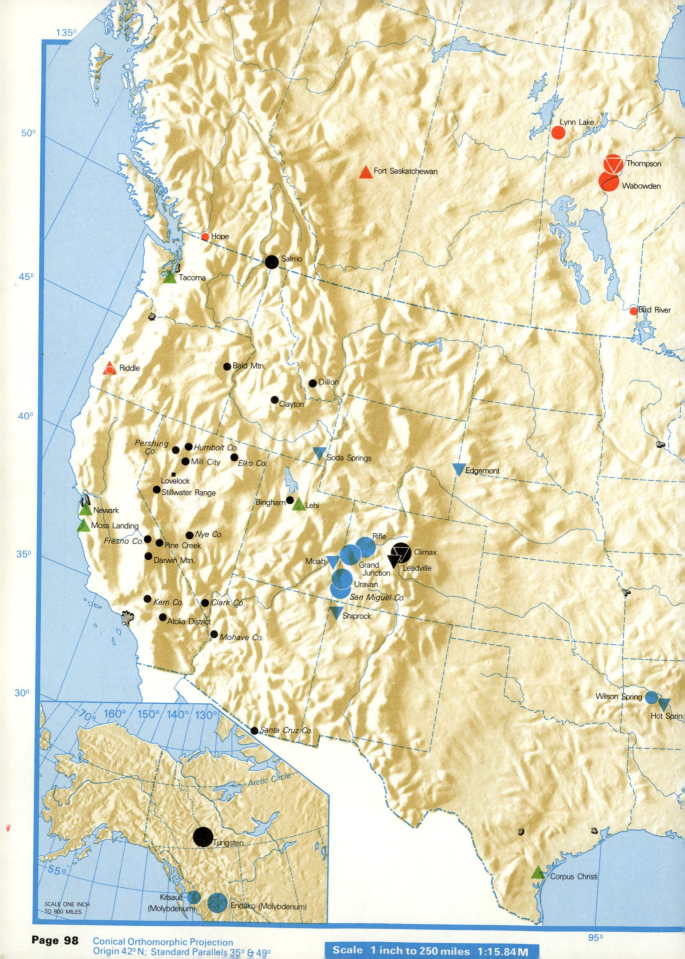

50°

Lynn Lake

Thompson

Wabowden

Fort Saskatchewan

Hope

45°

Salmo

Tacoma

Bird River

Riddle

Bald Mtn.

Dillon

40°

Clayton

Pershing Co.

Humbolt Co.

Mill City

Soda Springs

Edgemont

Elko Co.

Lovelock

Stillwater Range

Newark

Bingham

Lehi

Moss Landing

Nye Co.

Rifle

Climax

Fresno Co.

Pine Creek

Moab

Grand Junction

Leadville

35°

Darwin Mtn.

Uravan

San Miguel Co.

Kern Co.

Clark Co.

Atolia District

Shiprock

Mohave Co.

30°

Wilson Spring

Hot Sprin

70°

160°

150°

140°

130°

Santa Cruz Co.

Arctic Circle

55°

Tungsten

SCALE ONE INCH
TO 800 MILES

Kitsault
(Molybdenum)

Endako (Molybdenum)

Corpus Christi

Page 98 Conical Orthomorphic Projection
Origin 42°N; Standard Parallels 35° & 49°

Scale 1 inch to 250 miles 1:15.84M

95°

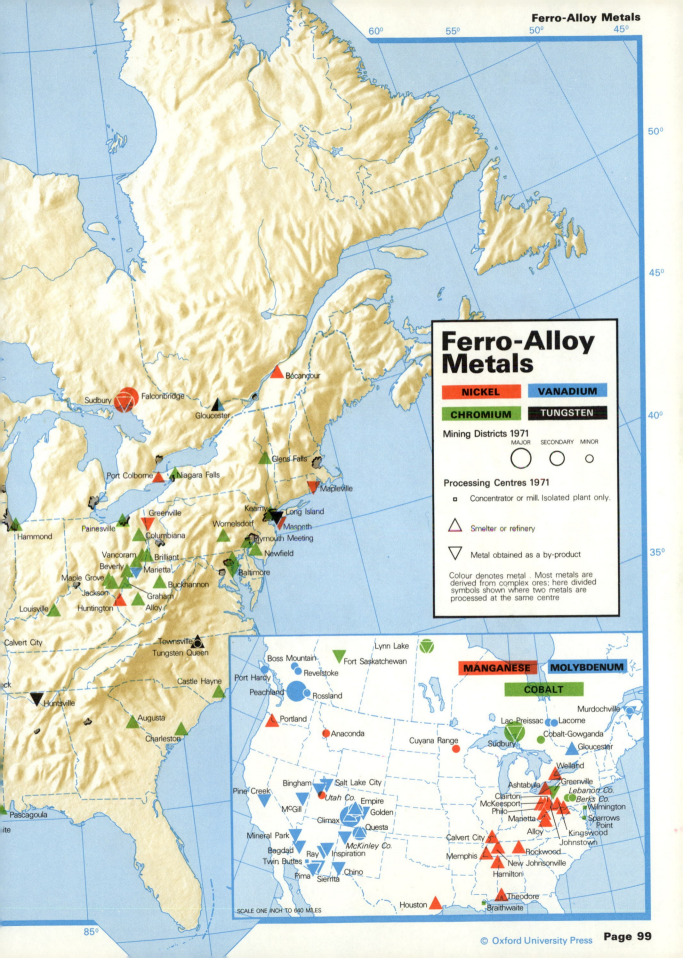

Ferro-Alloy Metals

NICKEL   **VANADIUM**
CHROMIUM   **TUNGSTEN**

Mining Districts 1971

MAJOR   SECONDARY   MINOR

Processing Centres 1971

Concentrator or mill. Isolated plant only.

Smelter or refinery

Metal obtained as a by-product

Colour denotes metal . Most metals are
derived from complex ores; here divided
symbols shown where two metals are
processed at the same centre

Sudbury   Falconbridge

Bécancour

Gloucester

Glens Falls

Port Colborne   Niagara Falls

Mapleville

Greenville   Kearny   Long Island

Painesville   Womelsdorf   Maspeth

Columbiana   Plymouth Meeting

Hammond   Newfield

Vancoram   Brilliant   Baltimore

Beverly   Marietta

Maple Grove   Buckhannon

Jackson   Graham

Louisville   Huntington   Alloy

Townsville
Tungsten Queen

Calvert City   Castle Hayne

Huntsville

Augusta

Charleston

Pascagoula

MANGANESE   **MOLYBDENUM**
COBALT

Lynn Lake   Murdochville

Boss Mountain   Fort Saskatchewan

Port Hardy   Revelstoke   Lac Preissac   Lacorne

Peachland   Rossland   Cobalt-Gowganda

Sudbury   Gloucester

Portland   Welland

Anaconda   Cuyana Range   Ashtabula   Greenville

Lebanon Co.

Clairton   Berks Co.

Bingham   Salt Lake City   McKeesport   Wilmington

Pine Creek   Utah Co.   Philo   Sparrows
    Empire   Marietta   Point

McGill   Golden   Alloy   Kingswood

Climax   Questa   Johnstown

Calvert City   Rockwood

Mineral Park   McKinley Co.   Memphis

Bagdad   Inspiration   New Johnsonville

Twin Buttes   Ray   Hamilton

Pima   Chino

Sierrita   Houston   Theodore

Braithwaite

SCALE ONE INCH TO 640 MILES

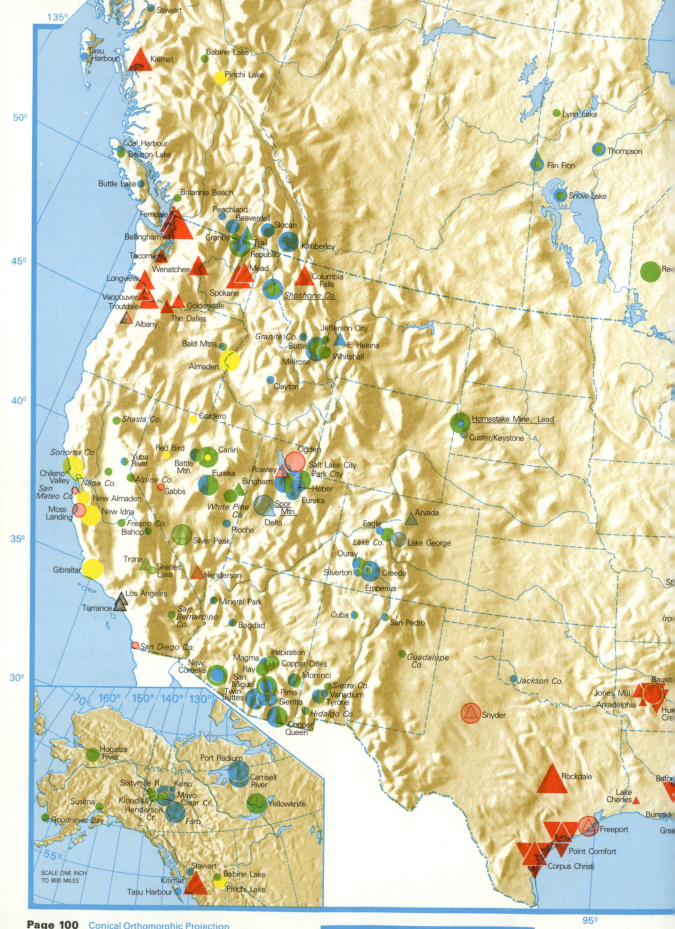

Stewart

Tasu
Harbour
Kitimat

Babine Lake

Pinchi Lake

Lynn Lake

Thompson

Flin Flon

Snow Lake

Coal Harbour
Benson Lake

Buttle Lake

Britannia Beach

Peachland
Beaverdell

Ferndale

Bellingham

Tacoma

Longview

Vancouver
Troutdale

Albany

Wenatchee

Granby
Slocan
Trail
Republic
Mead

Kimberley

Columbia
Falls
Shoshone Co.

Goldendale
The Dalles

Spokane

Bald Mtns.

Almaden

Granite Co.

Butte
Melrose

Whitehall

Jefferson City
E. Helena

Clayton

Shasta Co.

Cordero

Sonoma Co.

Chileno
Valley

San
Mateo Co.

Moss
Landing

Napa Co.

New Almaden

New Idria

Fresno Co.
Bishop

Yuba
River

Red Bird

Battle
Mtn.

Alpine Co.
Gabbs

Carlin

Eureka

Rowley

Bingham

White Pine
Co.

Pioche

Silver Peak

Ogden

Salt Lake City
Park City

Heber
Eureka

Spor
Mtn.
Delta

Homestake Mine, Lead

Custer/Keystone

Arvada

Eagle

Lake Co.
Lake George

Trona

Gibraltar

Searles
Lake

Henderson

Ouray

Silverton
Creede

Emperius

Los Angeles

Torrance

San
Bernardino
Co.

Mineral Park

Bagdad

Cuba

San Pedro

Guadalupe
Co.

San Diego Co.

New
Cornelia

Magma
Ray
San
Miguel
Twin
Buttes

Inspiration
Copper Cities
Morenci

Pima
Sierrita

Sierra Co.
Vanadium
Tyrone

Hidalgo Co.

Copper
Queen

Jackson Co.

Snyder

Bauxit

Jones Mill
Arkadelphia

Hu
Cre

Rockdale

Lake
Charles

Bator

Bumsid

Freeport

Point Comfort

Corpus Christi

Hogatza
River

Port Radium

Camsell
River

Sixtymile R
Keno
Mayo
Clear Cr.

Yellowknife

Susitna

Klondika
Henderson
Cr.

Faro

Goodnews Bay

Stewart

Kitimat

Tasu Harbour

Babine Lake

Pinchi Lake

SCALE ONE INCH
TO 800 MILES

Page 100 Conical Orthomorphic Projection
Origin 42° N; Standard Parallels 35° & 49°

Scale 1 inch to 250 miles 1:15.84 M

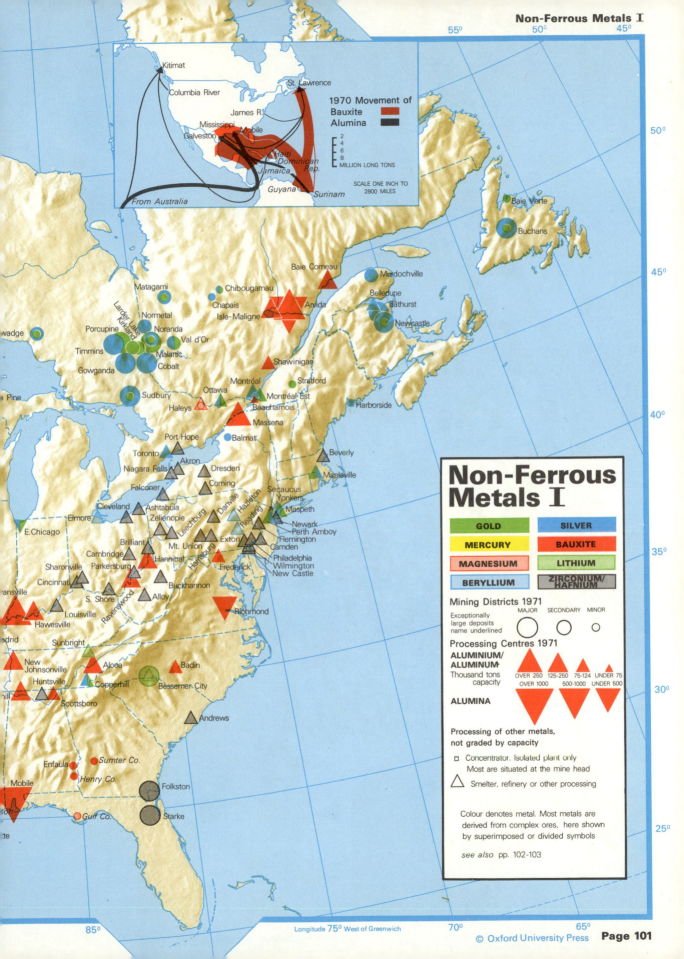

1970 Movement of Bauxite Alumina

2
4
6
8
MILLION LONG TONS

SCALE ONE INCH TO 2800 MILES

From Australia

Non-Ferrous Metals I

GOLD	SILVER
MERCURY	BAUXITE
MAGNESIUM	LITHIUM
BERYLLIUM	ZIRCONIUM/ HAFNIUM

Mining Districts 1971

Exceptionally large deposits name underlined

MAJOR   SECONDARY   MINOR

Processing Centres 1971

ALUMINIUM/ ALUMINUM
Thousand tons capacity

OVER 250   125-250   75-124   UNDER 75
OVER 1000   500-1000   UNDER 500

ALUMINA

Processing of other metals, not graded by capacity

▢   Concentrator. Isolated plant only
    Most are situated at the mine head

△   Smelter, refinery or other processing

Colour denotes metal. Most metals are derived from complex ores, here shown by superimposed or divided symbols

see also pp. 102-103

Map labels:

Kitimat
Columbia River
St. Lawrence
James R.
Mississippi
Galveston
Mobile
Haiti
Dominican Rep.
Jamaica
Guyana
Surinam

Baie Verte
Buchans

Matagami
Chibougamau
Chapais
Isle-Maligne
Anvida
Murdochville
Belledune
Bathurst
Newcastle
Baie Comeau

Larder Lake
Kirkland
Normetal
Porcupine
Noranda
Val d'Or
Timmins
Malartic
Gowganda
Cobalt
Sudbury
Shawinigan
Ottawa
Haleys
Stratford
Montréal
Montréal Est
Beauharnois
Massena
Harborside
Port Hope
Balmat
Beverly
Toronto
Akron
Dresden
Mapleville
Niagara Falls
Corning
Falconer
Secaucus
Yonkers
Cleveland
Ashtabula
Zelienople
Maspeth
Elmore
Leechburg
Danville
Hazleton
Newark
Perth Amboy
E.Chicago
Reading
Flemington
Brilliant
Mt. Union
Exton
Camden
Cambridge
Harrisburg
Philadelphia
Sharonville
Parkersburg
Hannibal
Frederick
Wilmington
New Castle
Cincinnati
Buckhannon
S. Shore
Alloy
Ravenswood
Louisville
Hawesville
Richmond
Sunbright
New Johnsonville
Alcoa
Badin
Huntsville
Copperhill
Bessemer City
Scottsboro
Andrews
Enfaula
Sumter Co.
Henry Co.
Folkston
Mobile
Gulf Co.
Starke
Larder Lake
wadge
Pine

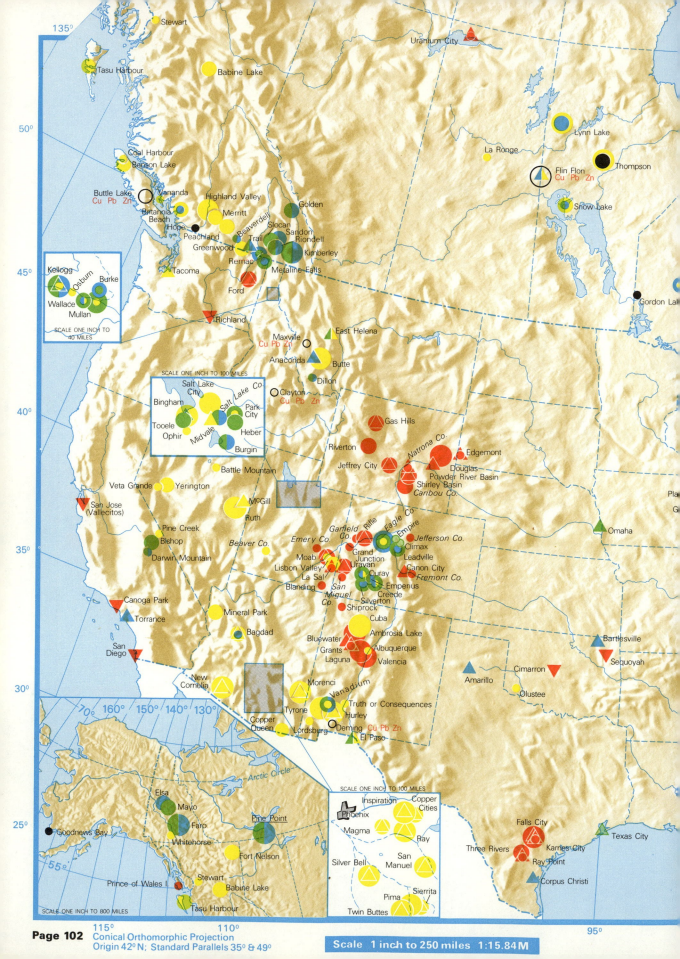

Conical Orthomorphic Projection
Origin 42° N; Standard Parallels 35° & 49°

Scale 1 inch to 250 miles 1:15.84M

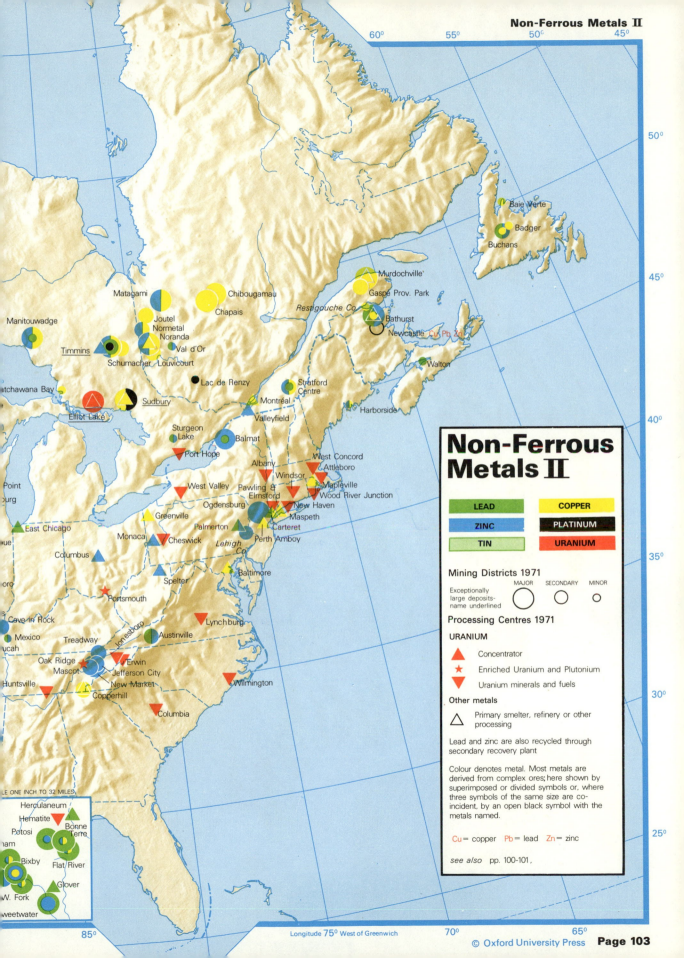

Matagami
Chibougamau
Chapais
Joutel
Normetal
Noranda
Val d'Or
Schumacher
Louvicourt
Manitouwadge
Timmins
Lac de Renzy
tchawana Bay
Sudbury
Elliot Lake
Sturgeon Lake
Port Hope
Balmat
Stratford Centre
Montréal
Valleyfield
Murdochville
Gaspé Prov. Park
Restigouche Co
Bathurst
Newcastle Cu Pb Zn
Walton
Harborside
Baie Verte
Badger
Buchans

Albany
West Concord
Attleboro
Windsor
Mapleville
Point
burg
West Valley
Pawling & Elmsford
Wood River Junction
Ogdensburg
New Haven
Maspeth
East Chicago
Greenville
Palmerton
Carteret
Monaca
Cheswick
Perth Amboy
Columbus
Spelter
Lehigh Co
Baltimore
oro
Portsmouth
Cave in Rock
Lynchburg
Mexico
Treadway
Jonesboro
Austinville
ucah
Oak Ridge
Erwin
Huntsville
Mascot
Jefferson City
New Market
Wilmington
Copperhill
Columbia

Herculaneum
Hematite
Bonne Terre
Potosi
ham
Bixby
Flat/River
Glover
W. Fork
weetwater

Non-Ferrous Metals II

LEAD	COPPER
ZINC	PLATINUM
TIN	URANIUM

Mining Districts 1971

Exceptionally large deposits-name underlined

MAJOR SECONDARY MINOR

Processing Centres 1971

URANIUM

▲ Concentrator

★ Enriched Uranium and Plutonium

▼ Uranium minerals and fuels

Other metals

△ Primary smelter, refinery or other processing

Lead and zinc are also recycled through secondary recovery plant

Colour denotes metal. Most metals are derived from complex ores; here shown by superimposed or divided symbols or, where three symbols of the same size are co-incident, by an open black symbol with the metals named.

Cu = copper Pb = lead Zn = zinc

see also pp. 100-101,

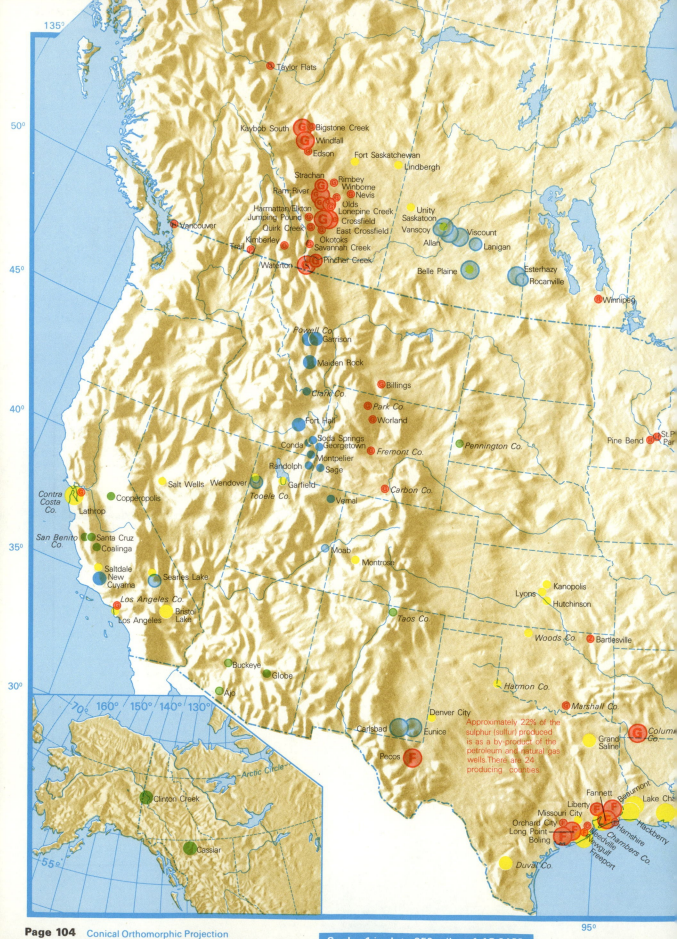

Taylor Flats

Kaybob South G Bigstone Creek
G Windfall
G Edson
Fort Saskatchewan
Lindbergh

Strachan Rimbey
Ram River Winborne
G Nevis
Olds
Harmattan/Elkton Lonepine Creek
Jumping Pound Crossfield
Quirk Creek East Crossfield
Vancouver Okotoks
Kimberley Savannah Creek
Trail Waterton G Pincher Creek

Unity
Saskatoon
Vanscoy
Allan Viscount
Lanigan

Belle Plaine
Esterhazy
Rocanville

Winnipeg

Powell Co.
Garrison

Maiden Rock

Clark Co.

Billings

Park Co.
Worland

Fort Hall

Soda Springs
Conda Georgetown
Montpelier
Randolph Sage

Fremont Co.

Pennington Co.

Pine Bend St.P
Par

Salt Wells Wendover Garfield

Tooele Co.

Vernal

Carbon Co.

Contra
Costa
Co.
Lathrop

Copperopolis

San Benito Santa Cruz
Co. Coalinga

Saltdale
New
Cuyama

Searles Lake

Los Angeles Co.
Los Angeles Bristol
Lake

Moab

Montrose

Taos Co.

Lyons Kanopolis
Hutchinson

Buckeye
Globe

Ajo

Woods Co.

Bartlesville

Harmon Co.

Marshall Co.

Denver City

Carlsbad
Eunice

Pecos F

Approximately 22% of the
sulphur (sulfur) produced
is as a by-product of the
petroleum and natural gas
wells. There are 24
producing counties.

Grand
Saline

Colum
Co. G

Fannett Beaumont
Liberty F F Lake Cha
Missouri City
Orchard City F Hamshire
Long Point F Hackberry
Boling F Needville Chambers Co.
Newgulf
Freeport

Duval Co.

Clinton Creek

Cassiar

Arctic Circle

70° 160° 150° 140° 130°

Scale 1 inch to 250 miles 1:15.84M

95°

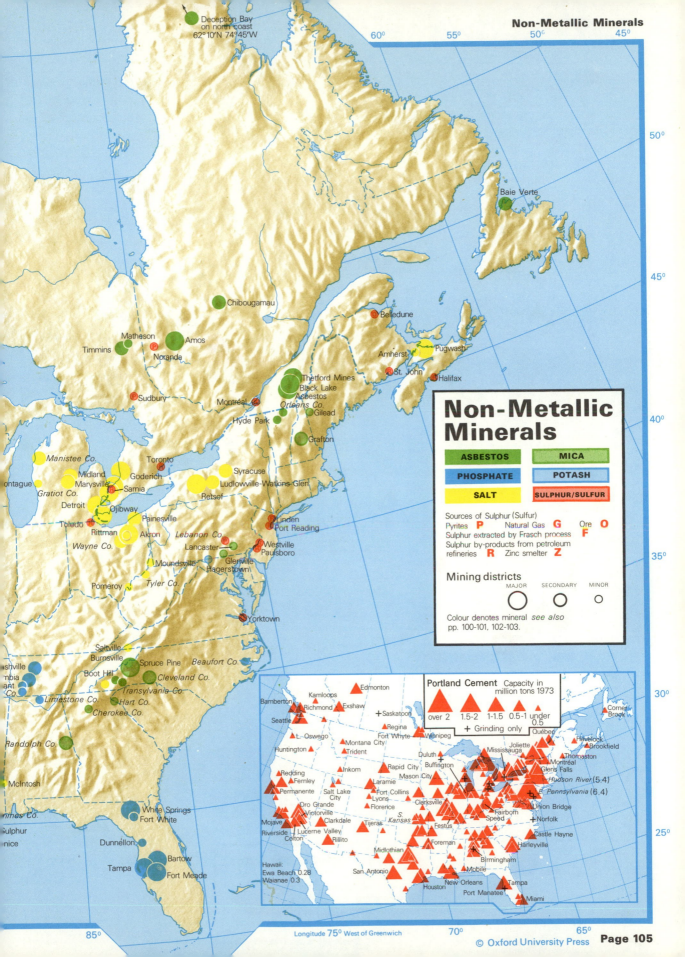

Deception Bay
on north coast
62°10'N 74°45'W

Baie Verte

Chibougamau

Belledune

Matheson
Timmins
Amos
Noranda
Pugwash
Amherst
St. John
Halifax

Thetford Mines
Black Lake
Asbestos
Sudbury
Montréal
Orleans Co.
Gilead
Hyde Park
Grafton

Manistee Co.
Toronto
Syracuse
Midland
Marysville
Goderich
Sarnia
Ludlowville-Watkins Glen
ontague
Gratiot Co.
Detroit
Retsof
Ojibway
Painesville
Linden
Port Reading
Toledo
Rittman
Akron
Lebanon Co.
Lancaster
Westville
Paulsboro
Wayne Co.
Moundsville
Glenville
Hagerstown
Pomeroy
Tyler Co.

Yorktown

Saltville
Burnsville
Spruce Pine
Beaufort Co.
shville
Boot Hill
Cleveland Co.
mbia
ant
Co.
Transylvania Co.
Limestone Co.
Hart Co.
Cherokee Co.

Randolph Co.

McIntosh

nes Co.
White Springs
Fort White
ulphur
nice
Dunnellon
Bartow
Tampa
Fort Meade

Non-Metallic Minerals

ASBESTOS	MICA
PHOSPHATE	POTASH
SALT	SULPHUR/SULFUR

Sources of Sulphur (Sulfur)
Pyrites **P**   Natural Gas **G**   Ore **O**
Sulphur extracted by Frasch process **F**
Sulphur by-products from petroleum
refineries **R**   Zinc smelter **Z**

Mining districts

MAJOR   SECONDARY   MINOR

Colour denotes mineral *see also*
pp. 100-101, 102-103.

Portland Cement Capacity in million tons 1973

over 2   1.5-2   1-1.5   0.5-1   under 0.5
+ Grinding only

Edmonton
Kamloops
Bamberton
Richmond
Exshaw
Saskatoon
Corner
Brook
Seattle
Regina
Fort Whyte
Winnipeg
Québec
Havelock
L. Oswego
Montana City
Duluth
Joliette
Mississauga
Brookfield
Thomaston
Montréal
Glen's Falls
Huntington
Trident
Buffington
Hudson River (5.4)
Redding
Rapid City
Mason City
E. Pennsylvania (6.4)
Fernley
Inkom
Laramie
Clarksville
Union Bridge
Permanente
Salt Lake City
Fort Collins
Lyons
Fairborn
Speed
Norfolk
Oro Grande
Florence
S. Kansas
Victorville
Clarkdale
Tijeras
Festus
Castle Hayne
Mojave
Lucerne Valley
Harleyville
Riverside
Colton
Rillito
Foreman
Midlothian
Birmingham
Mobile
San Antonio
Tampa
New Orleans
Port Manatee
Houston
Miami

Hawaii:
Ewa Beach 0.28
Waianae 0.3

Marquette Range

Ishpeming Negaunee
Tilden Township Palmer

SCALE ONE INCH TO 47 MILES

Tasu Harbour

JAPAN

Texada I.
Port Coquitlam (I)
Vancouver North Surrey
Victoria

Trail Kimberley
(blast furnace uses
by-product ore)

Seattle

Portland

McMinnville

Edmonton

Flin Flon

Calgary Forest Lawn

Regina

Selkirk (I)
Transcona

Br

Weiser

Lowman

Radersburg

SCALE ONE
INCH TO
47 MILES

Buhl Mountain
Iron
Kelly
Lake
Nashwauk Virginia Babbitt
Taconite Aurora
Eveleth Hoyt
Coleraine Chisholm Lakes
Keewatin Hibbing

Mesabi Range

Steep Rock
Lake

Tac
Ha

Two Harbors
Crosby Duluth

SCALE ONE INCH TO 67 MILES

Morton S. Chicago
Grove Chicago
Lemont Burns
Harbor
E. Chicago
Chicago Heights Gary (Q)

St. P

Black
River
Falls

Emeryville
Union City

Douglas
Co. Wabuska

Eureka
Co.

Geneva

Atlantic City

Sunrise

Albany Co.

Norfolk

Wil

Cedar City

Pitkin Co.

Kansas City

Alto

Granite

Sullivan

Iror

Kern
Co.
Los Angeles
Torrance
Long Beach Fontana
Etiwanda

Eagle Mt.

Pueblo

Tempe

Pampa

Sand Springs

Newport

Socorro Co.

El Paso

Morris Co.
Lone
Star Magnolia

Fort Worth
Midlothian

Longview Ja

Nacogdochee
Co.

160°

Ewa

Houston
Seguin Baytown

New

A

Hawaii

Hawaii

SCALE ONE INCH TO 133 MILES

Iron Ore Flow 1970

75
60
45
30
15
Million tons

Conical Orthomorphic Projection
Origin 42° N; Standard Parallels 35° & 49°

Scale 1 inch to 250 miles 1:15·84 M

135°

50°

45°

40°

35°

30°

25°

20°

115° 110° 95°

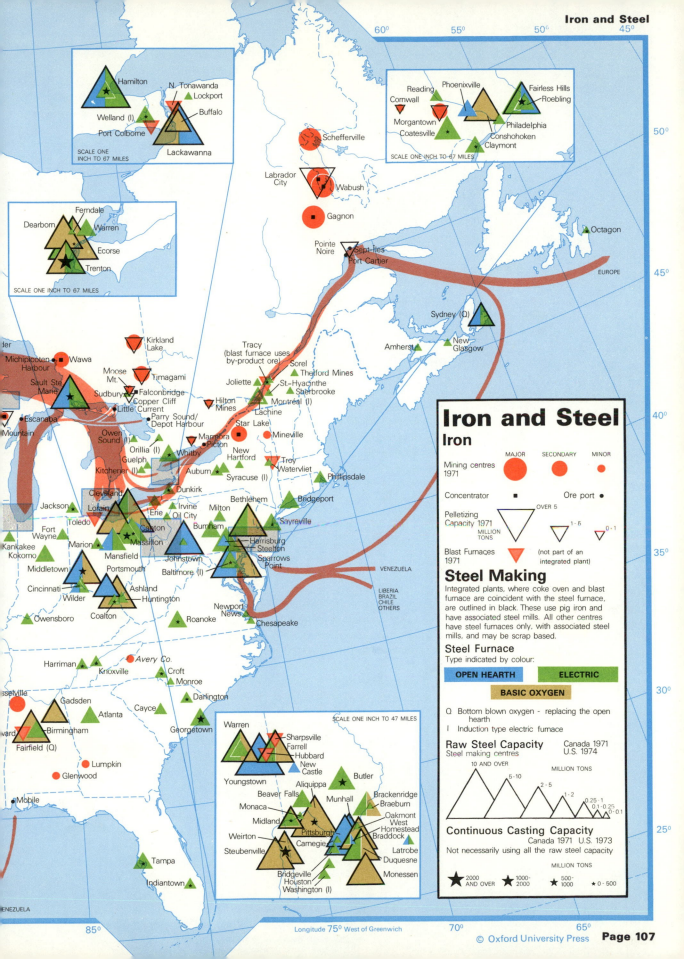

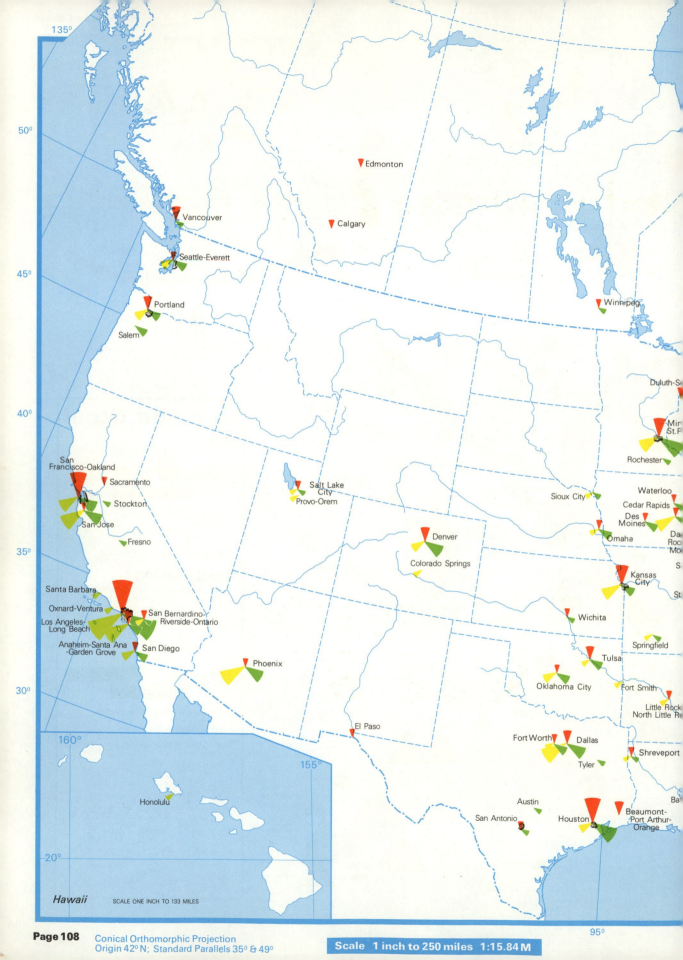

135°
50°
45°
40°
35°
30°

Edmonton

Vancouver

Calgary

Seattle-Everett

Winnipeg

Portland

Salem

Duluth-S

San
Francisco-Oakland

Sacramento

Salt Lake
City
Provo-Orem

Sioux City

Stockton

Min
St. P

San Jose

Rochester

Denver

Fresno

Waterloo
Cedar Rapids
Des
Moines

Santa Barbara

Colorado Springs

Omaha

Da
Roc
Mo

Oxnard-Ventura
Los Angeles-
Long Beach

San Bernardino-
Riverside-Ontario

Kansas
City

St

Anaheim-Santa Ana
-Garden Grove

San Diego

Wichita

Springfield

Phoenix

Tulsa

Oklahoma City

Fort Smith

Little Rock
North Little R

El Paso

Fort Worth

Dallas

Shreveport

Tyler

160°

155°

Ba

Austin

Honolulu

San Antonio

Houston

Beaumont-
Port Arthur-
Orange

20°

Hawaii   SCALE ONE INCH TO 133 MILES

Conical Orthomorphic Projection
Origin 42° N; Standard Parallels 35° & 49°   **Scale 1 inch to 250 miles 1:15.84 M**

95°

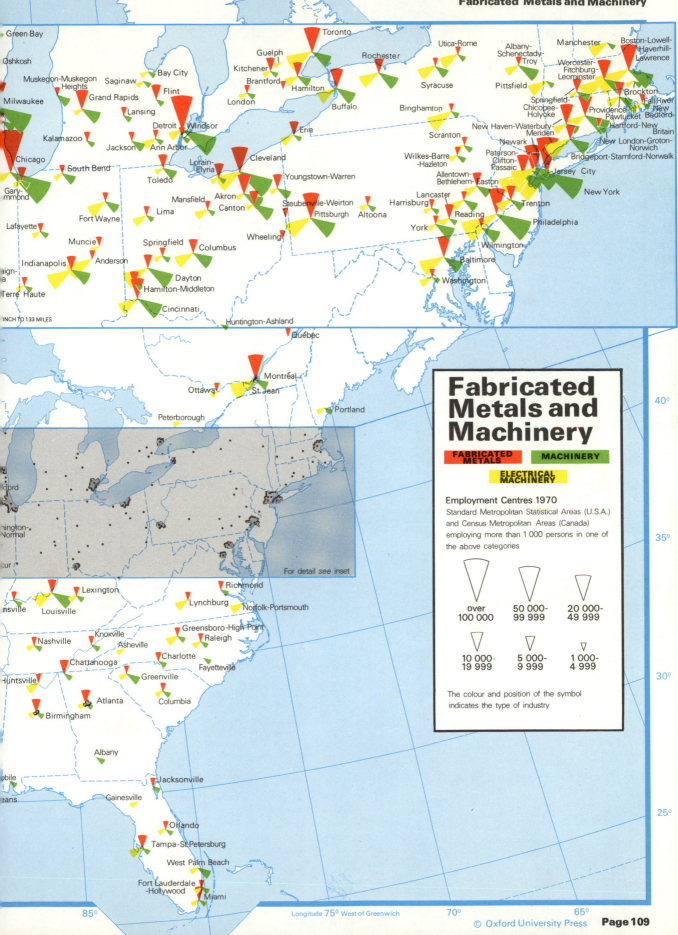

Green Bay
Oshkosh
Muskegon-Muskegon Heights
Saginaw
Bay City
Milwaukee
Grand Rapids
Flint
Lansing
Kalamazoo
Jackson
Ann Arbor
Detroit
Windsor
Chicago
South Bend
Gary-Hammond
Lorain-Elyria
Toledo
Cleveland
Lafayette
Fort Wayne
Mansfield
Akron
Canton
Youngstown-Warren
Lima
Muncie
Springfield
Columbus
Steubenville-Weirton
Pittsburgh
Altoona
Indianapolis
Anderson
Dayton
Wheeling
Champaign-a
Terre Haute
Hamilton-Middleton
Cincinnati
Huntington-Ashland

Toronto
Guelph
Kitchener
Brantford
London
Hamilton
Rochester
Buffalo
Erie
Utica-Rome
Syracuse
Binghamton
Scranton
Wilkes-Barre-Hazleton
Allentown-Bethlehem-Easton
Harrisburg
Lancaster
Reading
York
Wilmington
Baltimore
Washington

Albany-Schenectady-Troy
Pittsfield
Manchester
Boston-Lowell-Haverhill-Lawrence
Worcester-Fitchburg-Leominster
Brockton
Springfield-Chicopee-Holyoke
Providence
Pawtucket
Fall River
New Bedford
Hartford-New
New Haven-Waterbury-Meriden
New London-Groton-Norwich
Newark
Paterson-Clifton-Passaic
Bridgeport-Stamford-Norwalk
Jersey City
New York
Trenton
Philadelphia

INCH TO 133 MILES

Québec
Montréal
Ottawa
St. Jean
Peterborough
Portland

For detail *see* inset

Richmond
Lexington
Louisville
Lynchburg
Norfolk-Portsmouth
Nashville
Knoxville
Asheville
Greensboro-High Point
Raleigh
Chattanooga
Charlotte
Fayetteville
Huntsville
Greenville
Atlanta
Columbia
Birmingham
Albany
Mobile
Jacksonville
Gainesville
Orleans
Orlando
Tampa-St.Petersburg
West Palm Beach
Fort Lauderdale-Hollywood
Miami

ford
mington-Normal
tur
nsville

Fabricated Metals and Machinery

FABRICATED METALS   **MACHINERY**
ELECTRICAL MACHINERY

Employment Centres 1970
Standard Metropolitan Statistical Areas (U.S.A.)
and Census Metropolitan Areas (Canada)
employing more than 1 000 persons in one of
the above categories

over 100 000
50 000-99 999
20 000-49 999
10 000-19 999
5 000-9 999
1 000-4 999

The colour and position of the symbol
indicates the type of industry

40°
35°
30°
25°

Longitude 75° West of Greenwich   70°   65°
85°

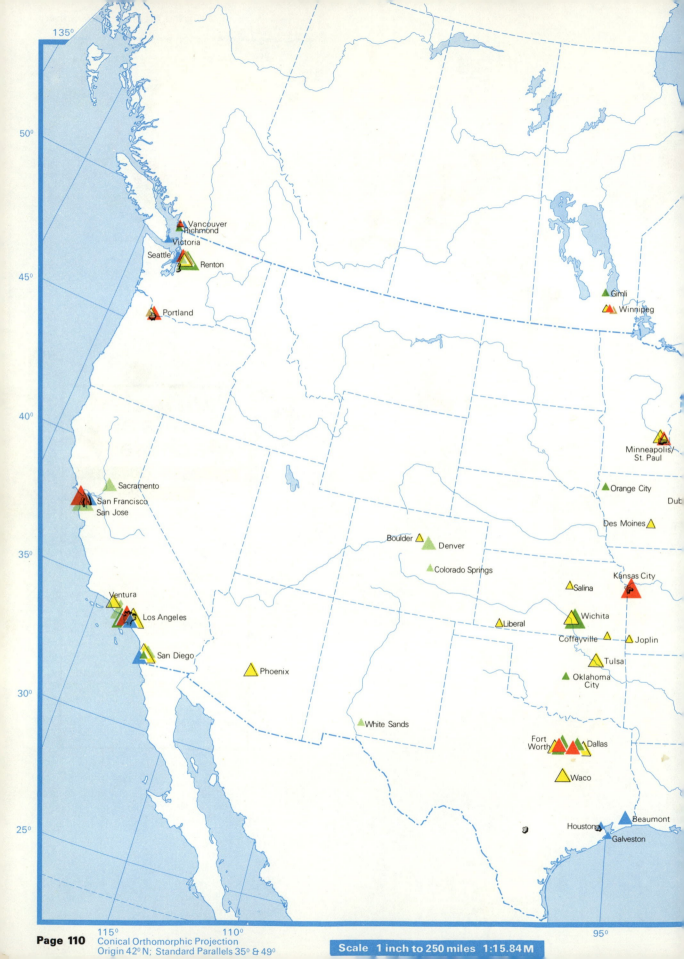

135°
50°
45°
40°
35°
30°
25°
115°
110°
95°

Vancouver
Richmond
Victoria
Seattle
Renton
Portland

Gimli
Winnipeg

Minneapolis/
St. Paul

Orange City
Dub

Des Moines

Sacramento
San Francisco
San Jose

Boulder
Denver

Colorado Springs

Kansas City

Salina

Wichita

Liberal

Coffeyville
Joplin

Tulsa

Ventura
Los Angeles

San Diego

Phoenix

Oklahoma
City

White Sands

Fort
Worth
Dallas

Waco

Houston
Beaumont
Galveston

Conical Orthomorphic Projection
Origin 42° N; Standard Parallels 35° & 49°

Scale 1 inch to 250 miles 1:15.84 M

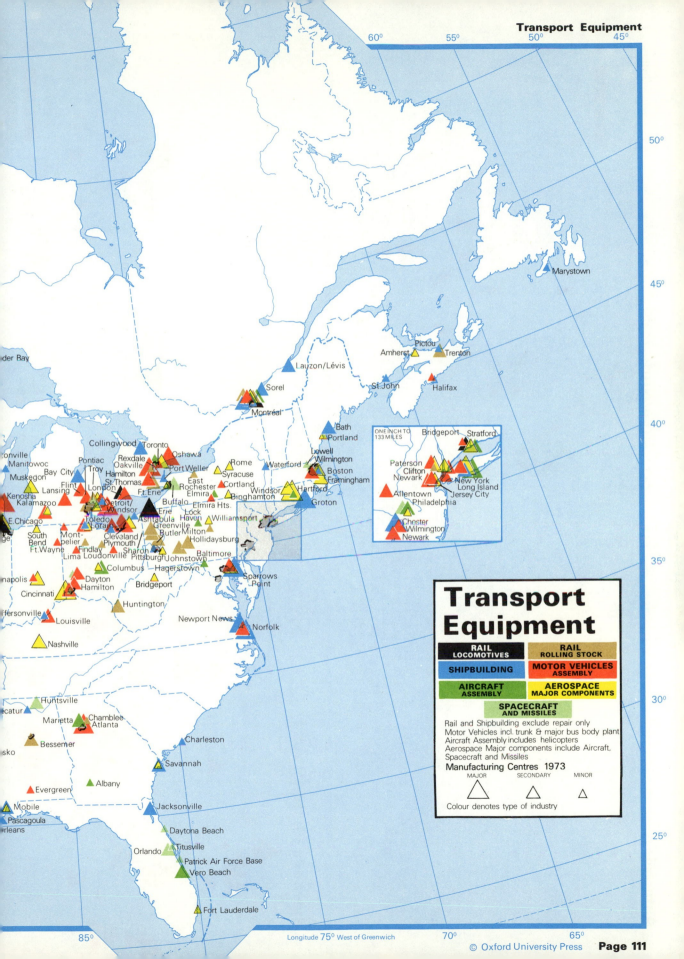

Marystown

Lauzon/Lévis

Sorel

Montréal

Amherst · Pictou
Trenton

St.John
Halifax

Bath
Portland

Lowell
Wilmington
Waterford
Boston
Framingham

Toronto
Collingwood
Rexdale
Pontiac
Oakville
Troy
Hamilton
Manitowoc
St Thomas
London
Ft.Erie
Bay City
Muskegon
Flint
Lansing
Kenosha
Kalamazoo
Detroit/
Windsor
E.Chicago
Buffalo
Toledo
Lorain
Ashtabula
Erie
South
Mont-
Bend
pelier
Cleveland
Ft.Wayne
Lima
Findlay
Plymouth
Sharon
Loudonville
Pittsburgh
Johnstown
Columbus
Hagerstown
Dayton
Hamilton
Bridgeport
Cincinnati
Huntington
ffersonville
Louisville

Oshawa
Port Weller
Rome
Syracuse
East
Rochester
Cortland
Elmira
Elmira Hts.
Binghamton
Windsor
Lock
Haven
Greenville
Butler
Milton
Holidaysburg
Baltimore
Williamsport
Hartford
Groton

Sparrows
Point

Nashville

Newport News

Norfolk

ONE INCH TO
133 MILES
Bridgeport
Stratford

Paterson
Clifton
Newark
New York
Long Island
Allentown
Jersey City
Philadelphia
Chester
Wilmington
Newark

Huntsville
ecatur
Marietta
Chamblee
Atlanta

Bessemer
sko

Charleston

Savannah

Evergreen
Albany

Mobile
Pascagoula
rleans

Jacksonville

Daytona Beach

Orlando
Titusville
Patrick Air Force Base
Vero Beach

Fort Lauderdale

der Bay
onville

indianapolis

Transport Equipment

RAIL LOCOMOTIVES	**RAIL ROLLING STOCK**
SHIPBUILDING	**MOTOR VEHICLES ASSEMBLY**
AIRCRAFT ASSEMBLY	**AEROSPACE MAJOR COMPONENTS**
SPACECRAFT AND MISSILES	

Rail and Shipbuilding exclude repair only
Motor Vehicles incl. trunk & major bus body plant
Aircraft Assembly includes helicopters
Aerospace Major components include Aircraft,
Spacecraft and Missiles

Manufacturing Centres 1973

MAJOR   SECONDARY   MINOR

Colour denotes type of industry

Page 111

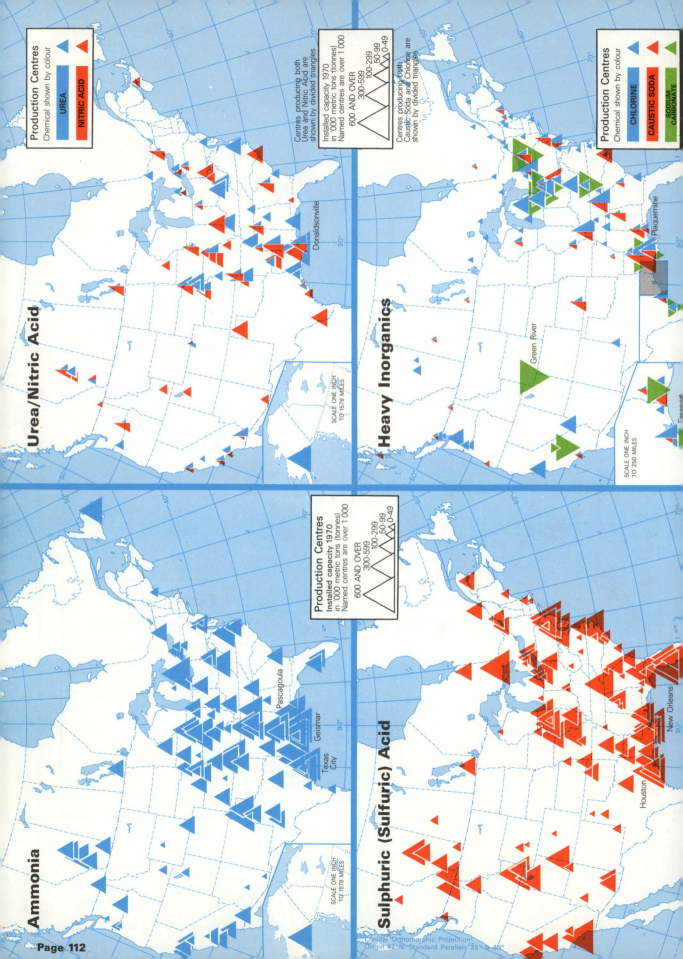

Urea/Nitric Acid

Donaldsonville

Centres producing both
Urea and Nitric Acid are
shown by divided triangles

Installed capacity 1970
in '000 metric tons (tonnes)
Named centres are over 1 000

600 AND OVER
300-599
100-299
50-99
0-49

Centres producing both
Caustic Soda and Chlorine are
shown by divided triangles

Heavy Inorganics

Plaquemine

Green River

Freeport

Ammonia

Pascagoula

Geismar

Texas City

Production Centres
Installed capacity 1970
in '000 metric tons (tonnes)
Named centres are over 1 000

600 AND OVER
300-599
100-299
50-99
0-49

Sulphuric (Sulfuric) Acid

New Orleans

Houston

Conical Orthomorphic Projection
Origin 42°N Standard Parallels 35° & 49°

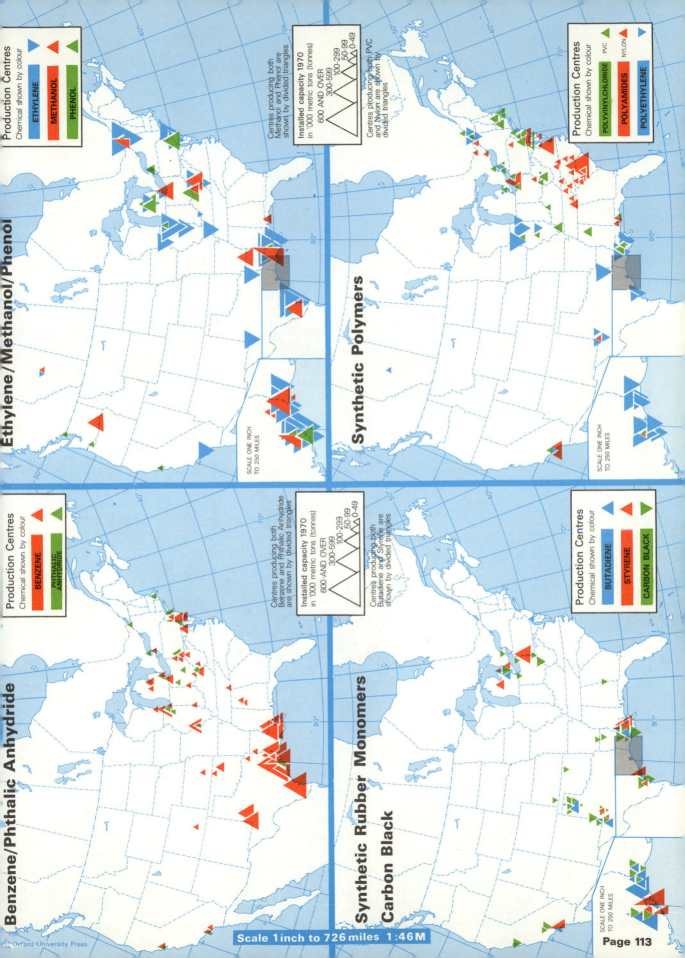

Ethylene / Methanol / Phenol

Production Centres
Chemical shown by colour

ETHYLENE	
METHANOL	
PHENOL	

Centres producing both
Methanol and Phenol are
shown by divided triangles

Installed capacity 1970
in '000 metric tons (tonnes)

600 AND OVER
300-299
100-299
50-99
0-49

Centres producing both PVC
and Nylon are shown by
divided triangles

SCALE ONE INCH
TO 250 MILES

Synthetic Polymers

Production Centres
Chemical shown by colour

POLYVINYLCHLORIDE	PVC
POLYAMIDES	NYLON
POLYETHYLENE	

SCALE ONE INCH
TO 250 MILES

Benzene/Phthalic Anhydride

Production Centres
Chemical shown by colour

BENZENE	
PHTHALIC ANHYDRIDE	

Centres producing both
Benzene and Phthalic Anhydride
are shown by divided triangles

Installed capacity 1970
in '000 metric tons (tonnes)

600 AND OVER
300-599
100-299
50-99
0-49

Centres producing both
Butadiene and Styrene are
shown by divided triangles

Synthetic Rubber Monomers
Carbon Black

Production Centres
Chemical shown by colour

BUTADIENE	
STYRENE	
CARBON BLACK	

SCALE ONE INCH
TO 250 MILES

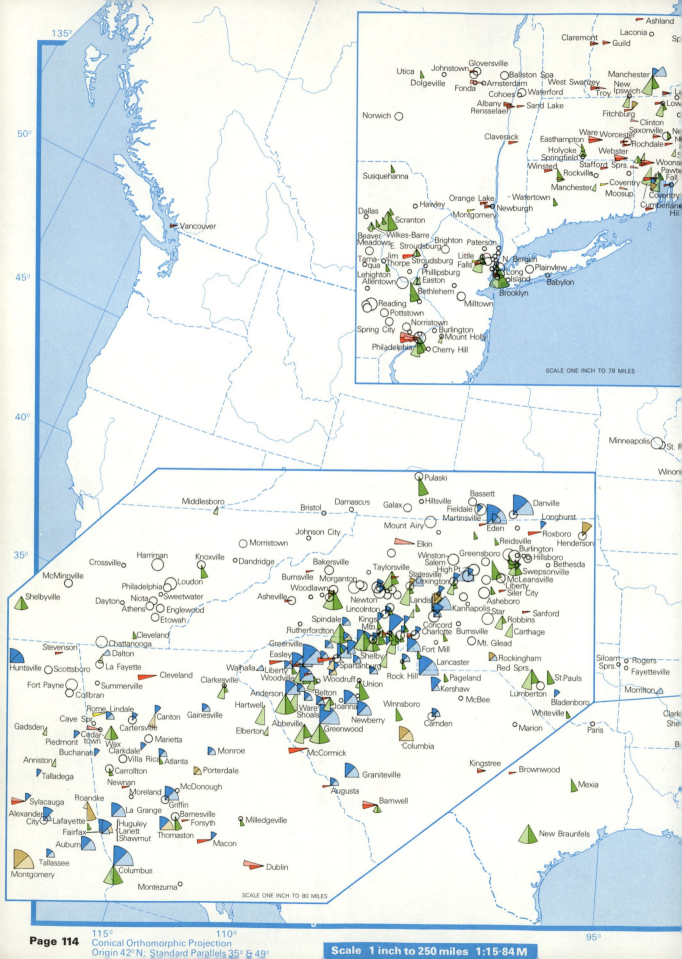

Conical Orthomorphic Projection
Origin 42° N; Standard Parallels 35° & 49°

Scale **1 inch to 250 miles** 1:15·84 M

SCALE ONE INCH TO 78 MILES

SCALE ONE INCH TO 80 MILES

Two Rivers
○ Sheboygan
○ Milwaukee
○ Kenosha

○ Jackson

◐ Chicago
△ Chicago Heights

Greenville
▷ Columbus ○ Bellefontaine
▶ Hamilton
○ Cincinnati

△ Louisville

Rockfield
○ Franklin
gfield
urg ▶ Lebanon
△ Nashville

○ Decatur
le ○ West Point
tte
○ Northport
kiusko ○ Prattville
△ Demopolis
on ○ Elba ◢ Dothan
nroeville ▶ Albany ○ West Green

Grand'Mère ◤ Montmorency
Plessisville ◣ St. Georges
Montréal Guilford
St.-Jérôme Drummond- Dexter
Lachute ville Corinna
Hawkesbury Clinton Ellsworth
Valleyfield Sherbrooke Waterville Augusta
St.-Jean Granby Lewiston
St.-Hyacinthe Westbrook
Perth

Midland
Lindsay
Toronto Scarborough Biddeford
Listowel Rochester
Hespeler ○ Auburn
London Hamilton Seneca Falls
Woodstock Depew
Five Corners Canisteo
Jamestown ○ Troy
Willoughby Salamanca Bloomsburg
Cleveland Solon Williamsport Hazleton
Lock Haven Berwick
Altoona New Holland
McConnellsburg Hagerstown
Grantsville Dover
Winchester Front Royal

Charlottesville Tappahannock
Waynesboro Scottsville
Covington
Petersburg
Lynchburg Emporia
Rocky Burnt Mills
Mount Ahoskie
Tarboro
Greenville

Delway
○ Wilmington

Mont Joli

Sussex
Stellarton
Truro
Windsor

Longitude 75° West of Greenwich

© Oxford University Press **Page 115**

Textiles
Production Centres 1973

COTTON SPINDLES	COTTON LOOMS
WOOL SPINDLES	WOOL LOOMS
MAN-MADE FIBRES SPINDLES	MAN-MADE FIBRES LOOMS
COTTON/MAN-MADE SPINDLES	COTTON/MAN-MADE LOOMS
WOOL/MAN-MADE SPINDLES	WOOL/MAN-MADE LOOMS

There is, in general, a marked difference in size between centres processing different fibres; mixed centres are classed by size & distinguished by colour. Colour denotes fibre.

	MAJOR	SECONDARY	MINOR
Cotton			
Spindles	over 250 000	100 000 to 250 000	50 000 to 99 000
Looms	over 5 000	2 000 to 5 000	1 000 to 1 900
Wool			
Spindles	over 15 000	7 500 to 15 000	2 000 to 7 500
Looms	over 200	100 to 200	50 to 99
Man-made Fibres			
Spindles	over 40 000	21 000 to 40 000	5 000 to 20 000
Looms	over 800	400 to 799	100 to 399
Knitting Machines	over 1,000	300 to 1,000	50 to 299

Employment Scale

— OVER 1,000,000
— 500,000 - 1,000,000
— 250,000 - 500,000
— 100,000 - 250,000
— 50,000 - 100,000
— 25,000 - 50,000
— 10,000 - 25,000
— 5,000 - 10,000
— LESS THAN 5,000

135°
50°
45°
40°
35°
30°
25°

115°   110°   95°

Edmonton

Calgary

Saskatoon
Regina

Vancouver
Victoria

Seattle-Everett
Tacoma

Spokane

Portland
Salem
Eugene

Great Falls

Billings

Winnipeg

Fargo-Moorhead

Duluth

Minneapolis/
St. Paul
Rochester

Santa Rosa
Vallejo-Napa   Reno
San
Francisco-
Oakland
Salinas-Monterey

Sacramento
Stockton
Modesto
San Jose
Fresno

Ogden
Salt Lake City
Provo-Orem

Denver

Colorado Springs
Pueblo

Sioux Falls

Sioux City

Omaha
Lincoln

Des
Moines

St. Joseph
Topeka

Waterloo
Ced
Rap
Davenport-R
Moline

Kansas
City
St. Lou

Bakersfield
Santa
Barbara
Oxnard-Ventura
Los Angeles-
Long Beach
San Bernardino-
Riverside-Ontario
Anaheim-Santa Ana-
Garden Grove
San Diego

Las Vegas

Albuquerque

Amarillo

Phoenix

Tucson

Wichita

Oklahoma City
Lawton

Tulsa

Spring

Ft. Smith
Little Rock-
North Little Rock

El Paso

Wichita Falls
Lubbock

Sherman-Denison
Dallas
Texarkana
Shreveport

Abilene
Midland
Odessa
San Angelo

Fort
Worth
Waco
Tyler
Monr

Austin

Bryan-College
Station
Houston

Beaumont-
Port/Arthur-
Orange

Ba

San Antonio

Lake
Charles
Galveston-Texas City

Lafa

Laredo

McAllen-Pharr
Brownsville-Harlingen

Corpus Christi

Page 116

Conical Orthomorphic Projection
Origin 42° N; Standard Parallels 35° & 49°

Scale   1 inch to 250 miles   1:15·84 M

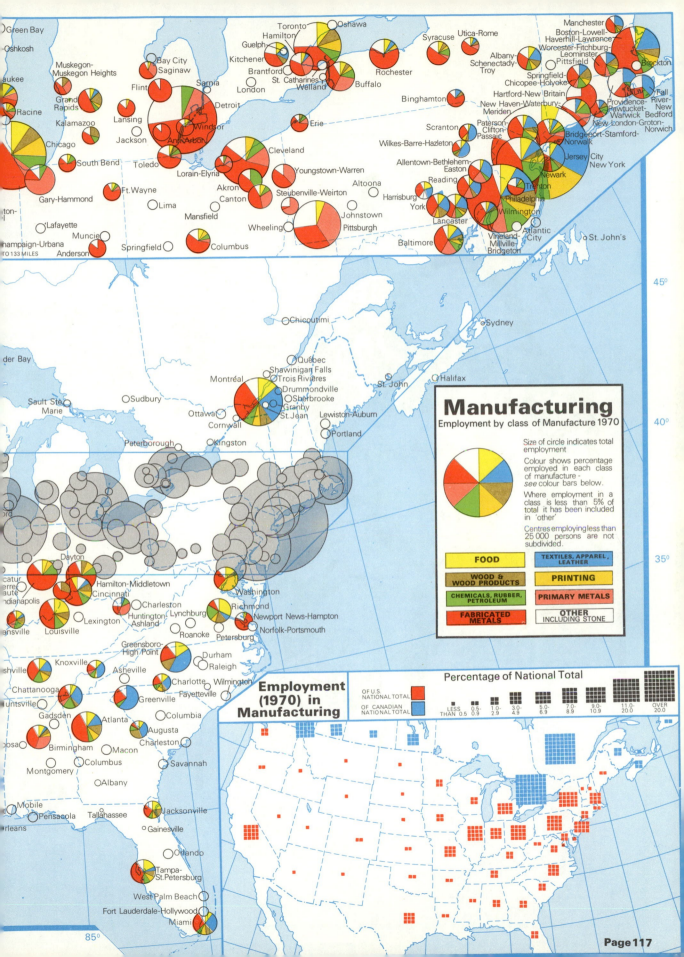

Manufacturing
Employment by class of Manufacture 1970

Size of circle indicates total employment

Colour shows percentage employed in each class of manufacture – *see colour bars below*.

Where employment in a class is less than 5% of total it has been included in 'other'

Centres employing less than 25 000 persons are not subdivided

FOOD	TEXTILES, APPAREL, LEATHER
WOOD & WOOD PRODUCTS	PRINTING
CHEMICALS, RUBBER, PETROLEUM	PRIMARY METALS
FABRICATED METALS	OTHER INCLUDING STONE

Employment (1970) in Manufacturing

Percentage of National Total

OF U.S. NATIONAL TOTAL
OF CANADIAN NATIONAL TOTAL

LESS THAN 0.5 | 0.5–0.9 | 1.0–2.9 | 3.0–4.9 | 5.0–6.9 | 7.0–8.9 | 9.0–10.9 | 11.0–20.0 | OVER 20.0

Page 117

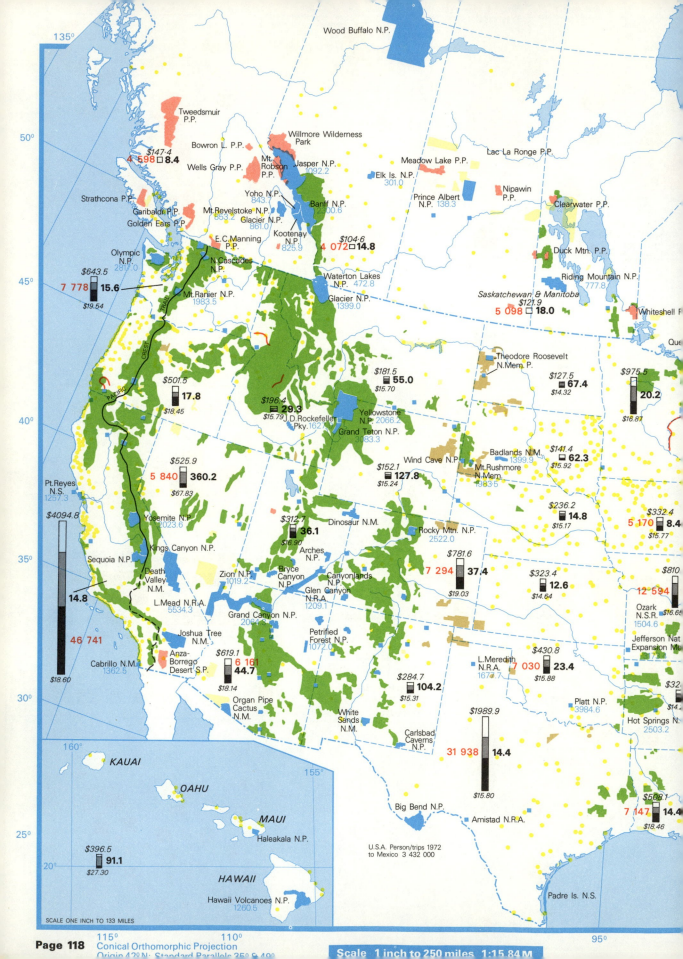

Wood Buffalo N.P.

Tweedsmuir P.P.
$147·4
4 598 ☐ 8.4

Bowron L. P.P.
Willmore Wilderness Park
Meadow Lake P.P.
Lac La Ronge P.P.

Wells Gray P.P.
Mt. Robson P.P.
Jasper N.P.
Elk Is. N.P. 301.0
Nipawin P.P.

Prince Albert N.P. 138.3
Clearwater P.P.

Strathcona P.P.
Yoho N.P. 843
Banff N.P. 2500.6

Garibaldi P.P.
Mt. Revelstoke N.P. 853.2
Glacier N.P. 861.0
Duck Mtn. P.P.

Golden Ears P.P.
E.C. Manning P.P.
Kootenay N.P. 825.9
Riding Mountain N.P. 777.8

Olympic N.P. 2817.0
N. Cascades N.P.
Waterton Lakes N.P. 472.8
4 072 ☐ 14.8
$104·6

$643.5
7 778 ■ 15.6
$19.54
Mt. Ranier N.P. 1983.5
Glacier N.P. 1399.0
Saskatchewan & Manitoba
$121.9
5 098 ☐ 18.0
Whiteshell P

Que

Theodore Roosevelt N.Mem.P.
$127.5
■ 67.4
$14.32
$975.5
■ 20.2
$16.87

$501.5
■ 17.8
$18.45
$181.5
■ 55.0
$15.70

$196.4
■ 29.3
$15.79
J.D. Rockefeller Pky. 162?
Yellowstone N.P. 2066.2
Grand Teton N.P. 3083.3

$525.9
5 840 ■ 360.2
$67.83
Wind Cave N.P.
$141.4
■ 62.3
$15.92
Badlands N.M. 1399.9

Pt. Reyes N.S. 1257.3
$152.1
■ 127.8
$15.24
Mt. Rushmore N.Mem. 1983.5

$4094.8
Yosemite N.P. 2023.6
$312.7
■ 36.1
$16.90
Dinosaur N.M.
Rocky Mtn. N.P. 2522.0
$236.2
■ 14.8
$15.17

$332.4
5 170 ☐ 8.4
$15.77

Sequoia N.P.
Kings Canyon N.P.
Death Valley N.M.
Arches N.P.
Bryce Canyon N.P.
Zion N.P. 1019.2
Canyonlands N.P.
Glen Canyon N.R.A. 1209.1
$781.6
7 294 ■ 37.4
$19.03
$323.4
■ 12.6
$14.64
$810
Ozark N.S.R. 1504.6 $16.6

14.8
L. Mead N.R.A. 5534.3
Grand Canyon N.P. 2064.3
Jefferson Nat Expansion Me ?

46 741
Joshua Tree N.M.
Petrified Forest N.P. 1072.0
$32

Cabrillo N.M. 1362.5
Anza-Borrego Desert S.P.
$619.1
6 161 ■ 44.7
$18.14
L. Meredith N.R.A. 1677.7
7 030 ■ 23.4
$430.8
$15.88
$14.
Hot Springs N. 2503.2

$18.60
Organ Pipe Cactus N.M.
White Sands N.M.
$284.7
■ 104.2
$15.31
Platt N.P. 3984.6

Carlsbad Caverns N.P.
$1989.9
31 938 ■ 14.4
$15.80

$508.1
7 147 ■ 14.4
$18.46

U.S.A. Person/trips 1972 to Mexico 3 432 000

Big Bend N.P.
Amistad N.R.A.

$396.5
■ 91.1
$27.30

Padre Is. N.S.

SCALE ONE INCH TO 133 MILES

Conical Orthomorphic Projection
Origin 42° N; Standard Parallels 35° & 49°

Scale 1 inch to 250 miles   1:15.84 M

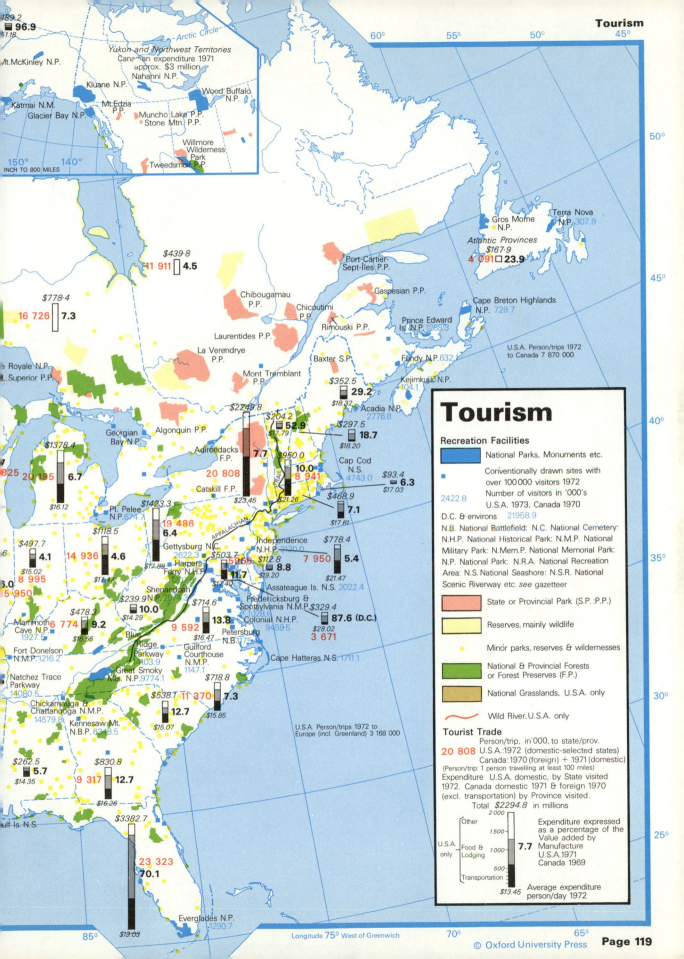

189.2
96.9
51.18

Mt. McKinley N.P.

Yukon and Northwest Territories
Canadian expenditure 1971
approx. $3 million
Nahanni N.P.

Kluane N.P.

Katmai N.M.
Glacier Bay N.P.

Mt. Edzia P.P.

Muncho Lake P.P.
Stone Mtn. P.P.

Wood Buffalo N.P.

Willmore Wilderness Park

Tweedsmuir P.P.

150° 140°

INCH TO 800 MILES

Arctic Circle

60°   55°   50°   45°

Gros Morne N.P.
Terra Nova N.P. 307.9

Atlantic Provinces
$167.9
4 091 ☐ **23.9**

$439.8
11 911 ☐ **4.5**

Chibougamau P.P.

Chicoutimi P.P.

Port-Cartier-
Sept-Îles P.P.

Gaspesian P.P.

Rimouski P.P.

Cape Breton Highlands N.P. 729.7

Prince Edward Is. N.P. 1288.3

$778.4
16 726 ☐ **7.3**

Laurentides P.P.

La Verendrye P.P.

Baxter S.P.

Fundy N.P. 632.1

U.S.A. Person/trips 1972
to Canada 7 870 000

Mont Tremblant P.P.

Kejimkujik N.P. 104.1

Royale N.P.
Superior P.P.

$2249.8

$352.5 **29.2**
$18.32

Acadia N.P. 2776.8

Algonquin P.P.

$204.2 ☐ **52.9**
$17.79

$297.5 ☐ **18.7**
$18.20

Georgian Bay N.P.

Adirondacks F.P.

$1378.4
825
20 195 **6.7**
$16.12

Catskill F.P.

7.7

$950.0 **10.0**
8 941
$21.26

Cap Cod N.S.
4743.0 **6.3**
$17.03

$93.4

$468.9 **7.1**
$17.61

Pt. Pelee N.P. 674.7

$1423.3
19 486 **6.4**

APPALACHIAN

$778.4
7 950 **5.4**
$21.47

Independence N.H.P. 3120.0

$497.7 **4.1**
$15.02

$1118.5
14 936 **4.6**
$17.41

Gettysburg N.C.
2622.3

Harpers Ferry N.H.P.

$503.7
5 966 **8.8**
$19.20

$112.8

6.0
5 950

8 995

Shenandoah N.P. 2514.9

$239.9 **10.0**
$14.29

Assateague Is. N.S. 2022.4

Fredericksburg & Spotsylvania N.M.P.
1028.6

$329.4 **87.6** (D.C.)
$28.02
3 671

Colonial N.H.P.
9459.5

$714.6 **13.8**

Mammoth Cave N.P. 1927.5

$478.3
6 774 **9.2**
$16.56

9 592

Petersburg N.B. 1175

Fort Donelson N.M.P. 1216.0

Blue Ridge Parkway

Guilford Courthouse N.M.P. 1147.1

Cape Hatteras N.S. 1711.1

Natchez Trace Parkway
14080.5

Great Smoky Mts. N.P. 9774.1

$718.8
11 370 **7.3**
$15.85

Chickamauga & Chattanooga N.M.P.
14579.8

$538.7 **12.7**
$15.07

Kennesaw Mt. N.B.P. 6348.5

$262.5 **5.7**
$14.35

$830.8
9 317 **12.7**
$16.26

Gulf Is. N.S.

$3382.7

23 323

70.1

Everglades N.P. 1290.7
$19.03

U.S.A. Person/trips 1972 to
Europe (incl. Greenland) 3 168 000

85°   Longitude 75° West of Greenwich   70°   65°

Tourism

Recreation Facilities

☐ (blue) National Parks, Monuments etc.

■ (small blue) Conventionally drawn sites with over 100 000 visitors 1972

2422.8 Number of visitors in '000's U.S.A. 1973, Canada 1970

D.C. & environs 21958.9

N.B. National Battlefield: N.C. National Cemetery: N.H.P. National Historical Park: N.M.P. National Military Park: N.Mem.P. National Memorial Park: N.P. National Park: N.R.A. National Recreation Area: N.S. National Seashore: N.S.R. National Scenic Riverway etc. *see gazetteer*

☐ (red) State or Provincial Park (S.P. :P.P.)

☐ (yellow) Reserves, mainly wildlife

• (yellow) Minor parks, reserves & wildernesses

☐ (green) National & Provincial Forests or Forest Preserves (F.P.)

☐ (olive) National Grasslands, U.S.A. only

~ (red) Wild River, U.S.A. only

Tourist Trade

Person/trip, in'000, to state/prov.
20 808 U.S.A.:1972 (domestic-selected states)
Canada:1970 (foreign) + 1971 (domestic)
(Person/trip: 1 person travelling at least 100 miles)
Expenditure U.S.A. domestic, by State visited 1972. Canada domestic 1971 & foreign 1970 (excl. transportation) by Province visited.
Total *$2294.8* in millions

2 000
Other
1 500
U.S.A. only
Food & Lodging
1 000
7.7
500
Transportation
$13.45

Expenditure expressed as a percentage of the Value added by Manufacture
U.S.A.1971
Canada 1969

Average expenditure person/day 1972

© Oxford University Press   **Page 119**

135°

50°

S/G Vancouver
Victoria
CFR
CDAL
Everett S/G C,O
Seattle
Tacoma

45°

Longview
Portland/ PP
Vancouver
Snake R.
Columbia R.

Two Harb
Duluth/Superior

40° Eureka

Minneapolis/
St. Paul

Early Dec.–
end March

PP

San
Francisco,
San Pablo
& Suisun Bays
PP

35°

End Nov.–
end March

Kansas City
Missouri R.

El Segundo
Los Angeles MP
PP

San Diego

Arkansas R.
Miss

30°

Gulf Intracoastal Waterway
SAME SCALE

Red R.
Ouachita R.

Volume of Trade
1971 (Canada)
1972 (U.S.A.)
(million short tons)

Bat
Rou
Lake
Charles

Beaumont/Port Arthur CFR
Houston CFR
Texas City/Galveston
Freeport

25°

5 15 25 35 45 55 65

Corpus
Christi M
PP

Gulf Intracoast

Brownsville

Page 120 Conical Orthomorphic Projection
Origin 42° N: Standard Parallels 35° & 49°

Scale 1 inch to 250 miles 1:15·84 M

115° 110° 95°

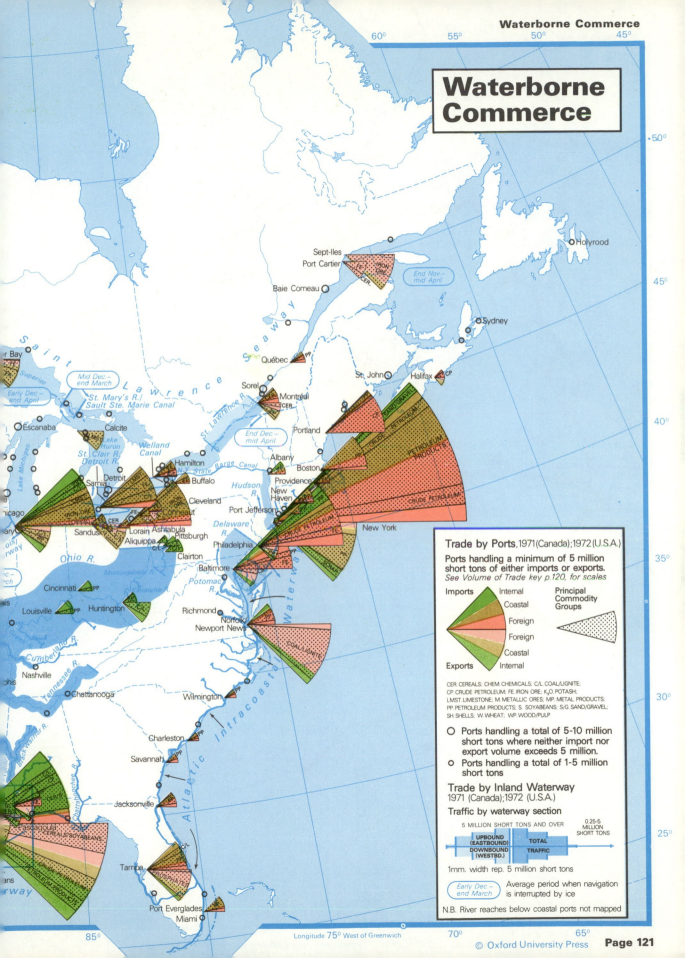

Waterborne Commerce

Trade by Ports, 1971 (Canada); 1972 (U.S.A.)

Ports handling a minimum of 5 million short tons of either imports or exports.
See Volume of Trade key p.120, for scales

Imports — Internal / Coastal / Foreign
Exports — Foreign / Coastal / Internal

Principal Commodity Groups

CER. CEREALS; CHEM. CHEMICALS; C/L. COAL/LIGNITE; CP. CRUDE PETROLEUM; FE. IRON ORE; K₂O. POTASH; LMST. LIMESTONE; M. METALLIC ORES; MP. METAL PRODUCTS; PP. PETROLEUM PRODUCTS; S. SOYABEANS; S/G. SAND/GRAVEL; SH. SHELLS; W. WHEAT; WP. WOOD/PULP

○ Ports handling a total of 5-10 million short tons where neither import nor export volume exceeds 5 million.
○ Ports handling a total of 1-5 million short tons

Trade by Inland Waterway
1971 (Canada); 1972 (U.S.A.)

Traffic by waterway section

5 MILLION SHORT TONS AND OVER — 0.25-5 MILLION SHORT TONS

UPBOUND (EASTBOUND) / TOTAL
DOWNBOUND (WESTBD.) / TRAFFIC

1mm. width rep. 5 million short tons

Early Dec – end March — Average period when navigation is interrupted by ice

N.B. River reaches below coastal ports not mapped

Longitude 75° West of Greenwich

© Oxford University Press **Page 121**

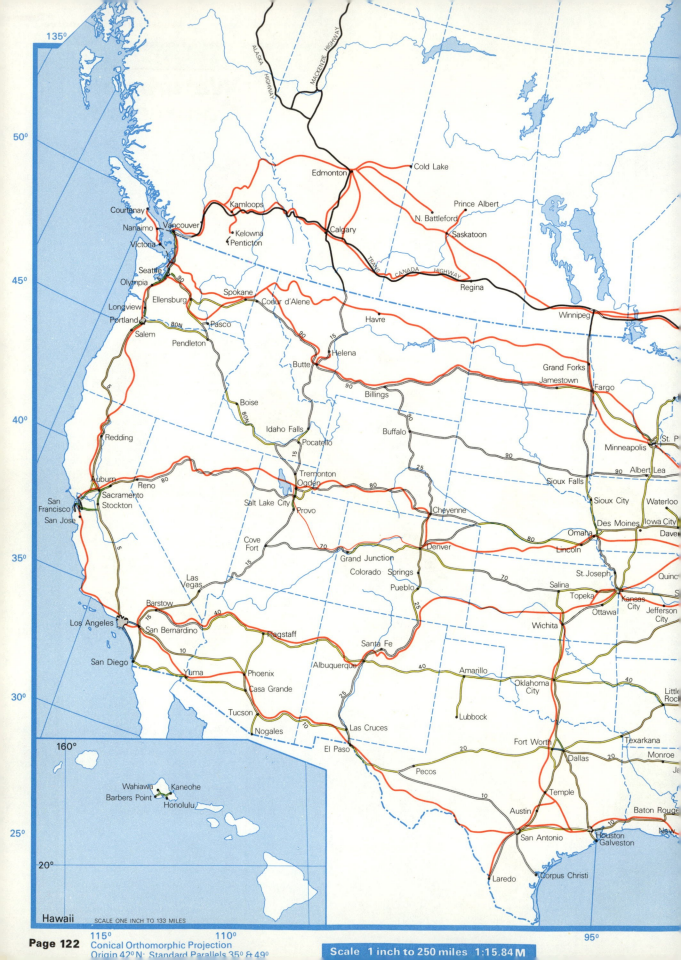

Conical Orthomorphic Projection
Origin 42° N; Standard Parallels 35° & 49°

Scale 1 inch to 250 miles 1:15.84 M

Hawaii

SCALE ONE INCH TO 133 MILES

ALASKA HIGHWAY

MACKENZIE HIGHWAY'

TRANS CANADA HIGHWAY

Edmonton
Cold Lake
Calgary
N. Battleford
Prince Albert
Saskatoon
Regina
Kamloops
Kelowna
Penticton
Courtenay
Vancouver
Nanaimo
Victoria
Seattle
Olympia
Longview
Portland
Salem
Ellensburg
Spokane
Coeur d'Alene
Havre
Winnipeg
Pasco
Pendleton
Helena
Butte
Boise
Billings
Grand Forks
Jamestown
Fargo
Idaho Falls
Pocatello
Buffalo
Minneapolis
St. P.
Albert Lea
Redding
Sioux Falls
Waterloo
Auburn
Reno
Sacramento
Stockton
Tremonton
Ogden
Salt Lake City
Provo
Cheyenne
Sioux City
Omaha
Des Moines
Iowa City
Dave
San Francisco
San Jose
Cove Fort
Grand Junction
Denver
Lincoln
St. Joseph
Quinc
Las Vegas
Colorado Springs
Pueblo
Salina
Topeka
Kansas City
Jefferson City
Barstow
Wichita
Ottawa
Los Angeles
San Bernardino
Flagstaff
Santa Fe
San Diego
Yuma
Phoenix
Casa Grande
Albuquerque
Amarillo
Oklahoma City
Little Rock
Tucson
Lubbock
Nogales
Las Cruces
El Paso
Fort Worth
Texarkana
Monroe
Pecos
Dallas
Ja
Temple
Austin
Baton Rouge
San Antonio
Houston
Galveston
New.
Laredo
Corpus Christi

Wahiawa
Kaneohe
Barbers Point
Honolulu

135°
160°
115°
110°
95°
50°
45°
40°
35°
30°
25°
20°

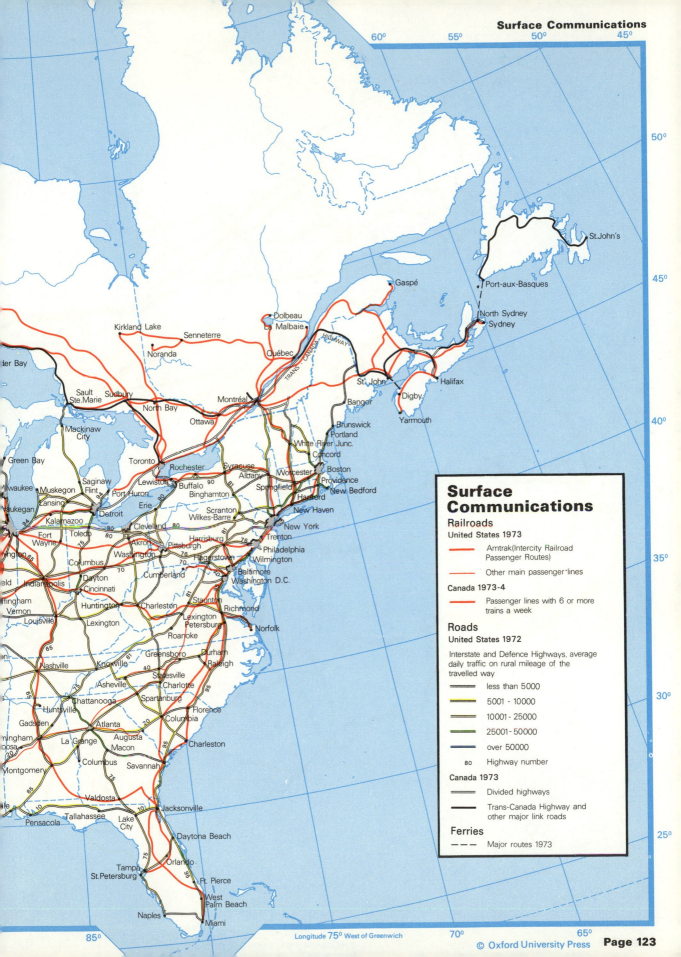

Surface Communications

Railroads

United States 1973

⸻ Amtrak (Intercity Railroad Passenger Routes)

⸻ Other main passenger lines

Canada 1973-4

⸻ Passenger lines with 6 or more trains a week

Roads

United States 1972

Interstate and Defence Highways, average daily traffic on rural mileage of the travelled way

⸻ less than 5000

⸻ 5001 - 10000

⸻ 10001 - 25000

⸻ 25001 - 50000

⸻ over 50000

80   Highway number

Canada 1973

⸻ Divided highways

⸻ Trans-Canada Highway and other major link roads

Ferries

– – – Major routes 1973

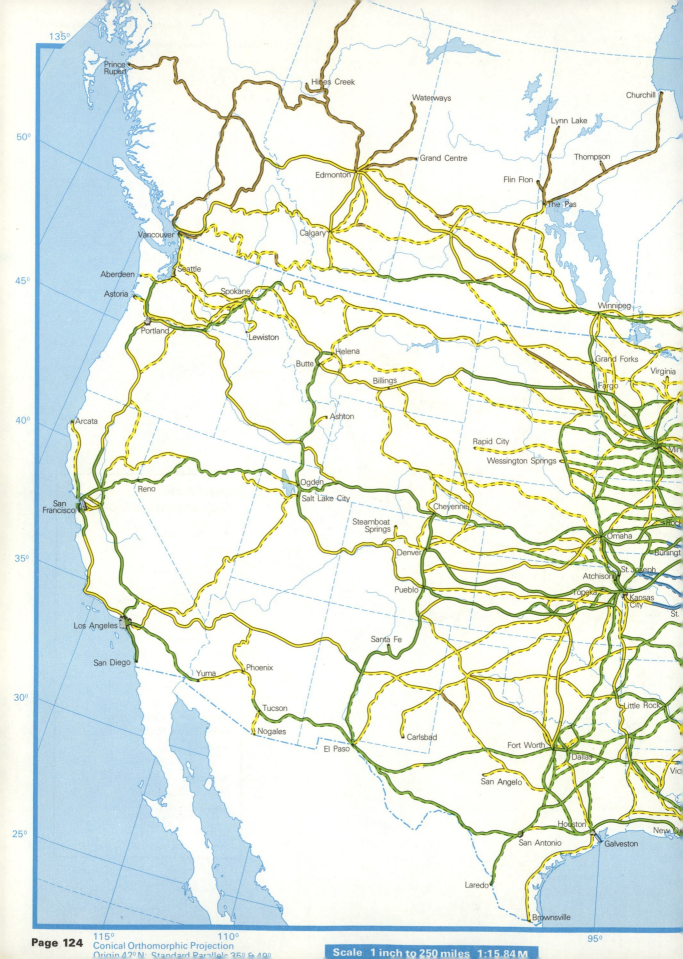

135°

50°

45°

40°

35°

30°

25°

Prince
Rupert

Hines Creek

Waterways

Churchill

Lynn Lake

Grand Centre

Thompson

Edmonton

Flin Flon

The Pas

Calgary

Vancouver

Seattle

Aberdeen

Spokane

Winnipeg

Astoria

Lewiston

Grand Forks

Portland

Helena

Virginia

Butte

Billings

Fargo

Arcata

Ashton

Rapid City

Wessington Springs

Reno

Ogden

Salt Lake City

Cheyenne

Min

San
Francisco

Steamboat
Springs

Omaha

Roc

Denver

Burlingt

Los Angeles

Pueblo

Atchison

St. Joseph

Topeka

Kansas
City

St.

Santa Fe

San Diego

Yuma

Phoenix

Little Rock

Tucson

Nogales

Carlsbad

El Paso

Fort Worth

Dallas

Vic

San Angelo

Houston

New O

San Antonio

Galveston

Laredo

Brownsville

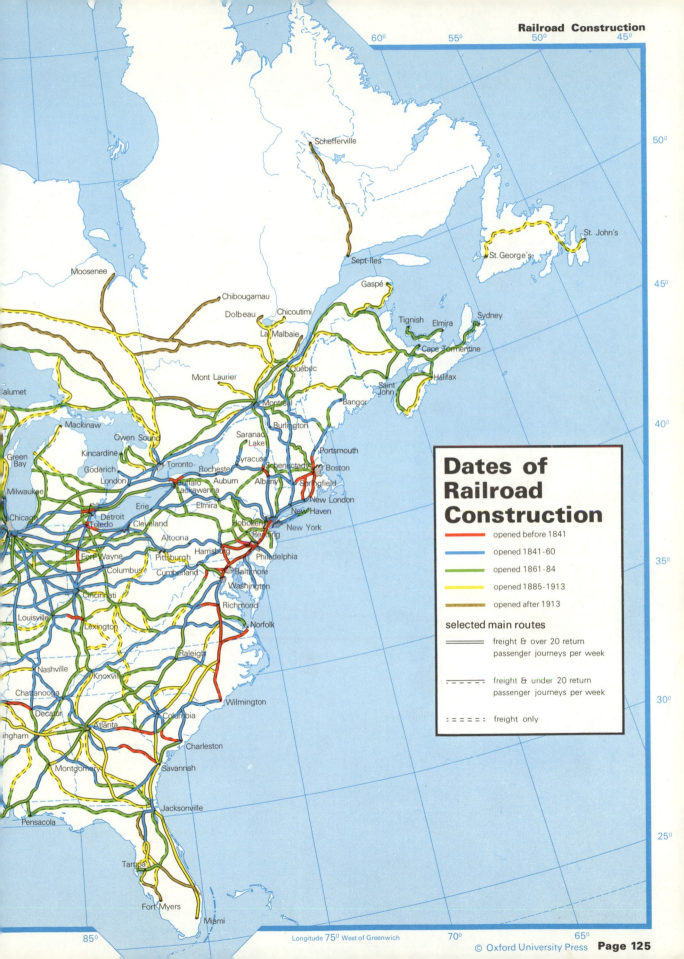

Dates of Railroad Construction

— opened before 1841
— opened 1841-60
— opened 1861-84
— opened 1885-1913
— opened after 1913

selected main routes

——— freight & over 20 return passenger journeys per week

‐ ‐ ‐ freight & under 20 return passenger journeys per week

= = = freight only

Schefferville
Moosenee
Chibougamau
Dolbeau
Chicoutimi
La Malbaie
Sept-Iles
Gaspé
Tignish
Elmira
Sydney
Cape Tormentine
Halifax
St. George's
St. John's
Mont Laurier
Québec
Saint John
Bangor
Montréal
Burlington
Portsmouth
Saranac Lake
Syracuse
Schenectady
Boston
Calumet
Mackinaw
Owen Sound
Kincardine
Goderich
London
Toronto
Rochester
Auburn
Albany
Springfield
New London
Green Bay
Milwaukee
Chicago
Erie
Elmira
New Haven
Detroit
Toledo
Cleveland
Hoboken
New York
Altoona
Reading
Fort Wayne
Pittsburgh
Harrisburg
Philadelphia
Columbus
Cumberland
Baltimore
Cincinnati
Washington
Louisville
Lexington
Richmond
Norfolk
Nashville
Knoxville
Raleigh
Chattanooga
Decatur
Wilmington
Atlanta
Columbia
ingham
Charleston
Montgomery
Savannah
Pensacola
Jacksonville
Tampa
Fort Myers
Miami

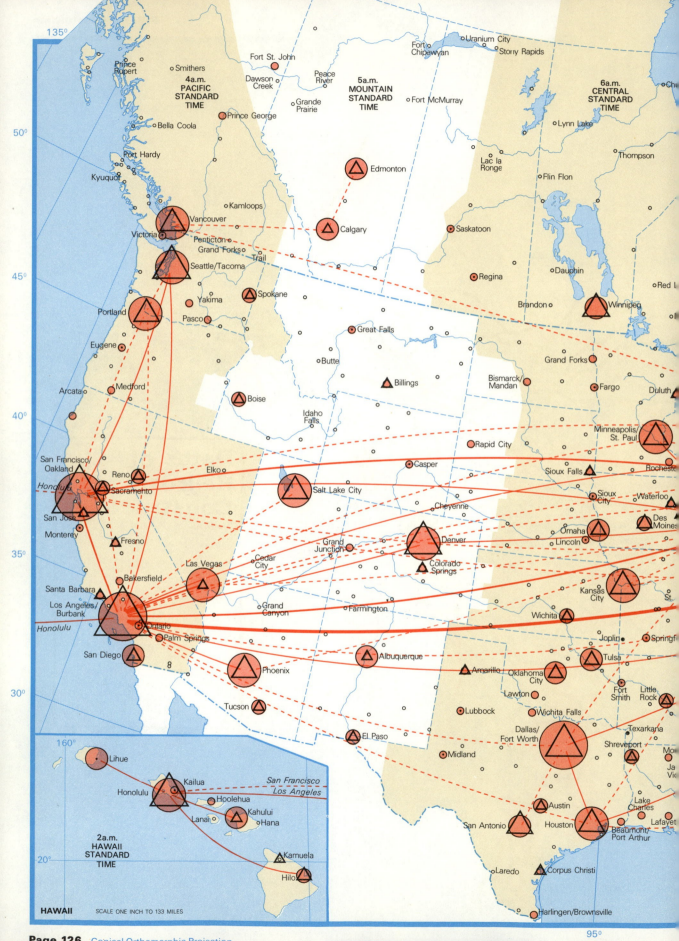

Conical Orthomorphic Projection
Origin 42° N: Standard Parallels 25° & 40°
Scale 1 inch to 250 miles 1:15,84M

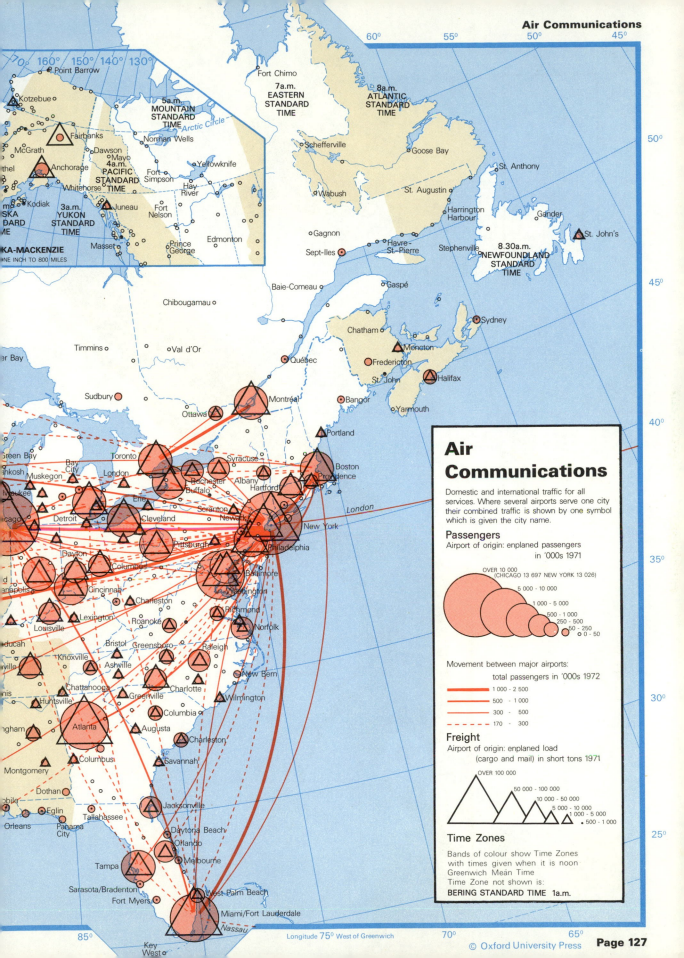

Air Communications

Domestic and international traffic for all
services. Where several airports serve one city
their combined traffic is shown by one symbol
which is given the city name.

Passengers

Airport of origin: enplaned passengers
in '000s 1971

OVER 10 000
(CHICAGO 13 697 NEW YORK 13 026)

5 000 - 10 000

1 000 - 5 000

500 - 1 000

250 - 500

50 - 250

0 - 50

Movement between major airports:

total passengers in '000s 1972

1 000 - 2 500

500 - 1 000

300 - 500

170 - 300

Freight

Airport of origin: enplaned load
(cargo and mail) in short tons 1971

OVER 100 000

50 000 - 100 000

10 000 - 50 000

5 000 - 10 000

1 000 - 5 000

500 - 1 000

Time Zones

Bands of colour show Time Zones
with times given when it is noon
Greenwich Mean Time
Time Zone not shown is:
BERING STANDARD TIME 1a.m.

© Oxford University Press

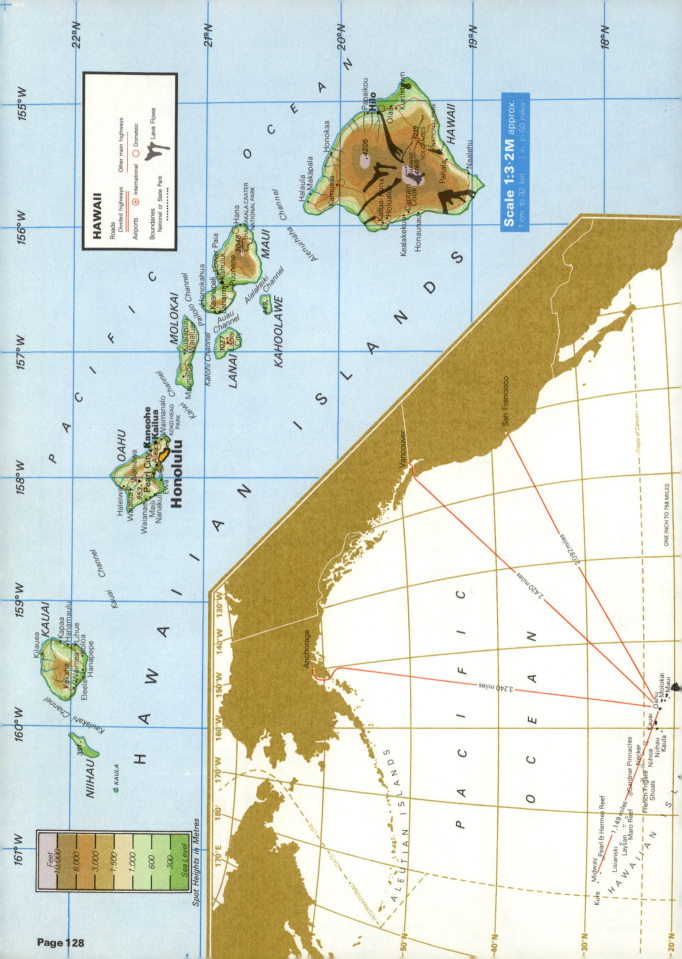

Gazetteer of the United States and Canada

Coordinates are given to the nearest degree, plus or minus, so that 47° 19′N 94° 47′W is read as 47N 95W

Urban plan references are given to the nearest ¼ degree

	Page	N	W
Abbeville: Alabama	27	32	85
Abbeville: Georgia	24	32	83
Abbeville: Louisiana	26	30	92
Abbeville: South Carolina	24	34	82
Abbotsford: British Columbia	38	49	122
Aberdeen: Maryland	17	40	76
Aberdeen: Mississippi	27	34	89
Aberdeen: North Carolina	24	35	79
Aberdeen: South Dakota	28	45	99
Aberdeen: Washington	39	47	124
Aberdeen L.: N.W.T.	44	65	99
Abert, L.: Oregon	36	43	120
Abilene: Kansas	28	39	97
Abilene: Texas	29	32	100
Abingdon: Virginia	16	37	82
Abington: Massachusetts	15	42	71
Abington: Pennsylvania	2	40	75¼
Abitibi: *r.* Ontario	11	50	82
Abitibi, L.: Ontario	11	49	80
Abloviak Fiord: Québec	45	60	65
Absaroka Ra.: Mont./Wyo.	28	45	110
Absecon: New Jersey	15	39	74
Academy: California	37	37	120
Acadia Nat. Park: Maine	11	44	68
Accotink: Virginia	17	39	77
Achille: Oklahoma	26	34	96
Acland Bay: N.W.T.	44	72	101
Acton: California	35	34	118
Acton: Ontario	18	44	80
Acton Vale: Québec	13	46	73
Acworth: Georgia	24	34	85
Ada: Ohio	19	41	84
Ada: Oklahoma	26	35	97
Adair, C.: N.W.T.	45	72	71
Adairsville: Georgia	24	34	85
Adak: Alaska	46	52	177
Adams: Massachusetts	15	43	73
Adams: New York	12	44	76
Adams: Wisconsin	20	44	90
Adams City: Colorado	3	39¾	105
Adams, L.: British Columbia	38	51	120
Adams, Mt.: Washington	39	46	121
Adams Sound: N.W.T.	45	73	85
Addison: New York	14	42	77
Addyston: Ohio	10	39	85
Adel: Georgia	25	31	83
Adel: Oregon	36	42	120
Adelaide Penin.: N.W.T.	44	68	98
Adelanto: California	35	35	117
Adin: California	36	41	121
Adirondack Forest Preserve: New York	13	44	74
Adirondack Mts.: New York	13	44	74
Admiralty Inlet: N.W.T.	45	73	86
Admiralty I.: N.W.T.	44	70	101
Adrian: Michigan	21	42	84
Afognak: *& i.* Alaska	43	58	153
Agassiz: British Columbia	38	49	122
Agattu I.: Alaska	60	52	174
Agawam: Massachusetts	15	42	73
Ager: California	36	42	122
Agness: Oregon	36	43	124
Aguadilla: Puerto Rico	27	18	67
Agua Fria: *r.*, Arizona	33	34	112
Aguanga: California	35	33	117
Aguanus: *r.*, Québec	9	51	62
Agu Bay: N.W.T.	45	70	88
Agujereada, Punta: Puerto Rico	27	19	67
Ahoskie: North Carolina	24	36	77
Aiea: Hawaii	128	21	158
Aiken: South Carolina	24	34	82
Aillik: Newfoundland	9	55	59
Air Force I.: N.W.T.	45	68	74
Aishihik: Yukon	40	62	138
Aishihik, L.: Yukon	40	61	137
Ajax: Ontario	12	44	79
Ajo: Arizona	33	32	113
Akhiok: Alaska	43	57	154
Akiachak: Alaska	43	61	162
Akiak: Alaska	43	61	161
Akimiski I.: N.W.T.	8	53	81
Aklavik: N.W.T.	44	68	135
Akpatok I.: N.W.T.	45	61	68
Akron: Ohio	19	41	82
Akron: Pennsylvania	14	40	76
Akulurak: Alaska	42	63	165
Akutan: Alaska	43	54	166
ALABAMA	27	—	—
Alabama: *r.*, Albama	27	31	88
Alachua: Florida	25	30	83
Alakanuk: Alaska	42	63	165
Alalakeiki Ch.: Hawaii	128	21	157
Alameda: California	6	37¾	122¼
Alameda Creek: California	6	37½	122
Alamo: California	6	37¾	122
Alamo: Tennessee	27	36	89
Alamo: *r.*, California	35	33	115
Alamogordo: New Mexico	29	33	106

	Page	N	W
Alamosa: Colorado	28	33	106
ALASKA	42/43	—	—
Alaska, Gulf of	43	59	145
Alaska Peninsula	43	56	159
Alaska Range	42/43	62	152
Alatna: Alaska	42	67	153
Alcatraz Is.: California	6	37¾	122½
Albany: California	6	38	122¼
Albany: Georgia	24	32	84
Albany: Indiana	21	40	85
Albany: New York	15	43	74
Albany: Oregon	39	45	123
Albemarle: North Carolina	24	35	80
ALBERTA	30	—	—
Albert Edward Bay: N.W.T.	44	70	102
Albert Falls: *dam*, Idaho	32	48	117
Albert Lea: Minnesota	10	44	93
Albertville: Alabama	27	34	86
Albion: California	37	39	124
Albion: Indiana	21	41	85
Albion: Michigan	21	42	85
Albion: New York	12	43	78
Albion: Pennsylvania	19	42	80
Albreda: British Columba	41	53	119
Albuquerque: New Mexico	29	35	107
Alcoa: Tennessee	24	36	84
Alden: New York	14	43	79
Aldine: Texas	3	30	95½
Aldergrove: British Columbia	38	49	122
Alderpoint: California	36	40	124
Aleknagik: *& lake*, Alaska	43	59	159
Alenuihaha Ch.: Hawaii	128	20	156
Alert: Northwest Territories	62	83	62
Alert Bay: B.C.	41	51	127
Aleutian Islands	60	53	174
Aleutian Range: Alaska	43	58	155
Alexander Arch.: Alaska	40/41	57	136
Alexander City: Alabama	27	33	86
Alexandra Falls: *sett.*, N.W.T.	30	60	116
Alexandria: Indiana	21	40	86
Alexandria: Louisiana	26	31	92
Alexandria: Ontario	13	45	75
Alexandria: Virginia	17	39	77
Alexandria City: Virginia	2	38¾	77
Algiers: Louisiana	3	30	90
Algoma: Wisconsin	20	45	87
Algonac: Michigan	19	43	83
Algonquin Prov. Park: Ontario	12	46	78
Alhambra: California	7	34	118¼
Alhambra: *r.*, California	6	38	122
Alice: Texas	22	28	98
Aliquippa: Pennsylvania	19	41	80
Alisal: California	37	37	122
Alison Park: *sett.*, Pennsylvania	5	40½	80
Alix: Alberta	30	52	113
Alkali L.: Nevada	36	42	120
Allakaket: Alaska	42	67	153
Allard, Lac: Québec	9	51	64
Allatoona L.: Georgia	24	34	85
Allegan: Michigan	21	43	86
Allegany: *& State Park*, N.Y.	14	42	79
Allegheny: *r.*, Pa./New York	11	42	79
Allegheny County Park: Pa.	5	40½	80
Allen: Oklahoma	26	35	96
Allendale: South Carolina	24	33	81
Allen Park: Michigan	5	42¼	83¼
Allens Mills: Pennsylvania	14	41	79
Allentown: Pennsylvania	14	41	76
Alliance: Nebraska	28	42	103
Alliance: Ohio	19	41	81
Allison: Pennsylvania	16	40	80
Allison Park: Pennsylvania	19	41	80
Alloy: West Virginia	16	38	81
Alma: Arkansas	26	35	94
Alma: Georgia	24	32	82
Alma: Michigan	20	43	85
Alma: Québec	8	49	72
Almanor: *& lake & dam*, Calif.	36	40	121
Almaville: Québec	13	47	73
Almont: Michigan	19	43	83
Almonte: Ontario	12	45	76
Alpaugh: California	34	36	119
Alpena: Michigan	18	45	83
Alpine: California	35	33	117
Alpine: Texas	29	30	104
Alsask: Saskatchewan	30	51	110
Alsek: *r.*, Yukon/B.C.	40	60	138
Altadena: California	7	34¼	118¼
Altamaha: *r.*, Georgia	34	32	82
Altamont: California	37	38	122
Altamont: New York	15	43	74
Altamont: Oregon	36	42	122
Altavista: Virginia	16	37	79
Alto: Texas	26	32	95
Alton: Illinois	10	39	90
Altoona: Alabama	27	34	86
Altoona: Pennsylvania	14	41	78
Alturas: California	36	42	121

	Page	N	W
Altus: Oklahoma	29	35	99
Alva: Kentucky	24	37	83
Alva: Oklahoma	29	37	99
Alvardo: California	6	37½	122
Alvarado: Texas	26	32	97
Alvin: Texas	26	29	95
Alymer, L.: Québec	12	46	71
Amadjuak L.: N.W.T.	45	65	71
Amado: Arizona	33	32	111
Amagansett: New York	15	41	72
Amarillo: Texas	29	35	102
Amasa: Michigan	20	46	88
Ambler: Alaska	42	67	158
Amboy: California	35	35	116
Amboy: Illinois	21	42	89
Ambridge: Pennsylvania	19	41	80
Amelia: Virginia	17	37	78
American Falls Res.: *& dam*, Idaho	32	43	113
American Fork: Utah	33	40	112
Americus: Georgia	24	32	84
Amery: Manitoba	31	57	94
Ames: Iowa	10	42	94
Amesbury: Massachusetts	15	43	71
Amherst: Massachusetts	15	42	73
Amherst: Nova Scotia	9	46	64
Amherst: Ohio	19	41	82
Amherst: Virginia	16	38	79
Amherstburg: Ontario	19	42	83
Amherst I.: Ontario	12	44	77
Amherst Junction: Wisconsin	20	44	89
Amisk L.: Saskatchewan	30	54	102
Amite: Louisiana	27	31	91
Amitoke Peninsula: N.W.T.	45	68	82
Amory: Mississippi	27	34	89
Amos: Québec	8	48	78
Amsterdam: New York	15	43	74
Amsterdam: Ohio	19	40	81
Amundsen Gulf: N.W.T.	44	70	124
Anacapa I.: California	34	34	119
Anaconda: Montana	32	46	113
Anacortes: Washington	38	49	123
Anacostia: *r.*, D.C./Maryland	2	38¾	77
Anaheim: California	7	33¾	117¾
Anahuac: Texas	26	30	95
Anaktuvuk Pass: Alaska	42	68	152
Ancaster: Ontario	19	43	80
Anchorage: Alaska	43	61	150
Anchor Bay: Michigan	5	42½	82¾
Anchor Point: *sett.*, Alaska	43	60	152
Andalusia: Alabama	27	31	87
Anderson: California	36	40	122
Anderson: Indiana	21	40	86
Anderson: South Carolina	24	35	83
Anderson: *r.*, N.W.T.	44	69	128
Anderson L.: B.C.	38	51	122
Andover: Massachusetts	15	43	71
Andover: New York	14	42	78
Andover: Ohio	19	42	81
Andreanof Is.: Alaska	60	52	175
Andrew Gordon Bay: N.W.T.	45	64	76
Andrews: Indiana	21	41	86
Andrews: North Carolina	24	35	84
Andrews: Oregon	36	42	119
Andrews: South Carolina	24	33	80
Androscoggin: *r.*, N.H./Maine	9	45	71
Angel Is.: *& State Park*, Calif.	6	37¾	122½
Angeles National Forest: Calif.	7	34¼	118
Angelina: *r.*, Texas	26	32	95
Angels Camp: California	37	38	121
Angier: North Carolina	24	36	79
Angijak I.: N.W.T.	45	66	62
Angikuni L.: N.W.T.	44	62	100
Angleton: Texas	26	29	95
Angola: Indiana	21	42	85
Angola: New York	19	43	79
Angoon: Alaska	40	58	135
Aniak: Alaska	43	62	160
Animas: *r.*, Colo./New Mexico	28	37	108
Anita: Pennsylvania	19	41	79
Aniwa: Wisconsin	20	45	89
Anmoore: West Virginia	16	39	80
Anna: Ohio	19	40	84
Annacis Island: British Columbia	6	49	123
Annandale: Virginia	2	38¾	77¼
Annapolis: Maryland	17	39	77
Annapolis Royal: Nova Scotia	9	45	66
Ann Arbor: Michigan	19	42	84
Ann, C.: Massachusetts	15	43	71
Annville: Pennsylvania	14	40	77
Anoka: Minnesota	3	45	93
Ansted: West Virginia	16	38	81
Anthony: Kansas	29	37	98
Anthony Chabot Regional Park: California	6	37¾	122
Anticosti I.: Québec	9	49	63
Antigo: Wisconsin	20	45	89
Antioch: California	37	38	122
Antlers: Oklahoma	26	34	96

	Page	N	W
Carnegie: Pennsylvania	**5**	40½	80
Carnwath: *r.*, N.W.T.	**44**	68	128
Caro: Michigan	**18**	43	83
Caroleen: North Carolina	**24**	35	82
Carpentersville: Illinois	**21**	42	88
Carpenterville: Oregon	**36**	42	124
Carpinteria: California	**34**	34	120
Carrabelle: Florida	**25**	30	85
Carrara: Nevada	**35**	37	117
Carrizo: *cr.*, California	**35**	33	116
Carrollton: Georgia	**24**	34	85
Carrollton: Ohio	**19**	41	81
Carrollton: Texas	**26**	33	97
Carrolltown: Pennsylvania	**14**	41	79
Carrot: *r.*, Saskatchewan	**30**	53	103
Carson: California	**7**	33¾	118¼
Carson: *r.*, Nevada	**37**	39	120
Carson City: Michigan	**20**	43	85
Carson City: Nevada	**37**	39	120
Carson Sink: Nevada	**33**	40	119
Cartago: California	**35**	36	118
Carteret: New Jersey	**15**	41	74
Cartersville: Georgia	**24**	34	85
Carthage: Indiana	**21**	40	86
Carthage: Missouri	**10**	37	94
Carthage: New York	**12**	44	76
Carthage: North Carolina	**24**	35	79
Carthage: Texas	**26**	32	94
Cartwright: Newfoundland	**9**	54	57
Cary: North Carolina	**24**	36	79
Caryville: Tennessee	**24**	36	84
Casa Grande: Arizona	**33**	33	112
Cashmere: Washington	**39**	48	120
Casitas Springs: California	**34**	34	119
Casmalia: California	**34**	35	121
Casper: Wyoming	**28**	43	106
Cass: *r.*, Michigan	**18**	43	83
Cass City: Michigan	**18**	44	83
Casselman: Ontario	**13**	45	75
Casselman: *r.*, Pa./Maryland	**16**	40	79
Cassiar: British Columbia	**40**	59	130
Cassiar Mts.: British Columbia	**40**	59	130
Cassopolis: Michigan	**21**	42	86
Castaic: California	**35**	35	119
Castella: California	**36**	41	122
Castile: New York	**14**	43	78
Castillo de San Marcos Nat. Mon.: Florida	**25**	30	81
Castlegar: British Columbia	**41**	49	118
Castle Rock: Washington	**39**	46	123
Castleton-on-Hudson: N.Y.	**15**	43	74
Castor: Alberta	**30**	52	112
Castro Valley: *town*, California	**6**	37¾	122
Castroville: California	**37**	37	122
Catahoula L.: Louisiana	**26**	32	92
Catawba Island: *sett.*, Ohio	**19**	42	83
Catawissa: Pennsylvania	**14**	41	76
Cathay: California	**37**	37	120
Cathlamet: Washington	**39**	46	123
Cat Island: Mississippi	**27**	30	89
Catlettsburg: Kentucky	**16**	38	83
Catlin: Illinois	**21**	40	88
Cataouatche, L.: Louisiana	**3**	29¾	90¼
Catskill: New York	**15**	42	74
Catskill Forest Preserve: N.Y.	**15**	42	75
Catskill Mtns.: New York	**15**	42	74
Cattaraugus: New York	**19**	42	79
Cattaraugus: *cr.*, New York	**14**	42	79
Caughnawaga: Québec	**2**	45½	73¾
Caumsett State Park: New York	**1**	41	73½
Cayey: Puerto Rico	**27**	18	66
Cayoosh Range: B.C.	**38**	50	122
Cayucos: California	**34**	35	121
Cayuga L.: New York	**14**	43	77
Cazenovia: New York	**14**	43	76
Cedar: *cr.*, North Dakota	**28**	46	102
Cedar: *r.*, Iowa	**10**	43	93
Cedar: *r.*, Washington	**6**	47½	122½
Cedar Bluff: Virginia	**16**	37	82
Cedarburg: Wisconsin	**20**	43	88
Cedar City: Utah	**33**	38	113
Cedar Falls: *town*, Iowa	**10**	43	92
Cedar Grove: W. Va.	**16**	38	81
Cedar L.: Manitoba	**31**	53	100
Cedar Rapids: Iowa	**10**	42	92
Cedar Springs: Michigan	**20**	43	86
Cedartown: Georgia	**27**	34	85
Cedarville: California	**36**	42	120
Cedarville: New Jersey	**14**	39	75
Celeste: Texas	**26**	33	96
Celina: Ohio	**21**	41	85
Celina: Texas	**26**	33	97
Center: Connecticut	**15**	41	73
Center: Texas	**26**	32	94
Center Hill Res.: Tennessee	**27**	36	86
Center Line: Michigan	**5**	42½	83
Center Moriches: New York	**15**	41	73
Centerville: Indiana	**21**	40	85
Centerville: Iowa	**10**	41	93
Centerville: Tennessee	**27**	36	87
Centerville: Texas	**26**	31	96
Centerville, L.: Minnesota	**3**	45¼	93
Central: Alaska	**42**	66	145
Central: New Mexico	**29**	33	108
Central: South Carolina	**24**	35	83
Central City: Colorado	**28**	40	106
Central City: Pennsylvania	**14**	40	79

	Page	N	W
Centralia: Illinois	**10**	39	89
Centralia: Washington	**39**	47	123
Central Lake: *sett.*, Michigan	**20**	45	85
Central Park: British Columbia	**6**	49¼	123
Central Park: New York	**1**	40¾	74
Central Valley: *town*, California	**36**	41	122
Centre: Alabama	**27**	34	86
Centreville: Maryland	**17**	39	76
Centreville: Michigan	**21**	42	86
Centreville: Mississippi	**26**	31	91
Ceres: California	**37**	38	121
Cerro Gordo: Illinois	**21**	40	89
Chabot, L.: California	**6**	37¾	120
Chacahoula: Louisiana	**27**	30	91
Chaco Canyon Nat. Mon.: New Mexico	**29**	36	108
Chadbourn: North Carolina	**24**	34	79
Chadron: Nebraska	**28**	43	103
Chagrin Falls: *town*, Ohio	**19**	41	81
Chaleur, Baie de: Québec/N.B.	**9**	48	66
Chalkyitsik: Alaska	**42**	67	144
Chalmette: Louisiana	**3**	30	90
Chalmette Natural History Pk.: La.	**3**	30	90
Chamberlain: South Dakota	**28**	44	99
Chamberlain, L.: Maine	**8**	46	69
Chambersburg: Pennsylvania	**14**	40	78
Chamouchouane: *r.*, Québec	**8**	49	73
Champagne: Yukon	**40**	61	137
Champaign: Illinois	**21**	40	88
Champlain: New York	**13**	45	73
Champlain, L.: Vt./New York	**13**	45	73
Chandalar: Alaska	**42**	68	149
Chandalar: *r.*, Alaska	**42**	67	147
Chandeleur Is.: Louisiana	**27**	30	89
Chandeleur Sound: Louisiana	**27**	30	89
Chandler: Arizona	**33**	33	112
Chandler: Oklahoma	**26**	36	97
Chandler: Québec	**9**	48	65
Chandler: Texas	**26**	32	95
Chaniliut: Alaska	**42**	63	163
Channel Is. Nat. Mon.: Calif.	**34**	34	119
Channing: Michigan	**20**	46	88
Chantrey Inlet: N.W.T.	**44**	68	96
Chanute: Kansas	**29**	38	95
Chapais: Québec	**8**	50	75
Chapel Hill: *town*, N.C.	**24**	36	79
Chapleau: Ontario	**10**	48	83
Chapman, C.: N.W.T.	**45**	69	89
Chardon: Ohio	**19**	42	81
Chariton: *r.*, Iowa/Missouri	**10**	40	93
Charles: *r.*, Massachusetts	**2**	42¼	71
Charles City: Iowa	**10**	43	93
Charles I.: N.W.T.	**45**	63	75
Charles Lee Tilden Regional Park: California	**6**	38	122¼
Charleston: Arkansas	**26**	35	94
Charleston: Illinois	**21**	40	88
Charleston: Mississippi	**27**	34	90
Charleston: South Carolina	**24**	33	80
Charleston: Tennessee	**24**	35	85
Charleston: West Virginia	**16**	38	82
Charleston Park: Nevada	**35**	36	116
Charlestown: New Hampshire	**13**	43	72
Charles Town: West Virginia	**17**	39	78
Charlevoix: Michigan	**20**	45	85
Charlotte: Michigan	**21**	43	85
Charlotte: North Carolina	**24**	35	81
Charlotte Harbor: Florida	**25**	27	82
Charlottesville: Virginia	**17**	38	78
Charlottetown: P.E.I.	**9**	46	63
Charlton City: Massachusetts	**15**	42	72
Charlton Depot: N.W.T.	**8**	52	79
Charlton I.: N.W.T.	**8**	52	80
Chartiers Creek: Pennsylvania	**5**	40½	80
Chase: British Columbia	**38**	51	120
Chase City: Virginia	**17**	37	78
Chatanika: Alaska	**42**	65	147
Chatham: Massachusetts	**15**	42	70
Chatham: Michigan	**20**	46	87
Chatham: New York	**15**	42	74
Chatham: Ontario	**19**	42	82
Chatham: Virginia	**16**	37	79
Chatham Strait: Alaska	**41**	56	134
Chatsworth: Georgia	**24**	35	85
Chattahoochee: Florida	**27**	31	85
Chattahoochee: *r.*, Ga./Ala.	**27**	31	85
Chattanooga: Tennessee	**27**	35	85
Chatuge: *dam.*, N.C./Georgia	**24**	35	84
Chaudière: *r.*, Québec	**13**	47	71
Chauncey: Ohio	**16**	39	82
Chautauqua L.: New York	**19**	42	79
Chazy: New York	**13**	45	73
Cheaha Mount: Alabama	**27**	33	86
Cheat: *r.*, West Virginia	**16**	40	80
Cheatham: *dam*, Tennessee	**23**	36	87
Cheat Mtn.: West Virginia	**16**	39	80
Cheboygan: Michigan	**20**	46	84
Checotah: Oklahoma	**26**	35	96
Chefornak: Alaska	**43**	60	164
Chehalis: & *r.*, Washington	**39**	47	123
Chelan: Washington	**39**	48	120
Chelan L.: Washington	**38/39**	48	120
Chelsea: Massachusetts	**2**	42¼	71
Chelsea: Michigan	**21**	42	84
Chemainus: British Columbia	**38**	49	124
Chenega: Alaska	**43**	60	148
Cheneyville: Louisiana	**26**	31	92

	Page	N	W
Chenik: Alaska	**43**	59	154
Chenoa: Illinois	**21**	41	89
Cheoah: *dam*, North Carolina	**24**	35	84
Cheraw: South Carolina	**24**	35	80
Cherikof I.: Alaska	**43**	56	156
Cherokee: Alabama	**27**	35	88
Cherokee: *dam*, Tennessee	**24**	36	83
Cherokees, L. of the: Okla.	**29**	37	95
Cherry Creek: Colorado	**3**	39¾	105
Cherry Creek Reservoir: Colo.	**3**	39¾	104¾
Cherry Hill: *sett.*, New Jersey	**2**	40	75
Cherry Hills Village: Colorado	**3**	39¾	105
Cherry Valley: *sett.*, New York	**15**	43	75
Chesaning: Michigan	**20**	43	84
Chesapeake: Ohio	**16**	38	82
Chesapeake: Virginia	**17**	37	76
Chesapeake: West Virginia	**16**	38	82
Chesapeake Bay: Md./Virginia	**17**	38	76
Cheshire: Connecticut	**15**	42	73
Cheshire: Massachusetts	**15**	43	73
Chester: California	**36**	40	121
Chester: Massachusetts	**15**	42	73
Chester: New York	**15**	41	74
Chester: Pennsylvania	**2**	39¾	75¼
Chester: South Carolina	**24**	35	81
Chester: Virginia	**17**	37	77
Chesterfield: South Carolina	**24**	35	80
Chesterfield Inlet: N.W.T.	**45**	63	92
Chesterfield Inlet: *sett.*, N.W.T.	**45**	63	91
Chesterland: Ohio	**19**	42	81
Chesterton: Indiana	**21**	42	87
Chestertown: Maryland	**17**	39	76
Chesterville: Ontario	**13**	45	75
Chestnut Hill: *sett.*, Pennsylvania	**2**	40	75¼
Chesuncook L.: Maine	**8**	46	69
Chevak: Alaska	**43**	62	166
Chevy Chase: Maryland	**2**	39	77
Cheyenne: Wyoming	**28**	41	105
Cheyenne: *r.*, South Dakota	**28**	44	102
Cheyenne Wells: Colorado	**29**	39	102
Chibougamau: Québec	**8**	50	74
Chicago: Illinois	**21**	42	88
Chicago Habor: Illinois	**4**	42	87½
Chicago Heights: Illinois	**21**	42	88
Chicago Sanitary and Ship Canal: Illinois	**4**	41¾	87¾
Chichagof I.: Alaska	**40**	58	136
Chickaloon: Alaska	**43**	62	148
Chickamauga L.: & *dam*, Tenn.	**27**	35	85
Chickasawhay: *r.*, Mississippi	**27**	31	89
Chickasha: Oklahoma	**29**	35	98
Chicken: Alaska	**42**	64	142
Chico: California	**37**	40	122
Chico: Washington	**39**	48	123
Chicopee: Massachusetts	**15**	43	73
Chicoutimi: Québec	**8**	48	71
Chief Joseph: *dam*, Wash.	**39**	48	120
Chignecto Bay: N.S./N.B.	**9**	46	65
Chignik: Alaska	**43**	56	158
Chignik Lagoon: *sett.*, Alaska	**43**	56	159
Chikaskia: *r.*, Kansas/Okla.	**29**	37	98
Chilcotin: *r.*, British Columbia	**41**	52	124
Childersburg: Alabama	**27**	33	86
Childress: Texas	**29**	34	100
Chilhowee: *dam*, Tennessee	**24**	35	84
Chilhowie: Virginia	**16**	37	82
Chilkoot: British Columbia	**40**	60	134
Chillicothe: Illinois	**21**	41	90
Chillicothe: Missouri	**10**	40	94
Chillicothe: Ohio	**16**	39	83
Chilliwack: British Columbia	**38**	49	122
Chiloquin: Oregon	**36**	43	122
Chilton: Wisconsin	**20**	44	88
China L.: California	**35**	36	118
China Lake: *sett.*, California	**35**	36	118
Chinchaga: *r.*, Alberta	**30**	58	119
Chincoteague: Virginia	**17**	38	75
Chincoteague B.: Maryland	**17**	38	75
Chiniak, C.: Alaska	**43**	58	152
Chino: California	**7**	34	117¾
Chipai L.: Ontario	**31**	53	88
Chipley: Florida	**27**	31	86
Chipola: *r.*, Fla./Alabama	**27**	31	85
Chippewa: *r.*, Michigan	**20**	44	84
Chippewa: *r.*, Wisconsin	**10**	45	91
Chippewa Falls: *town*, Wisconsin	**10**	45	91
Chistochina: Alaska	**43**	63	145
Chitina: Alaska	**43**	62	145
Chitina: *r.*, Alaska	**43**	61	144
Choate: British Columbia	**38**	49	121
Chocolate Mts.: California	**35**	33	115
Choctawhatchee: *r.*, Ala./Fla.	**27**	31	86
Cholame: California	**34**	36	120
Chomedey: Québec	**2**	45½	73¾
Choptank: *r.*, Maryland	**17**	39	76
Chorkbak Inlet: N.W.T.	**45**	65	74
Chowan: *r.*, North Carolina	**24**	36	77
Chowchilla: California	**37**	37	120
Chrisman: Illinois	**21**	40	88
Christiana: Pennsylvania	**14**	40	76
Christian I.: Ontario	**18**	45	80
Christiansburg: Virginia	**16**	37	80
Christie Bay: N.W.T.	**44**	63	111
Christina: *r.*, Alberta	**30**	56	111
Chualar: California	**37**	37	122
Chubbuck: California	**35**	34	115
Chuckawalla Mts.: California	**35**	34	115

	Page	N	W
Frankton: Indiana	21	40	86
Franktown: Nevada	37	39	120
Fraser: Michigan	5	42½	83
Fraser: *r.*, British Columbia	41	51	122
Fraser: *r.*, Newfoundland	9	57	64
Frederick: Maryland	17	39	77
Frederick: Oklahoma	29	34	99
Fredericksburg: Virginia	17	38	78
Fredericktown: Missouri	10	38	90
Fredericktown: Ohio	19	40	83
Fredericton: New Brunswick	9	46	67
Fredonia: New York	19	42	79
Fredrikshald Bay: N.W.T.	44	71	104
Freehold: New Jersey	15	40	74
Freeland: Michigan	20	44	84
Freeland: Pennsylvania	14	41	76
Freels, C.: Newfoundland	9	49	53
Freeman: Wisconsin	20	45	89
Freeport: Illinois	21	42	90
Freeport: New York	1	40¾	73½
Freeport: Pennsylvania	19	41	80
Freeport: Texas	26	29	95
Fremont: Michigan	20	43	86
Fremont: Nebraska	28	41	97
Fremont: North Carolina	24	36	78
Fremont: Ohio	19	41	83
French: *cr.*, Pennsylvania	9	42	80
French Broad: *r.*, N.C./Tenn.	24	36	83
French Camp: California	37	38	121
French Frigate Shoals: *is.*, Hawaii	128	24	167
Frenchglen: Oregon	36	43	119
French Gulch: California	36	41	123
Frenchman: *cr.*, Colo./Nebraska	28	41	102
Frenchman Flat: *dry lake*, Nev.	35	37	116
Frenchtown: New Jersey	14	41	75
Fresh Pond: Massachusetts	2	42¼	71
Fresno: California	37	37	120
Fresno: *r.*, California	37	37	120
Frewsburg: New York	19	42	79
Friant: California	37	37	120
Friars Point: *sett.*, Mississippi	27	34	91
Friday Harbor: Washington	38	49	123
Fridley: Minnesota	3	45	93¼
Friedens: Pennsylvania	17	40	79
Friendship: New York	14	42	78
Friendsville: Maryland	16	40	79
Fries: Virginia	16	37	81
Frio: *r.*, Texas	22	29	99
Frobisher Bay: N.W.T.	45	63	67
Frobisher Bay: *sett.*, N.W.T.	45	64	69
Frobisher L.: Saskatchewan	30	56	108
Front Royal: Virginia	17	39	78
Frostburg: Maryland	17	40	79
Frostproof: Florida	25	28	82
Froze Strait: N.W.T.	45	66	85
Fruitland: Maryland	17	38	76
Fryeburg: Maine	13	44	71
Fulford Harbour: B.C.	38	49	123
Fullerton: California	7	34	117¾
Fullerton: Kentucky	16	39	83
Fullerton, C.: N.W.T.	45	64	89
Fullerton Res.: California	7	34	118
Fulton: Mississippi	27	34	88
Fulton: Missouri	10	39	92
Fulton: New York	12	43	76
Fultonville: New York	15	43	74
Fundy, Bay of: N.S./N.B.	9	45	66
Fundy Nat. Pk.: New Brunswick	9	46	65
Fury and Hecla Str.: N.W.T.	45	70	85
Gabriel Str.: N.W.T.	45	62	66
Gadsden: Alabama	27	34	86
Gaffney: South Carolina	24	35	82
Gages Lake: Illinois	4	42¼	88
Gagnon: Québec	9	52	68
Gainesville: Florida	25	30	82
Gainesville: Georgia	24	34	84
Gainesville: Texas	26	34	97
Gaithersburg: Maryland	17	39	77
Gakona: Alaska	43	62	145
Galax: Virginia	16	37	81
Galena: Alaska	42	60	157
Galena: Illinois	10	42	90
Galena: Kansas	28	37	95
Galena Park: *sett.*, Texas	3	29¾	95¼
Galesburg: Illinois	10	41	90
Galeton: Pennsylvania	14	42	78
Galiano I.: B.C.	38	49	123
Galice: Oregon	36	43	124
Galion: Ohio	19	41	83
Gallatin: Tennessee	23	36	87
Gallatin: *r.*, Montana	28	45	111
Gallipolis: Ohio	16	39	82
Gallitzin: Pennsylvania	14	41	79
Galloo I.: New York	12	44	76
Galloway: Wisconsin	20	45	89
Gallup: New Mexico	29	36	109
Galt: California	37	38	121
Galt: Ontario	18	43	80
Galveston: Texas	26	39	95
Galveston Bay: Texas	26	30	95
Gambell: Alaska	60	64	172
Gambier I.: B.C.	38	49	123
Ganado St. Park: Texas	26	29	97
Gananoque: Ontario	12	44	76
Gander: *& r.*, Newfoundland	9	49	55
Gannett Peak: Wyoming	28	43	110
Garberville: California	36	30	124
Gardena: California	7	34	118¼
Garden City: Kansas	29	38	101
Garden City: Michigan	5	42¼	83¼
Garden City: New York	1	40¾	73¾
Garden City: South Carolina	24	34	79
Garden Grove: California	7	33¾	118
Garden I.: Michigan	20	46	86
Garden State Parkway: N.J.	15	40	74
Gardiner: Washington	38	48	123
Gardner: Illinois	21	41	88
Gardner: Massachusetts	15	43	72
Gardner Canal: B.C.	41	53	128
Gardner Pinnacles: *rocks*, Hawaii	128	25	168
Gardnerville: Nevada	37	39	120
Garfield: New Jersey	1	40¾	74
Garfield: Utah	33	41	112
Garibaldi: Oregon	39	46	124
Garibaldi Prov. Park: B.C.	38	50	123
Garland: Texas	26	33	97
Garnet Bay: N.W.T.	45	65	75
Garnett: Kansas	29	38	95
Garnier Bay: N.W.T.	45	74	92
Garrettsville: Ohio	19	41	81
Garrett: Indiana	21	41	85
Garrison: Montana	32	47	113
Garry Bay: N.W.T.	45	69	85
Garry L.: N.W.T.	44	66	100
Gary: Indiana	4	41½	87½
Gas City: Indiana	21	40	86
Gasconade: *r.*, Missouri	10	38	92
Gas Hills: Wyoming	28	44	109
Gaspé: Québec	9	49	65
Gaspé Passage: Québec	9	49	65
Gaspé Penin.: Québec	9	49	66
Gaspesian Prov. Park: Québec	9	49	66
Gassaway: West Virginia	16	39	81
Gaston, L.: Virginia	17	37	78
Gastonia: North Carolina	24	35	81
Gate City: Virginia	16	37	83
Gateshead I.: N.W.T.	44	71	100
Gatineau: *r.*, Québec	8	46	76
Gatineau Park: Ontario	12	45	76
Gatlinburg: Tennessee	24	36	83
Gauer L.: Manitoba	31	57	98
Gaukler Point: Michigan	5	42½	82¾
Gauley: *r.*, West Virginia	16	38	80
Gauley Bridge: W. Va.	16	38	81
Gaviota: California	34	34	120
Gearhart Mt.: Oregon	36	43	121
Geikie: *r.*, Saskatchewan	30	58	104
Geismar: Louisiana	26	30	91
Genesee: California	36	40	121
Geneva: Alabama	27	31	86
Geneva: Illinois	21	42	88
Geneva: Indiana	21	41	85
Geneva: New York	14	43	77
Geneva: Ohio	19	42	81
Geneva: Utah	33	40	112
Geneva, L.: Wisconsin	21	43	88
Geneva-on-the-Lake: Ohio	19	42	81
Genoa: Nevada	37	39	120
Genoa: Ohio	19	42	83
Gentilly: Louisiana	3	30	90
George: *r.*, Québec	9	57	65
George, L.: Florida	25	29	82
George, L.: New York	13	44	74
George River (Port-Nouveau-Québec): *sett.*, Québec	45	58	65
Georgetown: California	37	39	121
Georgetown: Connecticut	15	41	73
Georgetown: Delaware	17	39	75
Georgetown: Idaho	32	42	111
Georgetown: Illinois	21	40	88
Georgetown: Massachusetts	15	43	71
Georgetown: Ontario	12	44	80
Georgetown: South Carolina	24	33	79
GEORGIA	24/25	—	—
Georgiana: Alabama	27	32	87
Georgian Bay: Ontario	18	45	81
Georgian Bay Islands Nat. Pk.: Ontario	18	45	82
Georgia, Strait of: B.C.	38	49	124
Geraldton: Ontario	10	40	87
Gerber: California	36	40	122
Gerber Res.: Oregon	36	42	121
Gerdine, Mt.: Alaska	43	62	153
Gering: Nebraska	28	42	104
Gerlach: Nevada	36	41	119
Germantown: Ohio	21	40	84
Germantown: Pennsylvania	2	40	75¼
Gethsémani: Québec	9	50	61
Gettysburg: Pennsylvania	14	40	77
Geyserville: California	37	39	123
Gibbs Fiord: N.W.T.	45	71	72
Gibbstown: New Jersey	14	40	75
Gibsland: Louisiana	26	33	93
Gibson: California	36	41	122
Gibsonburg: Ohio	19	41	83
Gibson City: Illinois	21	40	88
Gibsonia: Pennsylvania	5	40¾	80
Gibsonville: North Carolina	24	36	80
Giddings: Texas	26	30	97
Gifford: *r.*, N.W.T.	45	71	83
Gifford Fiord: N.W.T.	45	70	82
Gig Harbor: Washington	39	47	123
Gila: *r.*, Arizona	33	33	109
Gila Bend: Arizona	33	33	113
Gila Cliff Dwellings Nat. Mon.: New Mexico	29	33	108
Gilbert, Mt.: B.C.	38	51	124
Gilbertville: Massachusetts	15	42	72
Gilford Park: New Jersey	15	40	74
Gillam: Manitoba	31	56	95
Gillett: Arkansas	26	34	91
Gillett: Wisconsin	20	45	88
Gillette: Wyoming	28	44	106
Gillian L.: N.W.T.	45	70	75
Gilman: Illinois	21	41	88
Gilmer: Texas	26	33	95
Gilroy: California	37	37	122
Gilroy Hot Springs: California	37	37	121
Girard: Ohio	19	41	81
Girard: Pennsylvania	19	42	80
Girdwood: Alaska	43	61	149
Giscome: British Columbia	41	54	122
Gjoa Haven: N.W.T.	44	69	96
Glace Bay: *town*, Nova Scotia	9	46	60
Glacier: British Columbia	41	51	118
Glacier Bay N.M.: Alaska	40	59	136
Glacier Creek: *sett.*, Yukon	40	64	141
Glacier National Park: B.C.	41	53	120
Glacier International Peace Park: Montana	32	49	114
Glacier Peak: Washington	38	48	121
Glacier View: *dam*, Montana	32	49	114
Gladewater: Texas	26	33	95
Gladstone: Michigan	20	46	87
Gladstone: Oregon	39	45	123
Gladwin: Michigan	20	44	84
Glamis: California	35	30	115
Glasgow: Kentucky	23	37	86
Glasgow: Montana	28	48	107
Glassboro: New Jersey	14	40	75
Glassmere: Pennsylvania	19	41	80
Glastonbury: Connecticut	15	42	73
Gleichen: Alberta	30	51	113
Glenbrook: Nevada	37	39	120
Glen Burnie: Maryland	17	39	77
Glen Canyon: *dam*, Arizona	33	37	111
Glencoe: Illinois	4	42¼	87¾
Glencoe: Minnesota	10	45	94
Glen Cove: New York	1	40¾	73¾
Glendale: Arizona	33	34	112
Glendale: California	7	34¼	118¼
Glendale: Colorado	3	39¾	105
Glendive: Montana	28	47	105
Glendora: California	7	34	117¾
Glen Ellen: California	37	38	123
Glen Ellyn: Illinois	4	42	88
Glen Lyon: Pennsylvania	14	41	76
Glenmora: Louisiana	26	31	93
Glenn: California	37	40	122
Glennallen: Alaska	43	62	146
Glennville: Georgia	24	32	82
Glen Ridge: New Jersey	1	40¾	74¼
Glen Rock: Pennsylvania	14	40	77
Glens Fall: *town*, N.Y.	13	43	74
Glenshaw: Pennsylvania	5	40½	80
Glenview: Illinois	4	42	87¾
Glenville: Pennsylvania	14	40	77
Glenville: West Virginia	16	39	81
Glenwood: Minnesota	10	46	95
Glenwood Springs: Colorado	28	40	107
Globe: Arizona	33	33	111
Gloster: Mississippi	26	31	91
Gloucester: Massachusetts	15	43	71
Gloucester: Virginia	17	37	77
Gloucester: Ohio	16	39	82
Gloucester City: New Jersey	2	40	75
Gloversville: New York	13	43	74
Gnadenhutten: Ohio	19	40	81
Goat I.: British Columbia	38	50	124
Goderich: Ontario	18	44	82
Godhavn: Greenland	45	69	54
Gods: *r.*, Manitoba	31	55	93
Gods L.: Manitoba	31	55	94
Gods Mercy, Bay of: N.W.T.	45	64	86
Goffs: California	35	35	115
Goffstown: New Hampshire	13	43	72
Gold Beach: Oregon	36	42	124
Golden: British Columbia	32	51	117
Golden: Colorado	28	40	105
Goldendale: Washington	39	46	121
Golden Ears Prov. Park: B.C.	38	50	122
Golden Gate: *str.*, California	6	37¾	122½
Golden Gate Nat. Recreation Area: California	6	37¾	122½
Golden Gate Park: California	6	37¾	122½
Golden Valley: Minnesota	3	45	93¼
Gold Hill: *sett.*, Oregon	32	42	123
Gold Mt.: Washington	39	48	123
Goldpines: Ontario	10	51	93
Goldsboro: North Carolina	24	35	78
Goldstone L.: California	35	35	117
Goleta: California	34	34	120
Golovin: Alaska	42	65	163
Gonzales: California	37	37	121
Gooding: Idaho	32	43	115
Goodland: Kansas	28	39	102
Goodman: Wisconsin	20	46	88
Goodnews (Mumtrak): *sett.*, Alaska	43	59	162

	Page	N	W
Goodsprings: Nevada	**35**	36	115
Goose: *r.*	**32**	42	114
Goose: *r.*, North Dakota	**28**	47	97
Goose Bay: *town*, Alaska	**43**	61	150
Goose Bay: *town*, Newfoundland	**9**	53	60
Goose L.: Oregon/California	**36**	42	120
Gorda: California	**34**	36	121
Gorda, Punta: *cape*, California	**36**	40	124
Gordon: Alaska	**42**	70	141
Gordon: Georgia	**24**	33	83
Gordon: Pennsylvania	**14**	41	76
Gordon Lake: *sett.*, Manitoba	**31**	49	100
Gordonsville: Virginia	**17**	38	78
Gore Bay: *town*, Ontario	**18**	46	82
Gorham: New Hampshire	**13**	44	71
Gorham: New York	**14**	43	77
Gorman: California	**35**	35	119
Goshen: California	**34**	36	119
Goshen: Indiana	**21**	42	86
Goshen: New York	**15**	41	74
Gothenburg: Nebraska	**28**	41	100
Gouin Reservoir: Québec	**8**	49	75
Gould: Arkansas	**26**	34	92
Gould City: Michigan	**20**	46	86
Gouverneur: New York	**13**	44	75
Gowanda: New York	**19**	42	79
Gowganda: Ontario	**11**	48	81
Graceville: Florida	**27**	31	86
Grafton: New Hampshire	**13**	44	72
Grafton: North Dakota	**28**	48	97
Grafton: Ohio	**19**	41	82
Grafton: West Virginia	**16**	39	80
Graham: Texas	**29**	33	99
Graham: West Virginia	**16**	39	82
Graham I.: B.C.	**41**	53	132
Graham Moore, C.: N.W.T.	**45**	73	76
Gramercy: Louisiana	**27**	30	91
Granby: Connecticut	**15**	42	73
Granby: Québec	**13**	45	73
Granby: *r.*, B.C.	**41**	50	119
Grand: *r.*, Michigan	**20**	43	85
Grand: *r.*, Missouri	**10**	40	94
Grand: *r.*, Ohio	**19**	42	81
Grand: *r.*, Ontario	**18**	43	80
Grand: *r.*, South Dakota	**28**	46	102
Grand Bank: *town*, Newfoundland	**9**	47	56
Grand Blanc: Michigan	**19**	43	84
Grand Calumet: Ontario	**12**	46	77
Grand Canyon: Arizona	**33**	36	113
Grand Canyon: *sett.*, Arizona	**33**	36	112
Grand Canyon Nat. Park: Ariz.	**33**	36	112
Grand Centre: Alberta	**30**	54	110
Grand Coulee: *dam*, Washington	**38**	48	119
Grand Calumet: Québec	**12**	46	77
Grande Prairie: Alberta	**30**	55	119
Grand Ronde: *r.*, Oregon	**32**	46	118
Grand Falls: *town*, N.B.	**9**	47	68
Grand Falls: *town*, Nfld.	**9**	49	56
Grand Forks: British Columbia	**41**	49	119
Grand Forks: North Dakota	**10**	48	97
Grand Gorge: New York	**15**	42	75
Grand Haven: Michigan	**20**	43	86
Grandin, L.: N.W.T.	**40**	64	119
Grand I.: Louisiana	**27**	29	90
Grand Island: *town*, Nebraska	**28**	41	98
Grand Junction: Colorado	**29**	39	109
Grand L.: Louisiana	**26**	30	91
Grand L.: Louisiana	**26**	30	93
Grand L.: Newfoundland	**9**	49	58
Grand L.: Ohio	**21**	41	85
Grand Ledge: Michigan	**21**	43	85
Grand Manan I.: N.B.	**9**	45	67
Grand'Mère: Québec	**13**	47	73
Grand Prairie: Texas	**26**	33	97
Grand Rapids: Manitoba	**31**	53	99
Grand Rapids: Michigan	**20**	43	86
Grand Rapids: Minnesota	**10**	47	94
Grand Saline: Texas	**26**	33	96
Grand Teton Nat. Park: Wyo.	**28**	44	111
Grand Traverse Bay: Michigan	**20**	45	86
Grandview: Manitoba	**31**	51	101
Grandview: Texas	**26**	32	97
Grandview: Washington	**39**	46	120
Grandville: Michigan	**20**	43	86
Granger: Washington	**39**	46	120
Grangeville: Idaho	**32**	46	116
Granite Falls: *sett.*, N.C.	**24**	36	81
Granite Mts.: California	**35**	34	115
Granite Mts.: California	**35**	35	116
Granite Peak: Montana	**28**	45	110
Granite Range: Nevada	**36**	41	120
Graniteville: California	**37**	39	121
Graniteville: South Carolina	**24**	34	82
Gran Quivira Nat. Mon.: New Mexico	**29**	34	106
Grant Park: Illinois	**4**	41¾	87½
Grant Point: N.W.T.	**44**	68	98
Grants: New Mexico	**29**	35	108
Grants Pass: Oregon	**36**	42	123
Grantsville: Maryland	**16**	40	79
Grant Town: West Virginia	**16**	40	80
Granville: New York	**13**	43	73
Granville: Ohio	**16**	40	83
Granville: Pennsylvania	**14**	41	78
Granville L.: Manitoba	**31**	56	100
Grapeland: Texas	**26**	32	96
Grapevine: California	**35**	35	119

	Page	N	W
Grass: *r.*, Manitoba	**31**	55	98
Grassflat: Pennsylvania	**14**	41	78
Grass Lake: *sett.*, California	**36**	42	122
Grass Narrows: Ontario	**10**	50	94
Grass Valley: *town*, California	**37**	39	121
Gravelbourg: Saskatchewan	**30**	50	107
Gravell Point: N.W.T.	**45**	67	77
Grayling: Michigan	**20**	45	85
Grays Harbor: Washington	**39**	47	124
Grayslake: Illinois	**4**	42¼	88
Grayson: Kentucky	**16**	38	83
Great Barrington: Massachusetts	**15**	42	73
Great Basin	**33**	40	116
Great Bear L.: N.W.T.	**40**	66	121
Great Bend: Kansas	**29**	38	99
Great Cacapon: W. Va.	**17**	40	78
Great Central: British Columbia	**43**	49	125
Great Central L.: B.C.	**38**	49	125
Great Falls: *sett.*, S.C.	**24**	35	81
Great Falls: *town*, Montana	**28**	48	111
Great Falls of the Potomac: Maryland	**2**	39	77¼
Great Kills Park: New York	**1**	40½	74
Great Meadows Nat. Wild Life Refuge: Massachusetts	**2**	42½	71¼
Great Neck: New York	**1**	40¾	73¾
Great Salt L.: Utah	**33**	41	113
Great Salt Lake Desert: Utah	**33**	41	113
Great Sand Dunes Nat. Mon.: Colorado	**28**	38	106
Great Slave L.: N.W.T.	**44**	61	114
Great Smoky Mts. Nat. Park: Tennessee/North Carolina	**24**	36	83
Great South Bay: New York	**1**	40¾	74¼
Great Whale: *r.*, Québec	**8**	55	76
Great Whale River: *sett.*, Qué.	**8**	55	78
Greely: Colorado	**28**	40	105
Green: *r.*, Illinois	**21**	42	89
Green: *r.*, Kentucky	**23**	38	87
Green: *r.*, Wyoming/Utah	**28**	40	110
Greenbackville: Virginia	**17**	38	75
Greenbank: Washington	**38**	48	123
Green Bay: Wis./Michigan	**20**	45	87
Green Bay: *town*, Wisconsin	**20**	45	88
Greenbelt: *sett. and park*, Md.	**2**	39	77
Greenbrier: *r.*, West Virginia	**16**	38	80
Greencastle: Indiana	**21**	40	87
Greencastle: Pennsylvania	**14**	40	78
Green Cove Springs: Florida	**25**	30	82
Greene: New York	**14**	42	76
Greeneville: Tennessee	**16**	36	83
Greenfield: California	**34**	35	119
Greenfield: California	**34**	36	121
Greenfield: Indiana	**21**	40	86
Greenfield: Massachusetts	**15**	43	73
Greenfield: Ohio	**16**	39	83
Greenfield: Tennessee	**22**	36	89
Green L.: Washington	**6**	47¾	122¼
Green L.: Wisconsin	**20**	44	89
Green Mts.: Vermont	**13**	44	73
Greenpark: Pennsylvania	**14**	40	77
Greenport: New York	**15**	41	72
Green River: Wyoming	**28**	42	109
Greens Bayou: Texas	**3**	29¾	95¼
Greensboro: Alabama	**27**	33	88
Greensboro: Georgia	**24**	34	83
Greensboro: Maryland	**17**	39	76
Greensboro: North Carolina	**24**	36	80
Greensburg: Pennsylvania	**19**	40	80
Green Springs: Ohio	**19**	41	83
Greentown: Indiana	**21**	40	86
Greenview: California	**36**	42	123
Greenville: Alabama	**27**	32	87
Greenville: California	**36**	40	121
Greenville: Florida	**25**	30	84
Greenville: Michigan	**20**	43	85
Greenville: Mississippi	**27**	33	91
Greenville: New Hampshire	**13**	43	72
Greenville: North Carolina	**24**	36	77
Greenville: Ohio	**21**	40	85
Greenville: Pennsylvania	**19**	41	80
Greenville: South Carolina	**24**	35	82
Greenville: Texas	**26**	33	96
Greenwich: Connecticut	**1**	41	73½
Greenwich: New Jersey	**14**	39	75
Greenwich: New York	**13**	43	74
Greenwich: Ohio	**19**	41	83
Greenwood: British Columbia	**41**	49	119
Greenwood: Indiana	**21**	40	86
Greenwood: Mississippi	**27**	34	90
Greenwood: New York	**15**	41	74
Greenwood: South Carolina	**24**	34	82
Greenwood Village: Colorado	**3**	39¼	105
Greer: South Carolina	**24**	35	82
Greer's Ferry Res.: *& dam*, Ark.	**26**	36	92
Greeson, L.: Arkansas	**26**	34	94
Grenada: California	**36**	42	123
Grenada: Mississippi	**27**	34	90
Grenada Res.: Mississippi	**27**	34	90
Gresham: Oregon	**39**	46	122
Gretna: Louisiana	**3**	30	90
Gridley: California	**37**	39	122
Griffin: Georgia	**24**	33	84
Griffith: Indiana	**21**	42	87
Griffith I.: N.W.T.	**45**	75	96
Griffith Park: California	**7**	34¼	118¼
Grimsby: *sett.*, Ontario	**19**	43	80

	Page	N	W
Grimshaw: Alberta	**30**	56	118
Grinnell Ice Cap: N.W.T.	**45**	62	67
Grise Fiord: *sett.*, N.W.T.	**61**	76	83
Groais I.: Newfoundland	**9**	51	55
Groesbeck: Texas	**26**	32	97
Grosse Point: Michigan	**5**	42½	83
Grosse Pointe: *sett.*, Michigan	**5**	42½	83
Grosse Pointe Park: *sett.*, Mich.	**5**	42½	83
Grosse Pointe Shores: *sett.*, Mich.	**5**	42½	83
Groswater Bay: Newfoundland	**9**	54	58
Groton: Connecticut	**15**	41	72
Groton: New York	**14**	43	76
Grottoes: Virginia	**17**	38	79
Groundhog: *r.*, Ontario	**11**	49	82
Grove City: Ohio	**16**	40	83
Grove City: Pennsylvania	**19**	41	80
Groveland: California	**37**	38	120
Groveport: Ohio	**16**	40	83
Grover City: California	**34**	35	121
Groveton: New Hampshire	**13**	45	72
Groveton: Texas	**26**	31	95
Grundy: Virginia	**16**	37	82
Grundy Lake Prov. Park: Ont.	**18**	46	81
Guadalupe: California	**34**	35	121
Guadalupe: *r.*, Texas	**22**	29	97
Gualala: California	**37**	39	124
Guano L.: Oregon	**36**	42	120
Guayama: Puerto Rico	**27**	18	66
Guelph: Ontario	**18**	44	80
Gueydan: Louisiana	**26**	30	93
Guilford: Connecticut	**15**	41	73
Guin: Alabama	**27**	34	88
Gulfport: Mississippi	**27**	30	89
Gulkana: Alaska	**43**	62	145
Gulliver: Michigan	**20**	46	86
Gunisao: *r.*, Manitoba	**31**	53	97
Gunnar: Saskatchewan	**30**	59	109
Gunnison: *& r.*, Colorado	**29**	39	107
Guntersville: *& lake & dam*, Ala.	**27**	34	86
Gurdon: Arkansas	**26**	34	93
Gustavus: Alaska	**40**	58	136
Gustine: California	**37**	37	121
Guthrie: Oklahoma	**26**	36	97
Guyandot: *r.*, West Virginia	**16**	38	82
Guymon: Oklahoma	**29**	37	102
Guyton: Georgia	**24**	32	81
Gwinn: Michigan	**20**	46	87
Gypsum Point: N.W.T.	**40**	62	115
Gypsumville: Manitoba	**31**	52	99
Gyrfalcon Is.: N.W.T.	**45**	59	69
Habay: Alberta	**30**	59	119
Hackamore: California	**36**	42	121
Hackberry: Louisiana	**26**	30	93
Hackensack: New Jersey	**1**	41	74
Hackensack: *r.*, New Jersey	**1**	40¾	74
Hackettstown: New Jersey	**14**	41	75
Haddam: Connecticut	**15**	41	73
Haddock: Georgia	**24**	33	83
Haddonfield: New Jersey	**2**	40	75
Hadley: Pennsylvania	**19**	41	80
Hadley Bay: N.W.T.	**44**	72	108
Hagaman: New York	**15**	43	74
Hagemeister I.: Alaska	**43**	58	161
Hagerstown: Indiana	**21**	40	85
Hagerstown: Maryland	**17**	40	78
Hagersville: Ontario	**19**	43	80
Hahira: Georgia	**25**	31	83
Haines: Alaska	**40**	59	135
Haines City: Florida	**25**	28	82
Haines Junction: Yukon	**40**	61	137
Haiwee: *& Res.*, California	**35**	36	118
Halaula: Hawaii	**128**	20	156
Haleakala Crater N. P.: Hawaii	**128**	20	156
Haleiwa: Hawaii	**128**	22	156
Hales Bar: *dam*, Tennessee	**27**	35	85
Haley: Ontario	**12**	46	77
Haleyville: Alabama	**27**	34	88
Half Moon Bay: *& sett.*, California	**6**	37½	122½
Halfway: *r.*, British Columbia	**41**	57	123
Haliburton: Ontario	**12**	45	79
Halifax: North Carolina	**24**	36	78
Halifax: Nova Scotia	**9**	45	64
Halifax: Pennsylvania	**14**	40	77
Halkett, C.: Alaska	**42**	71	152
Hallettsville: Texas	**26**	29	97
Hall L.: N.W.T.	**45**	69	82
Hall Lake: *sett.*, N.W.T.	**45**	69	81
Hall Penin.: N.W.T.	**45**	64	67
Halls: Tennessee	**27**	36	89
Halls Bayou: Texas	**3**	29¾	95¼
Halls Flat: California	**36**	41	121
Hallstead: Pennsylvania	**14**	42	76
Hallsville: Texas	**26**	33	95
Hamburg: Arkansas	**26**	33	92
Hamburg: California	**36**	42	123
Hamburg: New Jersey	**15**	41	75
Hamburg: New York	**19**	43	79
Hamburg: Pennsylvania	**14**	41	76
Hamilton: Alabama	**27**	34	88
Hamilton: Alaska	**42**	63	164
Hamilton: Indiana	**21**	42	85
Hamilton: New York	**14**	43	76
Hamilton: Ohio	**10**	39	85
Hamilton: Ontario	**19**	43	80
Hamilton City: California	**37**	40	122
Hamilton Inlet: Newfoundland	**9**	54	59

	Page	N	W
Hamilton, L.: Arkansas	**26**	34	93
Hamlet: North Carolina	**24**	35	80
Hamlin: Pennsylvania	**14**	41	75
Hamlin: Texas	**29**	33	100
Hammond: Indiana.	**4**	41¾	87½
Hammond: Louisiana	**27**	31	90
Hammondsport: New York	**14**	42	77
Hammonton: California	**37**	39	121
Hammonton: New Jersey	**14**	40	75
Hampton: New Hampshire	**15**	43	71
Hampton: South Carolina	**24**	33	81
Hampton: Virginia	**17**	37	76
Hamtramck: Michigan	**5**	42½	83
Hana: Hawaii	**128**	21	156
Hanamaulu: Hawaii	**128**	22	159
Hanapepe: Hawaii	**128**	22	160
Hancock: Maryland	**17**	40	78
Hancock: Michigan.	**10**	47	89
Hanford: California.	**34**	36	120
Hanging Rock St. Park: N.C.	**16**	36	80
Hanna: Alberta	**30**	52	112
Hannah Bay: Ontario	**8**	51	80
Hannibal: Missouri	**10**	40	91
Hannibal: Ohio	**16**	40	81
Hanover: New Hampshire	**13**	44	72
Hanover: Ohio	**16**	40	82
Hanover: Ontario	**18**	44	81
Hanover: Pennsylvania	**14**	40	77
Hansen Flood Control Basin: California	**7**	34¼	118½
Happy Camp: California	**33**	42	123
Harahan: Louisiana	**3**	30	90
Harbor Beach: *sett.*, Michigan	**18**	44	83
Harbor Springs: Michigan	**20**	45	85
Harbor Breton: Newfoundland	**9**	47	56
Hardin: Montana	**28**	46	108
Hardisty: Alberta	**30**	53	111
Hardisty L.: N.W.T.	**40**	65	118
Hardwick: Vermont.	**13**	45	72
Hare B.: Newfoundland	**9**	51	55
Hare Indian: *r.*, N.W.T.	**40**	66	128
Hare I.: Greenland	**45**	70	55
Harkers I.: *sett.*, North Carolina	**24**	35	77
Harkin Bay: N.W.T.	**45**	65	79
Harleyville: South Carolina	**24**	33	80
Harlingen: Texas	**22**	26	98
Harmony: California	**34**	35	121
Harmony: Pennsylvania	**19**	41	80
Harney L: Oregon	**32**	43	119
Harper L.: California	**35**	35	117
Harpers Ferry: West Virginia	**17**	39	78
Harper Woods: *sett.*, Michigan	**5**	42½	83
Harricanaw: *r.*, Québec	**8**	51	79
Harriet, L.: Minnesota	**3**	45	93¼
Harriman: Tennessee	**24**	36	85
Harriman St. Park: New York	**15**	41	74
Harrington: Delaware	**17**	39	76
Harrington Harbour: Québec	**9**	51	60
Harrisburg: Arkansas	**27**	36	91
Harrisburg: Pennsylvania.	**14**	40	77
Harrison Bay: Alaska	**42**	71	152
Harrisonburg: Virginia	**17**	38	79
Harrison, C.: Newfoundland	**9**	55	58
Harrison Hot Springs: B.C.	**38**	49	122
Harrison L.: British Columbia	**38**	50	122
Harriston: Ontario	**18**	44	81
Harrisville: Pennsylvania	**19**	41	80
Harrisville: West Virginia	**16**	39	81
Harrow: Ontario	**19**	42	83
Harrowby Bay: N.W.T.	**44**	70	128
Hart: Michigan	**20**	44	86
Hart: *r.*, Yukon	**40**	66	137
Hartfield: New York	**19**	42	80
Hartford: Alabama	**27**	31	86
Hartford: Arkansas	**26**	35	94
Hartford: Connecticut	**15**	42	73
Hartford: Michigan.	**21**	42	86
Hartford: Wisconsin	**20**	43	88
Hartford City: Indiana	**21**	40	85
Hartline: Washington	**39**	48	119
Hartselle: Alabama	**27**	34	87
Hartshorne: Oklahoma	**26**	35	96
Hartsville: South Carolina	**24**	34	80
Hartwell: Georgia	**24**	34	83
Hartwell Res.: *& dam*, S.C.	**24**	34	83
Havard: Illinois	**21**	42	89
Harvey: Illinois	**4**	41½	87¾
Harvey: North Dakota	**28**	48	100
Harwood: Ontario	**12**	44	78
Harwood Heights: *town*, Illinois	**4**	42	87¾
Haskell: Oklahoma	**26**	36	96
Haskell: Texas	**29**	33	100
Hastings: Michigan.	**21**	43	85
Hastings: Nebraska.	**28**	41	98
Hastings: Pennsylvania	**14**	41	79
Hatboro: Pennsylvania	**14**	40	75
Hatchie: *r.*, Tennessee	**27**	35	89
Hat Creek: *sett.*, California	**36**	41	122
Hathaway Pines: California	**37**	38	120
Hattiesburg: Mississippi	**27**	31	89
Havana: Florida	**25**	31	84
Havard: California	**35**	35	117
Havelock: New Brunswick	**9**	46	65
Havelock: North Carolina	**24**	35	77
Haverhill: Massachusetts	**15**	43	71
Havre: Montana	**28**	49	110
Havre de Grace: Maryland	**17**	40	76

	Page	N	W
Havre-St.-Pierre: Québec	**9**	50	64
Haw: *r.*, North Carolina	**24**	36	79
HAWAII	**128**	—	—
Hawaii: *i*, Hawaii	**128**	19	155
Hawaii Volcanoes N.P.: Hawaii	**128**	19	155
Hawaiian Is.	**128**	24	167
Hawes: California	**35**	35	117
Hawkesbury: Ontario	**13**	46	75
Hawkinsville: Georgia	**24**	32	83
Hawley: Pennsylvania	**14**	41	75
Haw River: *sett.*, N.C.	**24**	36	79
Hawthorne: California	**7**	34	118¼
Hawthorne: Nevada	**33**	39	119
Hawthorne: New Jersey	**1**	41	74¼
Hay: *r.*, Alberta/N.W.T.	**30**	60	117
Hay, C.: Northwest Territories	**44**	74	113
Hay, C.: Northwest Territories	**45**	74	80
Hayden: Arizona	**33**	33	111
Hayes: *r.*, Manitoba	**31**	56	98
Hayes: *r.*, Northwest Territories	**45**	67	93
Hayfork: California	**36**	41	123
Hay L.: Alberta	**30**	59	119
Haynesville: Louisiana	**26**	33	93
Hay River: *sett.*, N.W.T.	**30**	61	116
Hays: Kansas.	**28**	39	99
Hayward: California	**6**	38	122
Hazardville: Connecticut	**15**	42	73
Hazelhurst: Mississippi	**27**	32	90
Hazel Park: *sett.*, Michigan	**5**	42½	83
Hazelton: British Columbia	**41**	55	128
Hazen: Nevada	**37**	40	119
Hazen Strait: N.W.T.	**60/61**	77	110
Hazlehurst: Georgia	**24**	32	83
Hazleton: Pennsylvania	**14**	41	76
Headland: Alabama	**27**	31	85
Healdsburg: California	**37**	39	123
Healdton: Oklahoma	**26**	34	98
Healy: Alaska.	**42**	64	149
Hearne: Texas	**26**	31	97
Hearst: California	**37**	40	123
Hearst: Ontario	**10**	50	84
Heart: *r.*, North Dakota	**28**	47	102
Heath Point: Québec	**9**	49	62
Heavener: Oklahoma	**26**	35	95
H. E. Bailey Turnpike: Okla.	**29**	35	98
Heber: California	**35**	33	116
Heber: Utah	**33**	41	111
Heber Springs: Arkansas	**26**	35	92
Hebron: Indiana	**21**	41	87
Hecate Str.: British Columbia	**41**	53	131
Hector: California	**35**	35	116
Heflin: Alabama	**27**	34	86
Heinsburg: Alberta	**30**	54	110
Helena: Arkansas	**27**	35	91
Helena: California	**36**	41	123
Helena: Montana	**28**	47	112
Helendale: California	**35**	35	117
Hellertown: Pennsylvania.	**14**	41	75
Hells Canyon: Oregon/Idaho	**32**	42	117
Helm: California	**37**	37	120
Hematite: Missouri	**10**	38	91
Hemet: California	**35**	34	117
Hemlock: New York	**14**	43	78
Hemphill: Texas	**26**	31	94
Hempstead: New York	**1**	40¾	73½
Hempstead: Texas	**26**	30	96
Henderson: Kentucky	**23**	38	88
Henderson: Nevada	**35**	36	115
Henderson: North Carolina	**17**	36	78
Henderson: Tennessee	**27**	35	89
Henderson: Texas	**26**	32	95
Hendersonville: North Carolina	**24**	35	82
Henleyville: California	**36**	40	122
Henniker: New Hampshire	**13**	43	72
Henrietta: Texas	**29**	34	98
Henrietta Maria, C.: Ontario	**8**	55	82
Henry: Illinois	**21**	41	89
Henry, C.: Virginia	**17**	37	76
Henryetta: Oklahoma	**26**	35	96
Henry Kater, C.: N.W.T.	**45**	69	66
Heppner: Oregon	**39**	45	120
Herald: California	**37**	38	121
Herculaneum: Missouri	**10**	38	90
Hereford: Texas	**29**	35	102
Herendeen Bay: *sett.*, Alaska	**43**	56	161
Herkimer: New York	**13**	43	75
Herlong: California.	**36**	40	120
Herman: Pennsylvania	**19**	41	80
Hermansville: Michigan	**20**	46	88
Herminie: Pennsylvania	**19**	40	80
Hermiston: Oregon	**39**	46	119
Hernando: Mississippi	**27**	35	90
Herndon: California	**37**	37	120
Herndon: Virginia	**17**	39	77
Herring Cove: Alaska	**41**	55	131
Herschel: *& i.*, Yukon	**42**	70	139
Hershey: Pennsylvania	**14**	40	77
Hertford: North Carolina.	**17**	36	77
Hespeler: Ontario	**18**	43	80
Hesperia: California	**35**	34	117
Hess: *r.*, Yukon	**40**	63	133
Hetch Hetchy Aqueduct: Calif.	**37**	38	122
Hetch Hetchy Res.: California	**37**	38	120
Hewett, C.: N.W.T.	**45**	70	68
Hiawassee: *dam*, N.C.	**24**	35	84
Hiawatha: Kansas	**28**	40	96
Hibbing: Minnesota	**10**	47	93

	Page	N	W
Hickory: North Carolina	**24**	36	81
Hickory: Pennsylvania	**19**	40	80
Hicksville: New York	**1**	40¾	73½
Hicksville: Ohio	**21**	41	85
Higganum: Connecticut	**15**	42	73
Higgins L.: Michigan	**20**	45	85
High Bridge: New Jersey	**14**	41	75
High I.: Michigan	**20**	46	86
High Island: *sett.*, Texas	**26**	30	94
Highland County Park: Minnesota	**3**	44¾	93¼
Highland: Indiana	**4**	41½	87½
Highland-on-the-Lake: N.Y.	**19**	43	79
Highland Park: Illinois	**4**	42	87¾
Highland Park: Pennsylvania	**5**	40½	80
Highland Springs: Virginia	**17**	38	77
Highland Valley: B.C.	**38**	50	121
Highline Canal: Colorado	**3**	39½	105
High Point: *town.*, NC.	**24**	36	80
High Point State Park: N.J.	**15**	41	75
High Prairie: Alberta	**30**	56	116
High River: *town*, Alberta	**30**	51	114
Highrock L.: Manitoba	**31**	56	100
High Springs: Florida	**25**	30	83
Hildebrand: Oregon	**36**	42	121
Hill Island L.: N.W.T.	**30**	60	110
Hillsboro: Illinois	**10**	39	89
Hillsboro: New Hampshire	**13**	43	72
Hillsboro: North Carolina	**24**	36	79
Hillsboro: Oregon	**39**	46	123
Hillsboro: Texas	**26**	32	97
Hillsborough: *r.*, Florida	**25**	28	82
Hillsdale: Michigan	**21**	42	85
Hillsville: Virginia	**16**	37	81
Hilmar: California	**37**	37	121
Hilo: Hawaii	**128**	20	155
Hilton: New York	**12**	43	78
Hilts: California	**36**	42	123
Hinckley Res.: New York.	**13**	43	75
Hines: Oregon	**32**	44	119
Hines Creek: *sett.*, Alberta	**30**	56	119
Hinesville: Georgia	**24**	32	82
Hingham: Massachusetts	**2**	42¼	17
Hingham Bay: Massachusetts	**2**	42½	71
Hinkley: California	**35**	35	117
Hinsdale: Illinois	**4**	41¾	88
Hinsdale: New Hampshire	**13**	43	72
Hinton: Alberta	**30**	53	118
Hinton: West Virginia	**16**	38	81
Hi Vista: California.	**35**	35	118
Hiwassee: *r.*, Tenn./N.C.	**24**	35	85
Hoare Bay: N.W.T..	**45**	66	63
Hobart: Indiana	**21**	42	87
Hobbs: New Mexico	**29**	33	103
Hoboken: New Jersey	**1**	40¾	74
Hocking: *r.*, Ohio	**16**	39	82
Hodge: California	**35**	35	117
Hodge: Louisiana	**26**	32	93
Hodges, L.: California	**35**	33	117
Hodgson: Manitoba	**31**	51	98
Hogansville: Georgia	**27**	33	85
Hog I.: Michigan	**20**	46	85
Hoh: *r.*, Washington	**39**	48	124
Hohenwald: Tennessee	**27**	36	88
Holbrook: Arizona	**33**	35	110
Holdenville: Oklahoma	**26**	35	96
Holdrege: Nebraska	**28**	40	99
Holgate: Ohio.	**19**	41	84
Holikachuk: Alaska.	**42**	63	160
Holitna: *r.*, Alaska	**43**	61	158
Holland: Michigan	**21**	43	86
Holland: Oregon	**36**	42	124
Holland: Virginia	**17**	37	77
Hollandale: Mississippi	**27**	33	91
Hollidaysburg: Pennsylvania	**14**	40	78
Hollis: Alaska.	**41**	55	133
Hollister: California	**37**	37	121
Holliston: Massachusetts	**15**	42	71
Holly: Michigan	**19**	43	84
Holly Hill: *sett.*, South Carolina	**24**	33	80
Holly River State Park: W. Va.	**16**	39	80¼
Holly Springs: Mississippi	**27**	35	89
Hollywood: California	**7**	34	118¼
Hollywood: Florida	**25**	26	80
Holywood Res.: California	**7**	34	118
Holman Island: *sett.*, N.W.T.	**44**	71	118
Holston: *r.*, Tenn./Virginia	**24**	36	83
Holtville: California	**35**	33	115
Holualoa: Hawaii	**128**	20	156
Holy Cross: Alaska	**43**	62	160
Holyoke: Massachusetts	**15**	42	73
Home Bay: N.W.T..	**45**	69	67
Homer: Alaska	**43**	60	152
Homer: Illinois	**21**	40	88
Homer: Louisiana	**26**	33	93
Homer: New York	**14**	43	76
Homer City: Pennsylvania	**19**	41	79
Homerville: Georgia	**25**	31	83
Homestead: Florida.	**25**	25	80¾
Homewood: Illinois	**4**	41½	87
Honaunau: Hawaii	**128**	19	156
Honby: California	**35**	34	118
Honcut: California	**37**	39	122
Hondo: *r.*, California	**7**	34	118
Hondo: *r.*, New Mexico	**29**	33	105
Honea Path: South Carolina	**24**	34	82
Honeoye Falls: *sett.*, New York	**14**	43	78
Honesdale: Pennsylvania	**14**	42	75

	Page	N	W
Honeydew: California	36	40	124
Honey Grove: Pennsylvania	14	40	78
Honey Grove: Texas	26	34	96
Honey L.: California	36	40	120
Honokaa: Hawaii	128	20	155
Honokahua: Hawaii	128	21	157
Honolulu: Hawaii	128	21	158
Hood: *r.*, N.W.T.	44	67	110
Hood Canal: Washington	39	47	123
Hood, Mt.: Oregon	39	45	122
Hood River: *town*, Oregon	39	46	122
Hoonah: Alaska	40	58	135
Hoopa: California	36	41	124
Hooper Bay: *sett.*, Alaska	43	61	166
Hoopeston: Illinois	21	40	88
Hoosic: *r.*	15	43	73
Hoosick Falls: *town*, New York	15	43	73
Hoover: *dam*, Arizona/Nevada	33	36	115
Hoover Res.: Ohio	19	40	83
Hooversville: Pennsylvania	14	40	79
Hope: Alaska	43	61	150
Hope: Arkansas	26	34	94
Hope: British Columbia	38	49	121
Hopedale: Newfoundland	9	56	60
Hope, Point: Alaska	42	68	167
Hopes Advance Bay: Québec	45	59	70
Hopes Advance, C.: N.W.T.	45	61	70
Hopewell: New Jersey	15	40	75
Hopewell: Virginia	17	37	77
Hopewell Is.: N.W.T.	45	59	78
Hopkins: Minnesota	3	45	93¼
Hopkinsville: Kentucky	23	37	88
Hopland: California	37	39	123
Hopwood: Pennsylvania	16	40	80
Hoquiam: Washington	39	47	124
Horatio: Arkansas	26	34	94
Horicon: Wisconsin	20	43	89
Horn: *r.*, N.W.T.	40	62	118
Hornbrook: California	36	42	123
Hornby Bay: N.W.T.	40	66	118
Hornby I.: British Columbia	38	50	125
Hornell: New York	14	42	78
Horn I.: Mississippi	27	30	89
Horn Mts.: N.W.T.	40	62	120
Horse Creek: *sett.*, California	36	42	123
Horseheads: New York	14	42	77
Horse Heaven Hills: Wash.	39	46	120
Horse Is.: Newfoundland	9	50	56
Horse L.: California	36	41	121
Horseshoe Bay: *sett.*, B.C.	38	49	123
Horton: *r.*, N.W.T.	44	68	123
Horton L.: N.W.T.	44	68	122
Hortonville: Wisconsin	20	44	89
Hotham Inlet: Alaska	42	67	162
Hot Springs: *& Nat. Park*, Ark.	26	35	93
Hot Springs: South Dakota	28	43	103
Hot Springs: Virginia	16	38	80
Hottah L.: N.W.T.	40	65	118
Houghton: Washington	6	47¾	122¼
Houghton L.: Michigan	20	44	85
Houma: Louisiana	27	30	91
Housatonic: *r.*, Mass./Conn.	15	42	73
Houston: Mississippi	27	34	89
Houston: Pennsylvania	19	40	80
Houston: Texas	26	30	95
Houston Ship Channel: Texas	3	29¾	95¼
Houtzdale: Pennsylvania	14	41	78
Howell: Michigan	21	43	84
Hoxie: Arkansas	26	36	91
Hubbard: Ohio	19	41	81
Hubbard: Texas	26	32	97
Hubbard L.: Michigan	18	45	84
Hubbell: Wisconsin	10	47	88
Huddart Park: California	6	37¼	122¼
Hudson: Massachusetts	15	42	72
Hudson: Michigan	21	42	84
Hudson: New York	15	42	74
Hudson: Ohio	19	41	81
Hudson: Ontario	10	50	92
Hudson: *r.*, New York	11	42	74
Hudson Bay: N.W.T.	45	60	87
Hudson Bay: *town*, Sask.	30	53	102
Hudson Falls: *town*, New York	13	43	74
Hudson Hope: British Columbia	41	56	122
Hudson Strait: N.W.T./Québec.	45	63	73
Hughes: Alaska	42	66	154
Hughesville: Maryland	17	39	77
Hughesville: Pennsylvania	14	41	77
Hugo: Oklahoma	26	34	96
Hugo: Oregon	36	43	123
Hall: Massachusetts	2	42¼	71
Hull: Québec	12	45	76
Hullville: California	37	39	123
Humacao: Puerto Rico	27	18	66
Humber: *r.*, Ontario	5	43¾	79½
Humber Bay.: Ontario	5	43½	79½
Humboldt: Arizona	33	35	110
Humboldt: Saskatchewan	30	52	105
Humboldt: Tennessee	27	36	89
Humboldt: *r.*, Nevada	33	40	118
Hummels Wharf: Pennsylvania.	14	41	77
Humptulips: Washington	39	47	124
Hungry Horse: *res & dam*, Montana	32	48	114
Hungry Mother State Park: Va.	16	37	81
Hunter: New York	15	42	74
Hunters Point: California	6	37¾	122¼

	Page	N	W
Hunting Bayou: Texas	3	29¾	95¼
Huntingdon: Pennsylvania	14	41	78
Huntingdon: Québec	13	45	74
Huntingdon: Tennessee	27	36	88
Huntingdon I.: Newfoundland	9	54	57
Huntington: Indiana	21	41	86
Huntington: Massachusetts	15	42	73
Huntington: New York	1	41	73½
Huntington: Texas	26	31	95
Huntington: West Virginia	16	38	82
Huntington Beach: *town*, Calif.	7	33¾	118
Huntsville: Alabama	27	35	87
Huntsville: Arkansas	26	36	94
Huntsville: Ontario	12	45	79
Huntsville: Texas	26	31	96
Hurd, C.: Ontario	18	45	82
Hurley: New Mexico	29	33	108
Hurlock: Maryland	17	39	76
Huron: California	34	36	120
Huron: Ohio	19	41	83
Huron: South Dakota	28	44	98
Huron: *r.*, Michigan	19	42	83
Huron: *r.*, Ohio	19	41	83
Huron, Lake	18	—	—
Huron, Point: Michigan	5	42½	82¾
Hurricane: Alaska	42	63	150
Hurricane: *cr.*, Arkansas	26	34	92
Hurtsboro: Alabama	27	32	85
Huslia: Alaska	42	66	157
Hutchinson: Kansas	29	38	98
Huttig: Arkansas	26	33	92
Hyampom: California	36	41	123
Hyannis: Massachusetts	15	42	70
Hyattsville: Washington, D.C.	2	39	77
Hyadburg: Alaska	41	55	133
Hyde Park: New York	15	42	74
Hyde Park: Vermont	13	45	73
Hyder: Alaska	41	56	130
Hydesville: California	36	41	124
Hyland: *r.*, Yukon	40	61	129
Hyndman: Pennsylvania	14	40	79
Iberville: Québec	13	45	73
Ice Harbor: *dam*, Wash.	32	46	119
Ickesburg: Pennsylvania	14	40	77
Icy B.: Alaska	43	60	141
Idabel: Oklahoma	26	34	95
IDAHO	32	—	—
Idaho Falls: *town*, Idaho	32	44	112
Idria: California	34	36	121
Igiugig: Alaska	43	59	156
Igloolik: N.W.T.	45	69	82
Igo: California	36	41	123
Ikatan: Alaska	43	55	163
Ikpikpuk: *r.*, Alaska	42	70	155
Ile-à-la-Crosse: Saskatchewan	30	55	108
Ile-à-la-Crosse, Lac: Sask.	30	56	108
Iliamna L.: Alaska	43	60	155
Ilion: New York	14	43	75
ILLINOIS	10	—	—
Illinois: *r.*, Illinois	21	41	90
Illinois: *r.*, Oregon	36	42	124
Ilinois and Mich. Canal: Illinois	4	41¾	87¾
Ilwaco: Washington	39	46	124
Imlay City: Michigan	19	43	83
Immokalee: Florida	25	26	81
Imperial: California	35	33	116
Imperial: Pennsylvania	19	40	80
Imperial: *dam*, Calif./Arizona	33	33	115
Imperial Beach: *town*, Calif.	35	33	117
Imperial Valley: California	35	33	115
Imuruk L.: Alaska	42	66	163
Independence: California	35	37	118
Independence: Kansas	29	37	96
Independence: Louisiana	27	31	91
Independence: Oregon	39	45	123
Indian: *r.*, New York	12	44	76
INDIANA	10	—	—
Indiana: Pennsylvania	19	41	79
Indiana E.-W. Toll Road: Ind.	21	42	86
Indiana Harbor: Indiana	4	41½	87½
Indianapolis: Indiana	21	40	86
Indian Arm: *bay*, B.C.	6	49¼	122¾
Indian Cabins: Alberta	30	60	117
Indian Creek: Illinois	4	42¼	88
Indian Head: Pennsylvania	16	40	79
Indian House L.: Québec	9	56	65
Indian L.: New York	13	44	74
Indian L.: Ohio	19	40	84
Indianola: Mississippi	24	33	91
Indian River Bay: Delaware	17	39	75
Indian Springs: Nevada	35	37	116
Indio: California	35	34	116
Ingersoll: Ontario	19	43	81
Inglewood: California	7	34	118¼
Ingot: California	36	41	122
Inkom: Idaho	32	43	112
Inkster: Michigan	5	42¼	83¼
Inman: South Carolina	24	35	82
Innerkip: Ontario	19	43	81
Innisfail: Alberta	30	52	114
Inspiration: Arizona	33	33	111
Institute: West Virginia	16	38	82
Interlochen: Michigan	20	45	86
International Falls: *town*, Minn.	10	49	93
Intracoastal Waterway	26	—	—
Inugsuin Fiord: N.W.T.	45	70	69

	Page	N	W
Inuvik: Northwest Territories	44	68	134
Invermere: British Columbia	41	51	116
Inverness: California	37	38	123
Inverness: Florida	25	29	82
Inverness: Nova Scotia	9	46	61
Inyokern: California	35	36	118
Inyo Range: California	35	37	118
Ioco: British Columbia	6	49¼	122¾
Iola: Kansas	29	38	95
Iola: Wisconsin	20	45	89
Ione: California	37	38	121
Ionia: Michigan	20	43	85
Iota: Louisiana	26	30	93
IOWA	10	—	—
Iowa: *r.*, Iowa	10	43	94
Iowa City: Iowa	10	42	92
Ipperwash Prov. Park: Ontario	19	43	82
Ipswich: Massachusetts	15	43	71
Irish Hills: Michigan	19	43	84
Irondequoit: New York	12	43	78
Iron Mtn.: Idaho	32	43	117
Iron Mountain: *town*, Michigan	20	46	88
Iron Mountain: *sett.*, Missouri	10	38	91
Iron Mts.: Va./Tennessee	16	37	81
Iron River: *town*, Michigan	20	46	89
Iron Springs: Utah	33	38	113
Ironton: Ohio	16	39	83
Ironton: Utah	33	40	112
Ironwood: Michigan	10	46	90
Iroquis: Ontario	13	45	75
Iroquis: *r*, Illinois/Indiana	21	41	87
Irvine: Pennsylvania	19	42	79
Irvines Landing: B.C.	38	50	124
Irvington: New Jersey	1	40¾	74¼
Isabella: Michigan	20	46	87
Isabella Bay: N.W.T.	45	70	68
Isabella Res.: California	35	36	118
Isachsen: Northwest Territories	61	79	104
Ishpeming: Michigan	10	46	88
Iskut: *r.*, British Columbia	41	57	131
Island Beach State Park: N.J.	15	40	74
Island Falls: *sett.*, Ontario	11	50	81
Island L.: Manitoba	31	54	95
Island Mountain: *sett.*, Calif.	36	40	124
Island Pond: Vermont	13	45	72
Islands, Bay of: Newfoundland	9	49	58
Islands, Bay of: Ontario	18	46	82
Isle Royale Nat. Park: Michigan.	10	48	89
Iselton: California	37	38	122
Islington: Ontario	5	43¾	79½
Issaquah: Washington	39	48	122
Italy: Texas	26	32	97
Itasca: Illinois	4	42	88
Itasca: Texas	26	32	97
Itchen L.: N.W.T.	40	65	113
Ithaca: New York	14	42	77
Itta Bena: Mississippi	27	34	90
Iuka: Mississippi	27	35	88
Ivanof Bay: *town*, Alaska	43	56	159
Ivanpah: California	35	35	115
Ivishak: *r.*, Alaska	42	69	149
Ivoryton: Connecticut	15	41	72
Ivugivik: Québec	45	62	78
Jacinto City: Texas	3	29¾	95¼
Jackfish River: *sett.*, Alberta	30	59	113
Jackrabbit: Nevada	33	38	115
Jacks Mtn.: Pennsylvania	14	40	78
Jackson: Alabama	27	32	88
Jackson: California	37	38	121
Jackson: Georgia	24	33	84
Jackson: Louisiana	26	31	91
Jackson: Michigan	21	42	84
Jackson: Mississippi	27	32	90
Jackson: North Carolina	17	36	77
Jackson: Ohio	16	39	83
Jackson: Tennessee	27	36	89
Jackson: Wyoming	28	43	111
Jackson: *r.*, Virginia	16	38	80
Jackson Creek: *sett.*, Nevada	33	41	119
Jackson Park: Illinois	4	41¾	87½
Jacksonville: Alabama	27	34	86
Jacksonville: Arkansas	26	35	92
Jacksonville: Florida	25	30	82
Jacksonville: Illinois	10	40	90
Jacksonville: North Carolina	24	35	77
Jacksonville: Oregon	36	42	123
Jacksonville: Texas	26	32	95
Jacksonville Beach: *town*, Fla.	25	30	81
Jacques Cartier: Québec	2	45½	73½
Jacques Cartier Passage: Québec	9	50	63
Jacumba: California	35	33	116
Jaffrey: New Hampshire	13	43	72
Jal: New Mexico	29	32	103
Jalama: California	34	35	121
Jamaica Bay: New York	1	40¾	73¾
Jamaica Bay Wildlife Refuge: New York	1	40½	73¾
James: *r.*, N.D./S.D.	28	44	98
James: *r.*, Virginia	17	37	77
James Bay: Ontario/Québec	8	54	81
Jamesburg: New Jersey	15	40	74
James Ross Strait: N.W.T.	44	69	96
Jamestown: California	37	38	120
Jamestown: New York	19	42	79
Jamestown: North Dakota	28	47	99
Jamestown: Rhode Island	15	42	71

	Page	N	W
Kirkland: Washington	6	47¾	122¼
Kirkland Lake: *town*, Ontario	11	48	80
Kirksville: Missouri	10	40	93
Kirkwood: California	36	40	122
Kissimmee: Florida	25	28	81
Kissimmee: *r.*, Florida	25	27	81
Kississing L.: Manitoba	31	55	101
Kit Carson: California	37	39	120
Kitchener: Ontario	18	43	81
Kitimat: British Columbia	41	54	129
Kittanning: Pennsylvania	19	41	80
Kittery: Maine	15	43	71
Kivalina: Alaska	42	68	165
Kivitoo: N.W.T.	45	68	65
Kiwalik: Alaska	42	66	162
Klamath: California	36	42	124
Klamath: *r.*, California	36	41	124
Klamath Falls: *town*, Oregon	36	42	122
Klamath Falls Junction: Oregon	36	42	123
Klamath Marsh: Oregon	36	43	122
Klamath Mts.: California	36	41	123
Klawock: Alaska	41	56	133
Klemtu: British Columbia	41	53	129
Klickitat: *r.*, Washington	39	46	121
Klondike: California	35	35	116
Klondike: *r.*, Yukon	40	64	138
Kluane: Yukon	40	61	138
Kluane L.: Yukon	40	61	139
Kluane National Park: Yukon	40	60	139
Klukwan: Alaska	40	59	136
Knee L.: Manitoba	31	55	95
Knife: *r.*, North Dakota	28	47	102
Knight Inlet: B.C.	41	51	125
Knights Landing: California	37	39	122
Knightstown: Indiana	21	40	86
Knobley Mtn.: West Virginia	16	39	79
Knowlton: Québec	13	45	73
Knox: Indiana	21	41	87
Knox: Pennsylvania	19	41	80
Knox, C.: British Columbia	41	54	133
Knoxville: Tennessee	24	36	84
Koartak: Québec	45	61	70
Kobuk: Alaska	42	67	157
Kobuk: *r.*, Alaska	42	67	159
Koch I.: N.W.T.	45	70	78
Kodiak: Alaska	43	58	153
Kodiak Is.: Alaska	43	57	153
Kogaluk: *r.*, Québec	45	59	77
Kogaluk Bay: Québec	45	59	78
Kohler: Wisconsin	20	44	88
Koko Head Pk.: Hawaii	128	21	158
Kokolik: *r.*, Alaska	42	69	162
Kokomo: Indiana	21	41	86
Kokrines: Alaska	42	65	155
Kokrines Hills: Alaska	42	65	154
Koksoak: *r.*, Québec	45	58	69
Koliganek: Alaska	43	60	157
Koloa: Hawaii	128	22	159
Konawa: Oklahoma	26	35	97
Kootenai: *r.*, Idaho/Montana	32	49	115
Kootenai Falls: *dam*, Montana	32	49	116
Kootenay: *r.*, British Columbia	41	50	116
Kootenay L.: British Columbia	41	50	117
Kootenay National Park: B.C.	30	51	116
Koppel: Pennsylvania	19	41	80
Koraluk: *r.*, Newfoundland	9	56	63
Kosciusko: Mississippi	26	33	90
Koshkonong L.: Wisconsin	21	43	89
Kosmosdale: Kentucky	23	38	86
Kotcho L.: B.C.	30	59	121
Kotlik: Alaska	42	63	164
Kotzebue: Alaska	42	67	163
Kotzebue Sound: Alaska	42	67	163
Koukdjuak: *r.*, N.W.T.	45	67	72
Kountze: Texas	26	30	94
Kovik Bay: Québec	45	62	78
Koyuk: & *r.*, Alaska	42	65	161
Koyukuk: Alaska	42	65	158
Koyukuk: *r.*, Alaska	42	66	157
Krusenstern, C.: Alaska	42	67	164
Kruzof I.: Alaska	40	57	136
Kualapuu: Hawaii	128	21	157
Kugmallit Bay: N.W.T.	44	70	133
Kulik Lodge: Alaska	43	59	155
Kunghit I.: Britich Columbia	41	52	131
Kuparuk: *r.*, Alaska	42	70	149
Kure: *i.*, Hawaii	128	29	178
Kurtistown: Hawaii	128	20	155
Kusawa L.: Yukon	40	60	136
Kuskokwim: *r.*, Alaska	42	62	156
Kuskokwim Bay: Alaska	43	59	163
Kuskokwim Mts.: Alaska	42/43	62	157
Kuskokwim North Fork: *r.*, Alaska	42	64	153
Kwethluk: Alaska	43	61	162
Kwigillingok: Alaska	43	60	163
Kwiguk: Alaska	42	63	165
Kyburz: California	37	39	120
La Belle: Florida	25	27	81
Labelle: Québec	13	46	75
Laberge L.: Yukon	40	61	135
Labrador: *district*, Newfoundland	9	—	—
Labrador City: Newfoundland	8	53	67
La Canada: California	7	34¼	118¼
Lachine: Québec	2	45½	73¾
Lachute: Québec	13	46	74

	Page	N	W
Lac La Biche: *town*, Alberta	30	55	112
Lac la Hache: B.C.	41	52	121
Lac la Ronge: *sett., and Prov. Park*, Sask.	30	55	104
Lac-Mégantic: Québec	13	46	71
Lacolle: Québec	13	45	73
Lacombe: Alberta	30	53	114
Lacombe: Louisiana	27	30	90
Lacon: Illinois	21	41	89
Laconia: New Hampshire	13	44	71
Lacoochee: Florida	25	28	82
Lacorne: Québec	8	48	78
La Crosse: Wisconsin	10	44	91
Ladner: British Columbia	38	49	123
Ladonia: Texas	26	33	96
Ladysmith: British Columbia	38	49	124
Lafayette: Alabama	27	33	85
Lafayette: & *res.*, California	6	38	120
La Fayette: Georgia	27	35	85
Lafayette: Indiana	21	40	87
Lafayette: Louisiana	26	30	92
Lafayette, Mt.: N.H.	13	44	72
La Follete: Tennessee	24	36	84
La Grand: Oregon	32	45	118
La Grange: Georgia	27	33	85
La Grange: Illinois	4	41¾	87¾
Lagrange: Indiana	21	42	85
La Grange: North Carolina	24	35	78
La Grange: Texas	26	30	97
Laguna Beach: *town*, California	35	34	118
Lahontan Res.: Nevada	37	39	119
La Jolla: California	35	33	117
La Junta: Colorado	29	38	104
Lake Alpine: *sett.*, California	37	38	120
Lake Ariel: *sett.*, Pennsylvania	14	41	75
Lake Arthur: *town*, Louisiana	26	30	93
Lake Bluff: *sett.*, Illinois	4	42¼	87¾
Lake Borgne Canal: Louisiana	3	30	90
Lake Calumet Harbor: Illinois	4	43¾	87½
Lake Charles: *town*, Louisiana	26	30	93
Lake City: *town*, Florida	25	30	83
Lake City: *sett.*, Seattle	6	47¾	122¼
Lake City: *town*, South Carolina	24	34	80
Lake City: *sett.*, Tennessee	24	36	84
Lake Cowichan: *sett.*, B.C.	38	49	124
Lake Delton: *sett.*, Wisconsin	20	44	90
Lakefield: Ontario	12	44	78
Lake Forest: *town*, Illinois	21	42	88
Lake George: *sett.*, Colorado	28	39	105
Lake George: *sett.*, Michigan	20	44	85
Lake George: *sett.*, New York	13	43	74
La Habra: California	7	34	118
Lake Habour: *sett.*, N.W.T.	45	63	70
Lake Hills: *sett.*, Washington	6	47½	122¼
Lake Hughes: *sett.*, California	35	35	118
Lakehurst: New Jersey	15	40	74
Lake Isabella: *sett.*, California	35	36	118
Lake Jackson: *town*, Texas	26	29	95
Lakeland: Florida	25	28	82
Lakeland: Georgia	25	31	83
Lake Louise: *sett.*, Alberta	30	51	116
Lake Luzerne: *sett.*, New York	13	43	74
Lake Mead Nat. Rec. Area: Arizona/Nevada	33	36	114
Lake Mills: *town*, Wisconsin	20	43	89
Lake Minchumina: *sett.*, Alaska	42	64	152
Lake Odessa: *sett.*, Michigan	21	43	85
Lake Orion: *town*, Michigan	19	43	83
Lake Oswego: *sett.*, Oregon	36	45	123
Lake Park: *town*, Florida	25	27	80
Lake Placid: *town*, New York	13	44	74
Lakeport: California	37	39	123
Lake Providence: *town*, La.	26	33	91
Lake River: *town*, Ontario	8	55	83
Lakeshore: California	37	37	119
Lakeside: California	35	33	117
Lakeside: Michigan	21	42	87
Lakeview: California	35	34	117
Lakeview: Oregon	36	42	120
Lake Village: *town*, Arkansas	26	33	91
Lakeville: Connecticut	15	42	73
Lake Wales: *town*, Florida	25	28	82
Lakewood: California	7	33¾	118
Lakewood: Colorado	3	39¾	105
Lakewood: New Jersey	15	40	74
Lakewood: New York	19	42	79
Lakewood: Wisconsin	20	45	89
Lake Worth: *town*, Florida	25	27	80
Lake Zurich: *town*, Illinois	4	42¼	88
La Loche: Saskatchewan	30	57	109
La Loche Lac: Saskatchewan	30	57	110
La Malbaie: Québec	8	48	70
Lamar: Colorado	29	38	103
Lamar: South Carolina	24	34	80
La Martre, Lac: N.W.T.	40	63	118
Lambert: Mississippi	27	34	90
Lambertville: New Jersey	14	40	75
Lambertville: Pennsylvania	14	40	75
Lambton, C.: N.W.T.	44	71	123
Lame Deer: Montana	28	46	107
La Mesa: California	35	33	117
Lamesa: Texas	29	33	102
Lamoille: *r.*, Vermont	13	45	73
Lamont: California	35	35	119
Lahaina: Hawaii	128	21	157
Lanai: *i.*, Hawaii	128	21	157
Lanai City: Hawaii	128	21	157

	Page	N	W
Lanark: Illinois	21	42	90
Lanark: Ontario	12	45	76
Lancaster: California	35	35	118
Lancaster: New Brunswick	9	45	66
Lancaster: New Hampshire	13	44	72
Lancaster: New York	14	43	79
Lancaster: Ohio	16	40	83
Lancaster: Pennsylvania	14	40	76
Lancaster: South Carolina	24	35	81
Lancaster: Texas	26	33	97
Lancaster Sound: N.W.T.	45	74	85
Lander: Wyoming	28	43	109
Landisville: Pennsylvania	14	40	76
Landrum: South Carolina	24	35	82
Lanett: Alabama	27	33	85
Langell Valley: *sett.*, Oregon	36	42	121
Langeloth: Pennsylvania	19	40	80
Langhorne: Pennsylvania	14	40	75
L'Anguille: *r.*, Arkansas	27	35	91
Lanigan: Saskatchewan	30	52	105
Lansdale: Pennsylvania	14	40	75
Lansdowne House: Ontario	31	52	88
Lansing: Illinois	4	41½	87½
Lansing: Michigan	21	43	86
Laona: Wisconsin	20	46	89
La Panza: California	34	35	120
Lapeer: Michigan	19	43	83
La Poile B.: Newfoundland	9	48	59
La Porte: California	37	40	121
La Porte: Indiana	21	42	87
La Porte: Texas	26	30	95
La Potherie, Lac: Québec	45	59	72
La Prairie: Québec	2	45¼	73½
La Puente: California	7	34	118
La Quinta: Texas	22	28	98
Laramie: Wyoming	28	41	106
Laramie: *r.*, Wyoming	28	41	105
Larch: *r.*, Québec	8	57	72
Larder Lake: *sett.*, Ontario	11	48	80
Laredo: Texas	22	28	99
Larned: Kansas	29	38	99
La Ronge: Saskatchewan	30	55	105
La Ronge, Lac: Saskatchewan	31	55	105
Larsen Bay: *sett.*, Alaska	43	58	154
La Salle: Illinois	21	41	89
La Salle: Ontario	5	42¼	83
La Salle: Québec	2	45½	78½
Las Animas: Colorado	29	38	103
Las Cruces: California	34	35	120
Las Cruces: New Mexico	29	32	107
Las Plumas: California	37	40	121
Lasqueti I.: British Columbia	38	49	124
Lassen Peak: California	36	41	122
Lassen Volcanic Nat. Park: Calif.	36	40	122
L'Assomption: Québec	13	46	73
Last Mountain L.: Sask.	30	51	105
Las Vegas: Nevada	35	36	115
Las Vegas: New Mexico	29	36	105
Lathrop: California	37	38	121
Lathrop: Michigan	20	46	87
Lathrop Wells: Nevada	35	37	116
Latrobe: Pennsylvania	19	40	79
Latta: South Carolina	24	34	79
La Tuque: Québec	8	47	73
Laurel: Delaware	17	39	76
Laurel: Maryland	17	39	77
Laurel: Mississippi	27	32	89
Laurel: Montana	28	46	109
Laureldale: Pennsylvania	14	40	76
Laurel Ridge: West Virginia	16	49	80
Laurens: South Carolina	24	34	82
Laurentides Prov. Park: Québec	8	48	72
Laurinburg: North Carolina	24	35	79
Lauzon: Québec	13	47	71
Lava Beds Nat. Mon.: Calif.	36	42	122
Laval-des-Rapides: Québec	2	45½	73¾
La Verendrye Prov. Park: Qué.	8	47	77
La Verne: California	35	34	118
Lavonia: Georgia	24	34	83
Lavon Res.: Texas	26	33	96
Lawrence: Indiana	21	40	86
Lawrence: Kansas	28	39	95
Lawrence: Massachusetts	15	43	71
Lawrenceburg: Tennessee	27	35	87
Lawrenceville: Georgia	24	34	84
Lawrenceville: Virginia	17	37	78
Lawton: Oklahoma	29	35	98
Laysan: *i.*, Hawaii	128	26	172
Laytonville: California	37	40	123
Lead: South Dakota	28	44	104
Leadville: Colorado	28	39	106
Leaf: *r.*, Mississippi	27	32	89
Leaf (aux Feuilles): *r.*, Québec	45	58	73
Leaf Inlet (aux Feuilles): Québec	45	59	70
Leaksville: North Carolina	16	36	80
Leamington: Ontario	19	42	83
Leaside: Ontario	5	43¾	79¼
Leavenworth: Kansas	28	39	95
Leavenworth: Washington	39	48	121
Lebanon: Indiana	21	40	87
Lebanon: New Hampshire	13	44	72
Lebanon: Oregon	32	45	123
Lebanon: Pennsylvania	14	40	76
Lebanon: Tennessee	23	36	86
Lebec: California	35	35	119
Lecompte: Louisiana	26	31	92
Leduc: Alberta	30	53	114

	Page	N	W
Lower Post: B.C.	40	60	129
Lower Red L.: Minnesota	10	48	95
Lower Rouge: *r.*, Michigan	5	42¼	83½
Lowther I.: N.W.T.	44	75	98
Lowville: New York	12	44	76
Loyalsock: *cr.*, Pennsylvania	14	41	77
Loyalton: California	37	40	120
Lubbock: Texas	29	34	102
Lucas Channel: Ontario	18	45	82
Lucerne: California	37	39	123
Lucerne L.: California	35	35	117
Lucerne Valley: *sett.*, California	35	34	117
Lucia: California	34	36	122
Lucin: Utah	33	41	114
Lucknow: Ontario	18	44	82
Lucyville: Newfoundland	9	55	58
Ludington: *& St. Park*, Michigan	20	44	86
Ludlow: California	35	35	116
Ludlow: Vermont	13	43	73
Ludlowville: New York	14	43	77
Ludowici: Georgia	24	32	82
Lufkin: Texas	26	31	95
Lukens Mount: California	7	34¼	118¼
Lulu Island: British Columbia	6	49	123
Lumber City: Georgia	24	32	83
Lumberport: West Virginia	16	39	80
Lumberton: Mississippi	27	31	89
Lumberton: North Carolina	24	35	79
Lumby: British Columbia	41	50	119
Lumpkin: Georgia	27	32	85
Lund: British Columbia	43	50	125
Luray: Virginia	17	39	78
Lutcher: Louisiana	27	30	91
Luverne: Alabama	27	32	86
Lyell I.: British Columbia	41	53	131
Lykens: Pennsylvania	14	41	77
Lyles Wrigley: Tennessee	22	36	87
Lynch: Kentucky	16	37	83
Lynchburg: Virginia	16	37	79
Lynden: Washington	38	49	122
Lyndonville: New York	12	43	78
Lyndonville: Vermont	13	45	72
Lynn: Indiana	21	40	85
Lynn: Massachusetts	2	42½	71
Lynn Canyon Park: B.C.	6	49¼	123
Lynn Haven: Florida	27	30	86
Lynn Woods Res.: Massachusetts	2	42½	71
Lynn Lake: *sett.*, Manitoba	31	57	101
Lynx L.: N.W.T.	44	62	106
Lyon, C.: N.W.T.	44	70	123
Lyon Inlet: N.W.T.	45	66	84
Lyon Mountain: *sett.*, N.Y.	13	45	74
Lyons: Georgia	24	32	82
Lyons: Illinois	4	41¾	87¾
Lyons: Kansas	29	38	98
Lyons: New York	12	43	77
Lyons Falls: *sett.*, New York	13	44	75
Lytton: British Columbia	38	50	122
Lytton: California	37	39	123
Mabank: Texas	26	32	96
Mabton: Washington	39	46	120
McAdoo: Pennsylvania	14	41	76
McAlester: Oklahoma	26	35	96
McAllen: Texas	22	26	98
MacAlpine L.: N.W.T.	44	66	103
McArthur: Ohio	16	39	82
McBee: South Carolina	24	34	80
McBeth Fiord: N.W.T.	45	70	69
McBride: British Columbia	41	53	120
McCarthy: Alaska	43	61	143
McClean: Virginia	2	39	77¼
McCleary: Washington	39	47	123
McCloud: California	36	41	122
McCloud: *r.*, California	36	41	122
McClure L.: California	37	38	120
McColl: South Carolina	24	35	80
McComb: Mississippi	27	31	90
McComb: Ohio	19	41	84
McConnellsburg: Pennsylvania	14	40	78
McConnelsville: Ohio	16	40	82
McCook: Nebraska	28	40	101
McCormick: South Carolina	24	34	82
McDermitt: Nevada	33	42	118
Macdoel: California	36	42	122
McDonald: Pennsylvania	19	40	80
McDonough: Georgia	24	33	84
Macdougall L.: N.W.T.	44	66	99
MacFarlane: *r.*, Saskatchewan	30	58	108
McGee Bend: *dam*, Texas	26	31	94
McGehee: Arkansas	26	34	91
McGill: Nevada	33	39	115
McGrath: Alaska	42	63	156
McGraw: New York	14	43	76
McGregor: *r.*, B.C.	41	54	122
McHenry: Illinois	21	42	88
McIntosh: Alabama	27	31	88
McIntosh: South Dakota	28	46	101
Mackay L.: N.W.T.	44	64	111
McKeansburg: Pennsylvania	14	41	76
McKeesport: Pennsylvania	5	40¼	79¾
McKees Rocks: *sett.*, Pa.	5	40½	80
Mackenzie: British Columbia	41	55	123
McKenzie: Tennessee	27	36	89
Mackenzie: *r.*, N.W.T.	44	67	132
Mackenzie Bay: Yukon	44	69	137
Mackenzie, District of: N.W.T.	44	64	117

	Page	N	W
Mackenzie Mts.: Yukon/N.W.T.	40	64	130
Mackinac I.: Michigan	20	46	85
Mackinac, Straits of: Michigan	20	46	85
Mackinaw: *r.*, Illinois	21	41	89
Mackinaw City: Michigan	20	46	85
McKinley Bay: N.W.T.	44	70	131
McKinley, Mt.: Alaska	42	63	151
McKinley Park: Alaska	42	64	149
McKinney: Texas	26	33	97
McKittrick: California	34	35	120
McKnight: Pennsylvania	5	40½	80
McLennan: Alberta	30	56	117
McLeod: *r.*, Alberta	30	54	117
McLeod Bay: N.W.T.	44	63	110
McLeod Lake: *town*, B.C.	41	55	123
M'Clintock: Manitoba	31	58	94
M'Clintock Chan.: N.W.T.	44	72	102
McLoughlin Bay: N.W.T.	44	68	100
McLoughlin, Mt.: Oregon	36	42	122
M'Clure Strait: N.W.T.	46	75	120
McMillan: Michigan	20	46	86
Macmillan: *r.*, Yukon	40	63	135
McMinnville: Oregon	39	45	123
McMinnville: Tennessee	27	36	86
McMurray *see* Fort McMurray: Alberta	30	57	111
McNary: *dam*, Wash./Oregon	39	46	119
Macomb: Illinois	10	40	91
Macon: Georgia	24	33	84
Macon: Mississippi	27	33	89
McPherson: Kansas	29	38	98
McRae: Georgia	24	32	83
MacRae: Yukon	40	61	135
McTavish Arm: Great Bear L.: N.W.T.	40	66	119
McVicar Arm: Great Bear L.: N.W.T.	40	65	120
Mad: *r.*, California	36	41	124
Madawaska: *r.*, Ontario	12	45	77
Madeline: California	36	41	120
Madera: California	34	37	120
Madill: Oklahoma	26	34	97
Madison: Connecticut	15	41	73
Madison: Florida	25	30	84
Madison: Georgia	24	34	84
Madison: Indiana	10	39	85
Madison: North Carolina	16	36	80
Madison: Ohio	19	42	81
Madison: South Dakota	28	44	97
Madison: West Virginia	16	38	82
Madison: Wisconsin	20	43	89
Madison: *r.*, Montana	28	45	112
Madison Heights: *sett.*, Michigan	5	42½	83
Madisonville: Kentucky	23	37	88
Madisonville: Louisiana	27	30	90
Madisonville: Tennessee	24	36	84
Madisonville: Texas	26	31	96
Madras: Oregon	39	45	121
Madre, Laguna: Texas	22	27	97
Madrid: New York	13	45	75
Madrone: California	37	37	122
Madsen: Ontario	31	51	94
Magalia: California	36	40	122
Magazine Mt.: Arkansas	26	35	94
Magdalen Is.: Québec	9	47	62
Magee: Mississippi	27	32	90
Magnetawan: Ontario	18	46	80
Magnolia: Arkansas	26	33	93
Magnolia: Mississippi	27	31	91
Magnolia: North Carolina	24	35	78
Magog: Québec	13	45	72
Magpie L.: Québec	9	51	65
Maguse L.: N.W.T.	31	62	95
Maguse River: *sett.*, N.W.T.	31	61	94
Mahonoy City: Pennsylvania	14	41	76
Mahoning Creek Res.: Pa.	19	41	79
Mahood Creek: British Columbia	6	49	122¾
Mahwah: New Jersey	15	41	74
Maiden: North Carolina	24	36	81
Maidstone: Ontario	5	42¼	83
Maili: Hawaii	128	21	158
MAINE	8/9	—	—
Maine, Gulf of	11	43	70
Maitland: Ontario	12	45	76
Makapala: Hawaii	128	20	156
Makkovik: Newfoundland	9	55	59
Malaga: New Jersey	14	40	75
Malakoff: Texas	26	32	96
Mala Pascua, Cabo: Puerto Rico	17	18	66
Malartic: Québec	8	48	78
Malden: Massachusetts	2	42½	71
Malheur L.: Oregon	32	43	119
Mallory: West Virginia	16	38	82
Malone: New York	13	45	74
Malta: Montana	28	48	108
Malvern: Arkansas	26	34	93
Malvern: Ohio	19	41	81
Malvern: Pennsylvania	14	40	76
Mamaroneck: New York	1	41	73¾
Mammoth Caves Nat. Park: Ky.	23	37	86
Mammoth Lakes: *sett.*, Calif.	37	38	119
Mamou: Louisiana	26	32	92
Man: West Virginia	16	38	82
Manasquan: New Jersey	15	40	74
Manassas: Virginia	17	39	78
Manati: Puerto Rico	27	18	66
Manawa: Wisconsin	20	44	89

	Page	N	W
Manayunk: Pennsylvania	2	40	75¼
Mancelona: Michigan	20	45	85
Manchester: California	37	39	124
Manchester: Connecticut	15	42	73
Manchester: Georgia	24	33	85
Manchester: Massachusetts	15	43	71
Manchester: Michigan	21	42	84
Manchester: New Hampshire	13	43	71
Manchester: New York	14	43	77
Manchester: Pennsylvania	14	40	77
Manchester: Tennessee	27	35	86
Mandan: North Dakota	28	47	101
Mandeville: Louisiana	27	30	90
Mangum: Oklahoma	29	35	100
Manhattan: Kansas	28	39	97
Manhattan: New York	1	40¾	74
Manhattan Beach: *sett.*, Calif.	7	33¾	118½
Manheim: Pennsylvania	14	40	76
Manicouagan: *r.*, Québec	8	50	69
Manicouagan L.: *& dam*, Québec	8	52	69
Manicouagan Penin.: Québec	9	49	69
Manistee: *& r.*, Michigan	20	44	86
Manistique: Michigan	20	46	86
MANITOBA	31	—	—
Manitoba, Lake: Manitoba	31	51	99
Manitou I.: Michigan	10	47	88
Manitoulin I.: Ontario	18	46	82
Manitouwadge: Ontario	10	49	86
Manitowoc: Wisconsin	20	44	88
Maniwaki: Québec	12	46	76
Manix: California	35	35	117
Mankato: Minnesota	10	44	94
Manley Hot Springs: Alaska	42	65	151
Manlius: New York	14	43	76
Manning: South Carolina	24	34	80
Mannington: West Virginia	16	40	80
Manouane L.: Québec	8	51	71
Manse: Nevada	35	36	116
Mansel I.: N.W.T.	45	62	80
Mansfield: Georgia	24	34	84
Mansfield: Louisiana	26	32	94
Mansfield: Massachusetts	15	42	71
Mansfield: Ohio	19	41	83
Mansfield: Pennsylvania	14	42	77
Mansfield: Washington	39	48	120
Mansfield, Mt.: Vermont	13	45	73
Mansura: Louisiana	26	31	92
Manteca: California	37	38	121
Manteno: Illinois	21	41	88
Manton: Michigan	20	44	85
Mantua: Ohio	19	41	81
Manville: New Jersey	15	41	75
Many: Louisiana	26	32	93
Maple: Ontario	5	43¾	79½
Maple: *r.*, Michigan	20	43	85
Maple Creek: *town*, Sask.	30	50	109
Maple Shade: New Jersey	2	40	75
Maplewood: Minnesota	3	45	93
Marathon: Ontario	10	49	86
Marblehead: Massachusetts	2	42½	69¾
Marblehead: Ohio	19	42	83
Marble I.: N.W.T.	45	63	91
Marcellus: New York	14	43	76
Marcy, Mount: New York	13	44	74
Marengo: Illinois	21	42	89
Marfa: Texas	29	30	104
Margaret, C.: N.W.T.	45	70	92
Marian L.: N.W.T.	40	63	116
Marianna: Arkansas	27	35	91
Marianna: Florida	27	31	85
Maria Portage: Manitoba	31	54	95
Marias: *r.*, Montana	28	48	111
Maricopa: California	34	35	119
Marietta: Georgia	24	34	85
Marietta: Ohio	16	39	81
Marietta: Oklahoma	26	34	97
Marietta: Pennsylvania	14	40	77
Marieville: Québec	13	45	73
Marina: California	37	37	122
Marina del Rey: California	7	34	118½
Marine City: Michigan	19	43	83
Marinette: Wisconsin	20	45	88
Marin Pen.: California	6	37¾	122½
Marion: Alabama	27	33	87
Marion: Indiana	21	41	86
Marion: Iowa	10	42	92
Marion: Massachusetts	15	42	71
Marion: New York	12	43	77
Marion: North Carolina	24	36	82
Marion: Ohio	19	41	83
Marion: South Carolina	24	34	79
Marion: Virginia	16	37	82
Marion: Wisconsin	20	45	89
Marion, L.: South Carolina	24	34	80
Mariposa: California	37	38	120
Mark Tree: Arkansas	27	36	90
Markesan: Wisconsin	20	44	89
Markham: Ontario	5	43¾	79¼
Markham Bay: N.W.T.	45	63	72
Markleeville: California	37	39	120
Marks: Mississippi	27	34	90
Marksville: Louisiana	26	31	92
Marlboro: Massachusetts	15	42	72
Marlboro: New Hampshire	13	43	72
Marlboro: New York	15	42	74
Marlin: Texas	26	31	97
Marlinton: West Virginia	16	38	80

	Page	N	W
Penticton: British Columbia	38	49	120
Pentwater: Michigan	20	44	86
Pentz: California	37	40	122
Peoria: Illinois	21	41	90
Peotone: Illinois	21	41	88
Pepperwood: California	36	40	124
Pere Marquette: *r.*, Michigan	20	44	86
Perez: California	36	42	121
Péribonca: *r.*, Québec	8	49	71
Perkasie: Pennsylvania	14	40	75
Perris: California	35	34	117
Perry: Florida	25	30	84
Perry: Georgia	24	32	84
Perry: Michigan	21	43	84
Perry River: *sett.*, N.W.T.	44	68	102
Perrysburg: Ohio	19	42	84
Perryton: Texas	29	36	101
Perryville: Alaska	43	56	159
Perth: Ontario	12	45	76
Perth Amboy: New Jersey	1	40½	74
Peru: Illinois	21	41	89
Peru: Indiana	21	41	86
Pescadero: California	37	37	122
Peshtigo: *& r.*, Wisconsin	20	45	88
Petaluma: California	37	38	123
Petenwell Res.: Wisconsin	20	44	90
Peterborough: New Hampshire	13	43	72
Peterborough: Ontario	12	44	78
Peter Pond L.: Saskatchewan	30	56	109
Peters: California	37	38	121
Peters Canon Res.: California	7	33¾	117¾
Petersburg: Alaska	41	57	133
Petersburg: Michigan	19	42	84
Petersburg: Virginia	17	37	77
Petersburg: West Virginia	16	39	79
Peters Mt.: West Virginia	16	38	81
Petit Bois I.: Mississippi	27	30	88
Petitot: *r.*, B.C./Alberta	40	60	121
Petitskapau L.: Newfoundland	9	55	67
Petoskey: Michigan	20	45	85
Petrified Forest Nat. Park: Ariz.	33	35	110
Petrolia: California	36	40	124
Pewamo: Michigan	20	43	85
Phelan: California	35	34	118
Phelps: New York	14	43	77
Phenix City: Alabama	27	32	85
Philadelphia: Mississippi	27	33	89
Philadelphia: New York	12	44	76
Philadelphia: Pennsylvania	14	40	75
Philipsburg: Montana	32	46	113
Philipsburg: Pennsylvania	14	41	78
Philip Smith Mts.: Alaska	42	68	147
Phillips: California	37	39	120
Phillipsburg: Kansas	28	40	99
Phillipsburg: New Jersey	14	41	75
Philmont: New York	15	42	74
Philo: California	37	39	123
Philo: Ohio	16	40	82
Philpott Res.: Virginia	16	37	80
Phoenix: Arizona	33	34	112
Phoenix: New York	12	43	76
Phoenix: Oregon	36	42	123
Phoenixville: Pennsylvania	14	40	76
Picayune: Mississippi	27	31	90
Pickens: South Carolina	24	35	83
Pickle Crow: Ontario	31	52	90
Pickwick L.: Miss./Alabama	27	35	88
Pickwick Landing: *dam*, Tenn.	27	35	88
Picton: Ontario	12	44	77
Piedmont: Alabama	27	34	86
Piedmont: California	6	37¾	122¼
Piedmont: South Carolina	24	35	82
Piedmont: West Virginia	16	39	79
Piedmont Res.: Ohio	19	40	81
Piedras Blancas Point: Calif.	34	36	121
Pierrefonds: Québec	2	42½	73¾
Pierce: Florida	25	28	82
Piercy: California	36	40	124
Pierre: South Dakota	28	44	100
Pierreville: Québec	13	46	73
Pigeon: Michigan	18	44	83
Pigeon: *r.*, Minnesota	10	48	90
Pigeon Point: California	37	37	122
Pigs Eye, L.: Minnesota	3	45	93
Pikangikum L.: Ontario	31	52	94
Pikes Peak: Colorado	28	39	105
Pikeville: Kentucky	16	37	83
Pilarcitos Lake: California	6	37½	122½
Pillar Pt.: California	6	37½	122½
Pillsbury, L.: California	37	39	123
Pilot Mountain: *sett.*, N.C.	16	37	81
Pilot Point: Alaska	43	58	158
Pilot Point: *sett.*, Texas	26	33	97
Pilot Rock: *sett.*, Oregon	39	45	119
Pilot Station: Alaska	43	62	163
Pilottown: Louisiana	27	29	89
Pima: Arizona	33	33	110
Pincher Creek: *town*, Alberta	30	50	114
Pinconning: Michigan	20	44	84
Pine: *cr.*, Pennsylvania	14	41	77
Pine: *r.*, British Columbia	41	56	122
Pine: *r.*, Michigan	20	43	84
Pine Bluff: Arkansas	26	34	92
Pine Camp: New York	12	44	76
Pine Creek Res.: Oklahoma	26	34	95
Pinecrest: California	37	38	120
Pinedale: California	37	37	120

	Page	N	W
Pine Falls: *sett.*, Manitoba	31	51	96
Pine Flat Res.: *& dam*, Calif.	34	37	119
Pine Forest Mts.: Nevada	36	42	119
Pine Grove: Pennsylvania	14	41	76
Pinehouse L.: Saskatchewan	30	56	107
Pinehurst: North Carolina	24	35	79
Pinehurst: Oregon	36	42	122
Pine Island Sound: Florida	25	27	82
Pineland: Texas	26	31	94
Pine Pass: British Columbia	41	55	122
Pine Plains: New York	15	42	74
Pine Point: N.W.T.	30	61	114
Pint Point: *sett.*, N.W.T.	30	61	114
Pine Valley: *sett.*, California	35	33	117
Pineville: Kentucky	24	37	84
Pinnacles Nat. Mon.: California	34	37	121
Pinopolis: *dam*, South Carolina	24	33	80
Pinos, Mt.: California	34	35	119
Pinto: Maryland	17	40	79
Pioche: Nevada	33	38	115
Pioneer: California	37	38	121
Pipestone: *r.*, Ontario	31	52	91
Pipmuacan L.: Québec	8	50	70
Piqua: Ohio	19	40	84
Piru: California	35	34	119
Piru: *cr.*, California	35	35	119
Pismo Beach: *sett.*, California	34	35	121
Pistol River: *sett.*, Oregon	36	42	124
Pit: *r.* California	36	41	121
Pitkas Point: *sett.*, Alaska	43	62	163
Pitman: New Jersey	14	40	75
Pitt I.: British Columbia	41	54	130
Pitt River: *r.*, B.C.	6	49¼	122¾
Pittsboro: North Carolina	24	36	79
Pittsburg: California	37	38	122
Pittsburg: Kansas	29	37	95
Pittsburg: Texas	26	33	95
Pittsburgh: Pennsylvania	19	40	80
Pittsfield: Massachusetts	15	42	73
Pittsfield: New Hampshire	13	43	71
Pittsford: New York	12	43	78
Pittston: Pennsylvania	14	41	76
Pixley: California	34	36	119
Placentia: Newfoundland	9	47	54
Placentia B.: Newfoundland	9	48	54
Placerville: California	37	39	121
Plain City: Ohio	19	40	83
Plain Dealing: Louisiana	26	33	94
Plainfield: Connecticut	15	42	72
Plainfield: Illinois	21	42	88
Plainfield: New Jersey	1	40½	74½
Plainfield: Wisconsin	20	44	90
Plainview: Arkansas	26	35	93
Plainview: Texas	29	34	102
Plainville: Connecticut	15	42	73
Plainwell: Michigan	21	42	86
Planada: California	37	37	120
Plano: Illinois	21	42	89
Plano: Texas	26	33	97
Plant City: Florida	25	28	82
Plaquemine: Louisiana	26	30	91
Plaster City: California	35	33	116
Platinum: Alaska	43	59	162
Platte: *r.*, Nebraska	28	41	100
Platt National Park: Oklahoma	26	34	97
Plattsburgh: New York	13	45	73
Plattsmouth: Nebraska	28	41	96
Playgreen L.: Manitoba	31	54	98
Pleasant Gap: Pennsylvania	14	41	78
Pleasant Grove: California	37	39	121
Pleasant Hill: *town*, California	6	38	122
Pleasant Hills: Pennsylvania	5	40¼	80
Pleasanton: California	37	38	122
Pleasanton: Texas	22	29	99
Pleasantville: New Jersey	15	39	75
Pleasantville: New York	15	41	74
Plentywood: Montana	28	49	105
Plessisville: Québec	13	46	72
Pletipi L.: Québec	8	52	70
Plover: Wisconsin	20	44	90
Plush: Oregon	36	42	120
Plymouth: California	37	38	121
Plymouth: Indiana	21	41	86
Plymouth: Massachusetts	15	42	71
Plymouth: Michigan	5	42¼	83¾
Plymouth: Minnesota	3	45	93¼
Plymouth: New Hampshire	13	44	72
Plymouth: North Carolina	24	36	77
Plymouth: Ohio	19	41	83
Plymouth: Washington	39	46	119
Plymouth: Wisconsin	20	44	88
Pocatello: Idaho	32	43	112
Pocohontas: Virginia	17	37	78
Pocomoke: *r.*, Maryland	17	38	75
Pocomoke City: Maryland	17	38	76
Point Arena: *sett.*, California	37	39	124
Point Comfort: *sett.*, Texas	22	29	97
Pointe-aux-Trembles: *sett.*, Qué.	2	45¾	73½
Pointe-Claire: *town*, Québec	2	45½	73¾
Point Hope: *sett.*, Alaska	42	68	167
Point L.: Northwest Territories	40	65	113
Point Lay: *sett.*, Alaska	42	70	163
Point Pelee Nat. Pk.: Ontario	19	42	82
Point Pleasant: *town*, N.J.	15	40	74
Point Pleasant: *town*, W. Va.	16	39	82
Point Reyes Nat. Seashore: Calif.	37	38	123
Poisson Blanc, L.: Québec	12	46	76

	Page	N	W
Poland: Ohio	19	41	81
Polk: Pennsylvania	19	41	80
Polo: Illinois	21	42	90
Pomeroy: Ohio	16	39	82
Pomona: California	7	34	117¾
Pompano Beach: *town*, Florida	25	26	80
Pompton Lakes: New Jersey	1	41	74¼
Ponca City: Oklahoma	29	37	97
Ponce: Puerto Rico	27	18	67
Ponchatoula: Louisiana	27	30	90
Pond Fork: *r.*, West Virginia	16	38	82
Pond Inlet: N.W.T.	45	73	77
Pond Inlet: *sett.*, N.W.T.	45	73	78
Pondosa: California	36	41	122
Ponoka: Alberta	30	53	114
Pontchartrain, L.: Louisiana	27	30	90
Pontiac: Illinois	21	41	89
Pontiac: Michigan	19	43	83
Pontotoc: Mississippi	27	34	89
Pont-Rouge: Québec	13	47	72
Pont-Viau: *sett.*, Québec	2	45½	73¾
Poorman: Alaska	42	64	156
Pope: California	35	33	116
Poplar: *r.*, Manitoba	31	53	97
Poplar Bluff: Missouri	10	37	90
Porcher I.: B.C.	41	54	131
Porcupine: Ontario	11	49	81
Porcupine: *r.*, Yukon/Alaska	42	67	143
Portage: Alaska	43	61	149
Portage: Pennsylvania	14	40	79
Portage: Wisconsin	20	44	89
Portage-la-Prairie: Manitoba	31	50	98
Port Alberni: British Columbia	38	49	125
Portales: New Mexico	29	34	103
Port Alexander: Alaska	41	56	135
Port Alice: British Columbia	41	50	127
Port Allegany: Pennsylvania	14	42	78
Port Angeles: Washington	38	48	123
Port Arthur (*now* Thunder Bay): Ontario	10	48	89
Port Arthur: Texas	26	30	94
Port Austin: Michigan	18	44	83
Port-aux-Basques: Nfld.	9	48	59
Port Barre: Louisiana	26	31	92
Port Blandford: Newfoundland	9	48	54
Port Burwell: *bay*, Québec	45	60	65
Port Burwell: Ontario	19	43	81
Port Byron: New York	12	43	77
Port Cartier: Québec	9	50	67
Port Chester: New York	1	41	73¾
Port Chicago: California	37	38	122
Port Chilkoot: Alaska	40	59	135
Port Clarence: *bay*, Alaska	42	65	166
Port Clinton: Ohio	19	42	83
Port Colborne: Ontario	19	43	79
Port Coquitlam: B.C.	6	49¼	122¾
Port Credit: Ontario	5	43½	79½
Port Dalhousie: Ontario	19	43	79
Port Deposit: Maryland	17	40	76
Port Dover: Ontario	19	43	80
Port Edward: British Columbia	41	54	130
Port Edwards: Wisconsin	20	44	90
Portersville: Pennsylvania	19	41	80
Porterville: California	34	36	119
Port Everglades: Florida	25	26	80
Port Gibson: Mississippi	26	32	91
Port Henry: New York	13	44	73
Port Graham: Alaska	43	59	152
Port Hardy: British Columbia	41	51	128
Port Harrison: Québec	45	58	78
Port Heiden: Alaska	43	57	159
Port Hope: Ontario	12	44	78
Port Huron: Michigan	19	43	82
Port Jefferson: New York	15	41	73
Port Jervis: New York	15	41	75
Portland: Connecticut	15	42	73
Portland: Indiana	21	40	85
Portland: Maine	11	44	70
Portland: Michigan	21	43	85
Portland: Oregon	39	46	123
Port Logan: N.W.T.	45	72	93
Port Madison: *and bay*, Wash.	6	47¾	122½
Port Maitland: Ontario	19	43	80
Port Marion: Pennsylvania	16	40	80
Port Mellon: British Columbia	38	50	123
Port Menier: Québec	9	50	64
Port Moller: Alaska	43	56	161
Port Monmouth: New Jersey	14	40	74
Port Moody: British Columbia	6	49¼	122¾
Port Neches: Texas	26	30	94
Port Nelson: Manitoba	31	57	93
Portneuf: Québec	13	47	72
Port Norris: New Jersey	14	39	75
Port-Nouveau-Québec (George River): *sett.*, Québec	45	58	65
Portola: California	36	40	120
Port Orchard: *& chan.*, Wash.	6	47½	122¾
Port Radium: N.W.T.	40	66	118
Port Renfrew: B.C.	38	49	124
Port Rowan: Ontario	1	43	80
Port Royal: Virginia	17	38	77
Port St. Joe: Florida	27	30	85
Port San Luis Obispo: Calif.	34	35	121
Port Saunders: Newfoundland	9	51	57
Port Simpson: British Columbia	41	55	130
Portsmouth: New Hampshire	15	43	71
Portsmouth: Ohio	16	39	83

	Page	N	W
Portsmouth: Virginia	17	37	76
Port Stanley: Ontario	19	43	81
Port Sulphur: Louisiana	27	29	90
Port Townsend: Washington	38	48	123
Portville: New York	14	42	78
Port Washington: New York	1	40¾	73¾
Port Washington: Wisconsin	20	43	88
Port Weller: Ontario	19	43	79
Poste-de-la-Baleine *see* Great Whale River: *sett.*, Qué.	8	55	78
Postville: Newfoundland	9	55	60
Poteau: Oklahoma	26	35	95
Poteau: *r.*, Ark./Oklahoma	26	35	94
Poteet: Texas	22	29	99
Potholes Res.: Washington	39	47	119
Potomac: *r.*	17	39	78
Potomac R., N.Br.: W. Va./Md.	16	39	79
Potomac R., S. Br.: W. Va.	17	39	79
Potsdam: New York	13	45	75
Pottstown: Pennsylvania	14	40	76
Potwin: Kansas	29	38	97
Poughkeepsie: New York	15	42	74
Poulsbo: Washington	6	47¾	122¾
Poultney: Vermont	13	44	73
Pound: Wisconsin	20	45	88
Povungnituk: Québec	45	60	77
Povungnituk: *r.*, Québec	45	60	76
Poway: California	35	33	117
Powder: *r.*, Wyoming/Montana	28	45	106
Powell: Wisconsin	20	46	90
Powell: Wyoming	28	45	109
Powell, L.: Arizona/Utah	33	37	112
Powell River: *sett.*, B.C.	38	50	125
Powellton: West Virginia	16	38	81
Powers: Michigan	20	46	88
Powers: Oregon	36	43	124
Powhatan Point: *sett.*, Ohio	16	40	81
Poygan, L.: Wisconsin	20	44	89
Prado Flood Control Basin: Calif.	7	34	117¾
Prague: Oklahoma	26	35	97
Prairies, des: *r.*, Québec	2	45½	73½
Prairie Dog Town Fork: *r.*, Texas	29	35	101
Prairie du Sac: Wisconsin	20	43	90
Prairie Grove: Arkansas	26	36	94
Prather: California	37	37	120
Pratt: Kansas	29	38	99
Prattville: Alabama	27	32	87
Preeceville: Saskatchewan	30	52	103
Preissac, L.: Québec	8	48	78
Prescot I.: N.W.T.	44	73	97
Prescott: Arizona	33	35	112
Prescott: Arkansas	26	34	93
Prescott: Ontario	12	45	76
Presidio: California	6	37¾	122½
Presque Isle: Maine.	9	47	68
Presque Isle State Park: Pa.	19	42	80
Press Park: Louisiana	3	30	90
Preston: Idaho	32	42	112
Preston: Ontario	18	43	80
Prestonburg: Kentucky	16	38	83
Prettyboy Res.: Maryland	17	40	77
Price: Utah	33	40	111
Prichard:Alabama	27	31	88
Priest Rapids: *dam.* Wash.	39	47	120
Primrose L.: Saskatchewan	30	55	110
Prince Albert: Saskatchewan	30	53	106
Prince Albert Hills: N.W.T.	45	68	85
Prince Albert National Park: Saskatchewan	30	54	106
Prince Albert Penin.: N.W.T.	44	72	117
Prince Albert Sound: N.W.T.	44	70	115
Prince Charles I.: N.W.T.	45	68	76
PRINCE EDWARD ISLAND	9	—	—
Prince Edward Island Nat. Park	9	46	63
Prince George: B.C.	41	54	123
Prince Leopold I.: N.W.T.	45	74	90
Prince of Wales, C.: Québec	45	62	72
Prince of Wales I.: Alaska	41	56	133
Prince of Wales I.: N.W.T.	44	73	100
Prince of Wales Strait: N.W.T.	44	73	118
Prince Regent Inlet: N.W.T.	45	73	90
Prince Rupert: B.C.	41	54	130
Princess Anne: Maryland.	17	38	76
Princess Royal I.: B.C.	41	53	129
Princeton: British Columbia	38	49	121
Princeton: Illinois	21	41	89
Princeton: New Jersey	15	40	75
Princeton: West Virginia	16	37	81
Prince William Sound: Alaska	43	61	147
Prineville: Oregon	32	44	121
Proberta: California	36	40	122
Proctor: British Columbia	41	50	117
Proctor: Vermont	13	44	73
Prophet: *r.*, British Columbia	40	58	123
Prospect: Ohio	19	40	83
Prospect: Oregon	36	43	123
Prospect: Pennsylvania	19	41	80
Prospect Heights: *town*, Illinois	4	42	88
Prospect Park: *town*, New York	1	40¾	74
Prosser: Washington	39	46	120
Proven: Greenland	45	73	56
Providence: Rhode Island	15	42	71
Provincetown: Massachusetts	15	42	70
Provo: Utah	33	40	112
Provost: Alberta	30	52	110
Prudhoe B.: *& sett.*, Alaska	42	70	148
Prunedale: California	37	37	122

	Page	N	W
Puce: Ontario	5	42¼	82¾
Puckaway, L.: Wisconsin	20	44	89
Pueblo: Colorado	29	38	105
Puerco: *r.*, New Mexico/ Arizona	29	35	109
Puget Sound: Washington	38/39	48	122
Pulaski: New York	12	44	76
Pulaski: Pennsylvania	19	41	80
Pulaski: Tennessee.	27	35	87
Pulaski: Virginia	16	37	81
Pulaski: Wisconsin	20	45	88
Pulga: California	36	40	121
Pulgas Ridge: California	6	37½	122¼
Pullman: Washington	32	47	117
Punta Gorda: Florida	25	27	82
Punxsutawney: Pennsylvania	14	41	79
Purcellville: Virginia	17	39	78
Purvis: Mississippi	27	31	89
Putnam: Connecticut	15	42	72
Puunene: Hawaii	128	21	156
Putunia: Québec	45	62	74
Puyallup: Washington	39	47	122
Pymantuning Res.: Pennsylvania.	19	42	80
Pyramid: Nevada	36	40	120
Pyramid L.: Nevada	36	40	120
Quabbin Res.: Massachusetts	15	42	72
Quadra I.: British Columbia	38	50	125
Quail Mts.: California	35	36	117
Quakertow: Pennsylvania.	14	40	75
Quantico: Virginia	17	39	77
Qu'Appelle: *r. & dam*, Saskatchewan	31	51	102
Quarryville: Pennsylvania	14	40	76
Quartz Hill: *town*, California	35	35	118
Quartz Mountain: *sett.*, Oregon	36	42	121
QUÉBEC	8	—	—
Québec: Québec	13	47	71
Queen Charlotte: B.C.	41	53	132
Queen Charlotte Is.: B.C..	41	53	132
Queen Charlotte Sound: B.C.	41	51	130
Queen Charlotte Str.: B.C.	41	51	128
Queen Elizabeth Park: B.C.	6	49¼	123
Queen Maud G.: Northwest Territories	44	68	103
Queens: New York	1	40¾	74
Queenstown: Maryland	17	39	76
Queets: Washington	39	48	124
Quesnel: British Columbia	41	53	123
Quesnel L.: British Columbia	41	52	121
Questa: New Mexico	29	37	106
Quetico Prov. Park: Ontario	10	48	92
Quibell: Ontario	10	50	93
Quilcene: Washington	39	48	123
Quill Lakes: Saskatchewan	31	52	104
Quinault: *r.*, Washington	39	48	124
Quinault, L.: Washington	39	47	124
Quincy: California	36	40	121
Quincy: Florida	25	31	85
Quincy: Illinois	10	40	91
Quincy: Massachusetts	2	42¼	71
Quincy: Michigan	21	42	85
Quincy: Washington	39	47	120
Quincy Bay: Massachusetts	2	42¼	71
Quinebaug: *r.*, Mass./Conn.	15	42	72
Quinhagak: Alaska	43	60	162
Quinton: Oklahoma	26	35	95
Quitman: Georgia	25	31	84
Quitman: Mississippi	27	32	89
Quitman: Texas	26	33	95
Quoich: *r.*, N.W.T.	45	65	95
Quorn: Ontario	10	49	91
Qutdligssat: Greenland	45	70	53
Raccoon: *r.*, Iowa	10	42	95
Raccoon: *r.*, Ohio	16	39	82
Raccoon Point: Louisiana	26	29	91
Race, C.: Newfoundland	9	47	53
Racine: Wisconsin	21	43	88
Radec: California	35	34	117
Radford: Virginia	16	37	81
Radisson: Saskatchewan	30	52	107
Radville: Saskatchewan	30	49	104
Rae: Northwest Territories	40	63	116
Rae: *r.*, Northwest Territories	44	68	116
Raeford: North Carolina	24	35	79
Rae Isthmus: N.W.T.	45	67	88
Rae Strait: N.W.T.	45	69	95
Ragland: Alabama	27	34	86
Rainbow: Alaska	43	61	150
Rainier: Oregon	39	46	123
Rainier, Mt.: Washington	39	47	122
Rainy: *r.*, Ontario/Manitoba	10	49	94
Rainy L.: Minn./Ontario	10	49	93
Rainy River: *town.* Ontario	10	49	95
Raisin: *r.*, Michigan	19	42	84
Raleigh: North Carolina	24	36	79
Ramona: California.	35	33	117
Rampart: Alaska	42	65	150
Ramsey: New Jersey	15	41	74
Rancheria: Yukon	40	60	131
Rancocas Creek: New Jersey	2	40	75
Rand: West Virginia	16	38	82
Randleman: North Carolina	24	36	80
Randolph: Massachusetts	15	42	71
Randolph: New York	19	42	79
Randolph: Utah	33	42	111

	Page	N	W
Randolph: Vermont	13	44	7
Randsburg: California	35	35	11
Rankin Inlet: N.W.T.	45	63	9
Rankin Inlet: *sett.*, N.W.T.	45	63	9
Rantoul: Illinois	21	40	8
Rapid City: South Dakota	28	44	10
Rapid River: *sett.*, Michigan	20	46	8
Rappahannock: *r.*, Virginia	17	38	7
Raquette: *r.*, New York	13	44	7
Raquette L.: New York	13	44	7
Rarden: Ohio	16	39	8
Raritan: r., New Jersey	1	40½	7
Raritan Bay: New Jersey	1	40½	7
Rat: *r.*, Manitoba	31	56	9
Rat Is.: Alaska	60	52	178
Raton: New Mexico	29	37	10
Rat River: *sett.*, N.W.T.	30	61	11
Ratz, Mt.: British Columbia	40	57	13
Ravendale: California	36	41	12
Ravenna: California	35	34	11
Ravenswood: West Virginia	16	39	8
Rawdon: Québec	13	46	7
Rawlins: Wyoming	28	42	10
Ray: Arizona	33	33	11
Ray, C.: Newfoundland	9	48	5
Raymond: Alberta	30	50	11
Raymond: California	37	37	12
Raymond: Washington	39	47	12
Raymondville: Texas	22	27	9
Ray Mts.: Alaska	42	66	15
Rayne: Louisiana	26	30	9
Rayville: Louisiana	26	32	9
Reading: Massachusetts	15	43	7
Reading: Michigan	21	42	8
Reading: Pennsylvania	14	40	7
Read Island: *sett.*, N.W.T.	44	69	11
Red: *r.*	22	31	9
Red Bank: New Jersey	15	40	74
Red Bay: *sett.*, Alabama	27	34	8
Red Bluff: California	36	40	122
Redcliff: Colorado	28	40	106
Red Deer: Alberta	30	52	114
Red Deer: *r.*, Alberta	30	51	112
Red Deer: *r.*, Saskatchewan	30	53	103
Red Deer L.: Manitoba	31	53	101
Red Devil: Alaska	43	62	157
Redding: California	36	41	122
Redfield: South Dakota	28	45	99
Redkey: Indiana	21	40	85
Red Lake: *r.*, Minnesota	10	48	96
Red L.: Ontario	31	51	94
Redlands: California	35	34	117
Red Lion: Pennsylvania	14	40	77
Red Mesa: Arizona.	33	37	109
Redmond: Oregon	32	44	121
Redmond: Utah	33	39	112
Redmond: Washington	6	47¾	122
Red Mountain: *sett.*, California.	35	35	118
Redonda Is.: British Columbia	38	50	125
Redondo Beach: *town*, Calif.	7	33¾	118
Redoubt Volcano: Alaska	43	61	15
Red River of the North	10	48	97
Red Springs: North Carolina	24	35	79
Redwater: Alberta	30	54	113
Redway: California.	36	40	124
Red Valley: *sett.*, California	37	39	123
Red Wing: Minnesota	10	45	93
Redwood: Mississippi	27	32	91
Redwood City: California	6	37½	122
Redwood Estates: California	37	37	122
Redwood Falls: *town*, Minn.	10	45	95
Redwood Regional Park: California	6	37¾	122
Reed City: Michigan	20	44	86
Reedley: California	34	37	119
Reeds Gap; Pennsylvania	14	40	78
Reedville: Virginia	17	38	76
Regina: Saskatchewan	30	51	105
Rehoboth Bay: Delaware	17	39	75
Rehoboth Beach: *sett*,. Del.	17	39	75
Reidsville: Georgia	24	32	82
Reidsville: North Carolina	16	36	80
Reindeer Depot: N.W.T.	44	69	134
Reindeer L.: Man./Sask.	30/31	58	102
Reindeer Station: Alaska	42	66	161
Reisterstown: Maryland	17	39	77
Reltier, L.: Minnesota	3	45¼	93
Remington: Indiana	21	41	87
Renfrew: Ontario	12	45	77
Reno: Nevada	37	40	120
Reno: Pennsylvania	19	41	80
Renovo: Pennsylvania	14	41	78
Rensselaer: Indiana	21	41	87
Rensselaer: New York	15	43	74
Renton: Washington	6	47½	122
Republic: Washington	32	49	119
Republican:*r.*, Nebr./Kansas	28	40	98
Repulse Bay: *sett.*, N.W.T.	45	67	86
Requa: California	36	42	124
Reseda: California	7	39¼	118½
Reserve: Louisiana	27	30	91
Resolute: Northwest Territories	45	75	95
Resolution I.: N.W.T.	45	62	65
Resolution Island: *sett.*, N.W.T.	45	62	65
Retsof: New York	14	43	78
Reusens: Virginia	16	37	79
Revelstoke: British Columbia	41	51	118

	Page	N	W
Revere: Massachusetts	2	42½	71
Revere Beach: Massachusetts	2	42½	71
Rexburg: Idaho	32	44	112
Reyes, Point: California	37	38	123
Reynolds: Georgia	24	33	84
Reynoldsville: Pennsylvania	14	41	79
Rhinebeck: New York	15	42	74
Rhinelander: Wisconsin	20	46	89
RHODE ISLAND	15	—	—
Rice, L.: Minnesota	3	45¼	93¼
Rice L.: Ontario	12	44	78
Richard Collinson Inlet: N.W.T.	44	72	114
Richards L.: N.W.T.	44	69	135
Richardson: Texas	26	33	97
Richardson: *r.*, Alberta	30	58	111
Richardson I.: N.W.T.	40	66	118
Richardson Is.: N.W.T.	44	58	110
Richardson Mts.: Yukon	42	68	137
Richelieu: *r.*, Québec	13	46	73
Riche Point: Newfoundland	9	51	57
Richfield: Minnesota	3	35	93¼
Richfield: Utah	33	39	112
Richfield Springs: New York	14	43	75
Richford: Vermont	13	45	73
Richgrove: California	34	36	119
Richibucto: New Brunswick	9	47	65
Richland: Georgia	27	32	85
Richland: Washington	39	46	119
Richlands: Virginia	16	37	82
Richmond: British Columbia	6	49	123½
Richmond: California	6	38	122¼
Richmond: Indiana	21	40	85
Richmond: Kentucky	23	38	84
Richmond: Michigan	19	43	83
Richmond: New York	1	40½	74¼
Richmond: Pennsylvania	2	40	75
Richmond: Québec	13	46	72
Richmond: Texas	26	30	96
Richmond: Virginia	17	38	77
Richmond Beach: *sett.*, Wash.	6	47¾	122½
Richmond Gulf: Québec	8	56	76
Richmond Heights: *sett.*, Washington	6	47¾	122¼
Richmond Hill: *town*, Ontario	6	43¾	79½
Rich Mt.: West Virginia	16	39	80
Rich Passage: Washington	6	47½	122½
Richton: Mississippi	27	31	89
Richwood: Ohio	19	40	83
Richwood: West Virginia	16	38	81
Rico: Colorado	29	38	108
Riddle: Oregon	32	43	123
Rideau: *r.*, Ontario	12	45	76
Rideau L.: Ontario	12	45	76
Ridgecrest: California	35	36	118
Ridgefield: Connecticut	15	41	74
Ridgeland: South Carolina	24	33	81
Ridgely: Maryland	17	39	76
Ridgetown: Ontario	19	42	82
Ridgeway: Ohio	19	41	84
Ridgway: Pennsylvania	14	41	79
Ridgewood: Illinois	4	41½	88
Ridgewood: New Jersey	1	41	74¼
Riding Mountain Nat. Park: Manitoba	31	51	100
Ridley Creek State Park: Pennsylvania	2	40	75¼
Rifle: Colorado	28	40	108
Rigaud: Québec	13	45	74
Rigolet: Newfoundland	9	54	59
Rillito: Arizona	33	32	111
Rimbey: Alberta	30	53	114
Rimouski: Québec	9	48	69
Rio Dell: California	36	41	124
Rio Grande: *r.*	29	30	105
Riondel: British Columbia	41	50	117
Rio Vista: California	37	38	122
Ripley: Mississippi	27	35	89
Ripley: New York	19	42	80
Ripley: Tennessee	27	36	90
Ripley: West Virginia	16	39	82
Ripon: California	37	38	121
Ripon: Wisconsin	20	44	89
Rison: Arkansas	26	34	92
Ritter, Mt.: California	37	38	119
Rittman: Ohio	19	41	82
Rivanna: *r.*, Virginia	17	38	78
Riverbank: California	37	38	121
Riverdale: New Jersey	15	41	74
River Forest: *town*, Illinois	4	42	87¾
Riverhead: New York	15	41	73
Riverhurst: Saskatchewan	30	51	107
River Jordan: *sett.*, B.C.	38	48	124
River Rouge: Michigan	5	42¼	83¼
River Rouge Park: Michigan	5	42¼	83¼
Riverside: California	35	34	117
Riverside: Illinois	4	41¾	87¾
Riverside: New Jersey	2	40	75
Riverside: Ontario	5	42¼	83
Rivers Inlet: B.C.	41	52	127
Riverton: Manitoba	31	51	97
Riverton: Wyoming	28	43	108
Riverton Heights: *sett.*, Wash.	6	47½	112¼
Rivesville: West Virginia	16	40	80
Rivière Bersimis: *sett.*, Québec	8	49	69
Rivière du Loup: Québec	9	48	70
Roanoke: Alabama	27	33	85
Roanoke: Illinois	21	41	89

	Page	N	W
Roanoke: Virginia	16	37	80
Roanoke: *r.*, Va./N.C.	16/17	37	79
Roanoke Rapids: N.C.	17	36	78
Roanoke Rapids L.: N.C.	17	37	78
Roaring Spring: Pennsylvania	14	40	78
Robbins: California	37	39	122
Robbinsdale: Minnesota	3	45	93¼
Robbinsville: New Jersey	15	40	75
Robersonville: North Carolina	24	36	77
Robert Brown, C.: N.W.T.	45	68	81
Robert, C.: Ontario	18	46	83
Roberval: Québec	8	49	72
Robesonia: Pennsylvania	14	40	76
Robinson: Pennsylvania	19	40	79
Robinson: Yukon	40	60	135
Robson, Mount: Alberta/B.C.	41	53	119
Robstown: Texas	22	28	98
Rochdale: Massachusetts	15	42	72
Rochelle: Georgia	24	32	83
Rochelle: Illinois	21	42	89
Rocher River: *sett.*, N.W.T.	30	61	113
Rochester: Indiana	21	41	86
Rochester: Michigan	19	43	83
Rochester: Minnesota	10	44	92
Rochester: New Hampshire	11	43	71
Rochester: New York	12	43	78
Rochester: Pennsylvania	19	41	80
Rock: *r.*, Illinois/Wisconsin	21	42	89
Rockaway: Oregon	39	46	124
Rockaway Beach: New York	1	40½	74
Rockaway Inlet: New York	1	40½	74
Rock Creek: *sett.*, B.C.	38	49	119
Rock Creek Park: D.C.	2	40	75¼
Rockdale: Texas	26	31	97
Rock Falls: *town*, Illinois	21	42	90
Rockford: Illinois	21	42	89
Rockford: Michigan	20	43	86
Rockford: Ohio	21	41	85
Rock Hill: *town*, S.C.	24	35	81
Rockingham: North Carolina	24	35	80
Rock Island: *dam*, Washington	39	47	120
Rock Island: *town*, Illinois	10	42	91
Rockland: Massachusetts	15	42	71
Rockland: Ontario	13	46	75
Rockland: *dam*, Texas	26	31	94
Rocklin: California	37	39	121
Rockmart: Georgia	27	34	85
Rockport: California	36	40	124
Rockport: Massachusetts	15	43	71
Rock Springs: Wyoming	28	42	109
Rockville: California	37	38	122
Rockville: Connecticut	15	42	72
Rockville: Indiana	21	40	87
Rockville: Maryland	17	39	77
Rockville Centre: New York	1	40¾	73¾
Rockwall: Texas	26	33	96
Rockwell: North Carolina	24	36	80
Rockwood: Maine	9	46	70
Rockwood: Pennsylvania	16	40	79
Rockwood: Tennessee	24	36	85
Rocky Ford: Colorado	29	38	104
Rocky Hill: *sett.*, Connecticut	15	42	73
Rocky Mount: *town*, N.C.	24	36	78
Rockymount: Virginia	16	37	80
Rocky Mountain Arsenal: Colo.	3	39¾	104¾
Rocky Mountain House: Alta.	30	52	115
Rocky Mt. Nat. Park: Colorado	28	40	106
Rocky Mountains	32	—	—
Rocky Point: *sett.*, New York	15	41	73
Rocky Reach: *dam*, Washington	39	48	120
Rodessa: Louisiana	26	33	94
Roebling: New Jersey	15	40	75
Roes Welcome Sound: N.W.T.	45	65	87
Roff: Oklahoma	26	35	97
Rogers City: Michigan	20	45	84
Rogers L.: California	35	35	118
Rogers, Mount: Virginia	16	37	82
Rogersville: Tennessee	24	36	83
Roggan River: *sett.*, Québec	8	54	79
Rogue: *r.*, Oregon	36	43	124
Rogue River: *sett.*, Oregon	36	42	123
Rojo, Cabo: Puerto Rico	27	18	67
Rolla: Missouri	10	38	92
Rolling Fork: Mississippi	27	33	91
Rolling Prairie: Indiana	21	42	87
Romain, C.: South Carolina	24	33	79
Romaine: *r.*, Québec	9	51	63
Romano, C.: Florida	25	26	82
Romanzof, C.: Alaska	43	62	166
Rome: Georgia	27	34	85
Rome: New York	13	43	75
Romeo: Michigan	19	43	83
Romney: West Virginia	17	39	79
Romulus: Michigan	19	42	83
Ronceverte: West Virginia	16	38	80
Rondeau Prov. Park: Ontario	19	42	82
Rondout Res.: New York	15	42	74
Ronkonkoma: New York	15	41	73
Roosevelt: *dam*, Arizona	33	34	111
Root Portage: Ontario	10	51	91
Rosamond: California	35	35	118
Rosamond L.: California	35	35	118
Roscoe: Pennsylvania	19	40	80
Roseau: *r.*, Minn./Manitoba	10	49	96
Roseboro: North Carolina	24	35	79
Rosebud: Texas	26	31	97
Roseburg: Oregon	32	42	123

	Page	N	W
Rosedale: Mississippi	27	34	91
Roselle: Illinois	4	42	88
Rosemead: California	7	34	118
Rosenberg: Texas	26	30	96
Rosetown: Saskatchewan	30	52	108
Roseville: California	37	39	121
Roseville: Michigan	5	42½	83
Roseville: Minnesota	3	45	93¼
Rosewood: California	36	40	123
Ross: *r.*, Yukon	40	62	131
Rossignol L.: Nova Scotia	9	44	65
Rossiter: Pennsylvania	14	41	79
Ross Barnet Res.: Mississippi	27	32	90
Ross L.: Washington	38	49	121
Rossland: British Columbia	41	49	118
Ross River: *sett.*, Yukon	40	62	132
Rossville: Georgia	27	35	85
Rossville: Illinois	21	40	88
Rosthern: Saskatchewan	30	53	106
Roswell: Georgia	24	34	84
Roswell: New Mexico	29	33	105
Rouge: *r.*, Michigan	5	42½	83¼
Rouge: *r.*, Ontario	5	43¾	79¼
Rouge: *r.*, Québec	13	46	75
Round Hill Park: Pennsylvania	5	40½	79¾
Round L.: Ontario	12	46	78
Round Mountain: *sett.*, Calif.	36	41	122
Roundup: Montana	28	46	109
Rouseville: Pennsylvania	19	41	80
Rouyn: Québec	8	48	79
Rowes Run: Pennsylvania	16	40	80
Rowland: North Carolina	24	35	79
Rowley I.: N.W.T.	45	69	79
Roxboro: North Carolina	17	36	79
Roxbury: Massachusetts	2	42¼	71
Roxbury: New York	15	42	75
Roxton: Texas	26	34	96
Royale, Isle: Michigan	10	48	89
Royal Oak: Michigan	5	42½	83¼
Royersford: Pennsylvania	14	40	76
Royston: Georgia	24	34	83
Rubicon: *r.*, California	37	39	121
Ruby: Alaska	42	65	156
Ruby Ranges: Yukon	40	61	138
Rugby: North Dakota	28	48	100
Ruggs: Oregon	39	45	120
Ruleville: Mississippi	27	34	91
Rum: *r.*, Minnesota	10	46	94
Rumsey: California	37	39	122
Rumson: New Jersey	15	40	74
Running Springs: California	35	34	117
Rupert: Idaho	32	43	114
Rupert: *r.*, Québec	8	51	78
Rupert House: Québec	8	52	79
Rural Valley: *sett.*, Pennsylvania	19	41	79
Rushville: Indiana	21	40	85
Rushville: New York	14	43	77
Rusk: Texas	26	32	95
Russells: Kansas	28	39	99
Russell: Kentucky	16	39	83
Russell: Manitoba	31	51	101
Russell Fork: *r.*, Kentucky	16	37	82
Russell Inlet: N.W.T.	44	70	130
Russell I.: N.W.T.	44	74	99
Russell Point: N.W.T.	44	74	115
Russellville: Alabama	27	35	88
Russellville: Arkansas	26	35	93
Russian: *r.*, California	37	39	123
Russian Mission: Alaska	43	62	161
Ruston: Louisiana	26	33	93
Ruth: California	36	40	123
Ruth: Nevada	33	39	115
Rutherfordton: North Carolina	24	35	82
Rutland: Vermont	13	44	73
Ryan: California	35	36	117
Ryde: California	37	38	122
Sabine: *r.*, Texas/Louisiana	26	31	94
Sable, C.: Florida	25	25	81
Sable, C.: Nova Scotia	9	43	66
Sable I.: Nova Scotia	9	44	60
Sacandaga Res.: New York	13	43	74
Sachigo: *r.*, Ontario	31	54	91
Sachs Harbour: N.W.T.	44	72	125
Sachs Harbour: *sett.*, N.W.T.	44	72	125
Sackets Habor: New York	12	44	76
Saco: Maine	11	44	70
Sacramento: *& r.*, California	37	39	122
Sacramento Mts.: New Mexico	29	33	105
Safford: Arizona	33	33	110
Sagamore: Massachusetts	15	42	71
Sage: California	35	34	117
Sage: Wyoming	28	42	111
Sag Harbor: New York	15	41	72
Saginaw: Michigan	20	43	84
Saginaw: *r.*, Michigan	20	44	84
Saginaw Bay: Michigan	18	44	83
Sagola: Michigan	20	46	88
Saguaro Nat. Mon.: Arizona	33	32	111
Saguenay: *r.*, Québec	8	48	70
St. Albans: Newfoundland	9	48	56
St. Albans: Vermont	13	45	73
St. Albans: West Virginia	16	38	82
St. Andrews Bay: Florida	27	30	86
Ste.-Anne-de-Bellevue: Québec	2	45½	74
St. Anthony: Idaho	32	44	112
St. Anthony: Newfoundland	9	51	56

	Page	N	W
St.-Augustin: *sett. & r.*, Québec	9	52	59
St. Augustine: Florida	25	30	81
St. Augustine-Saguenay: Québec	9	51	59
St.-Basile: Québec	13	47	72
St. Boniface: Manitoba	31	50	97
St. Catharines: Ontario	19	43	79
St.-Césaire: Québec	13	45	73
St. Charles: Illinois	21	42	88
St. Charles: Michigan	20	43	84
St. Clair: Michigan	19	43	83
St. Clair: Pennsylvania	14	41	76
St. Clair: *r.*, Michigan/Ontario	19	43	82
St. Clair, L.: Michigan/Ontario	19	43	83
St. Clair Shores: Michigan	5	42½	83
St. Clairsville: Ohio	16	40	81
St. Cloud: Florida	25	28	81
St. Cloud: Minnesota	10	46	94
St. Croix: *r.*, Wis./Minnesota	10	46	93
St. Elias, Mt.: Alaska	43	60	141
St. Elias Mts.: Yukon	40	61	139
St.-Eugene: Ontario	13	46	74
St.-Eustache: Québec	2	45½	74
St.-Félicien: Québec	8	49	72
St.-Félix-de-Valois: Québec	13	46	73
Ste.-Foy: Québec	13	47	71
St. Francis: *r.*, Ark./Mo.	22	36	91
St.-François: *r.*, Québec	13	46	73
St.-François, L.: Québec	13	46	71
St.-Gabriel-de-Brandon: Québec	13	46	73
Ste.-Geneviève: Québec	2	45½	74
St. George: Alaska	60	57	170
St. George: New Brunswick	9	45	67
St. George: South Carolina	24	33	81
St. George: Utah	33	37	114
St. George, C.: Florida	27	30	85
St. George, Pt.: California	36	42	124
St. George's: Newfoundland	9	48	59
St.-Georges: Québec	13	46	71
St. George's B.: Newfoundland	9	48	59
St. George Sound: Florida	25	30	84
St. Helena Sound: S.C.	24	32	80
St. Helens: Oregon	39	46	123
St. Helens, Mt.: Washington	39	46	122
St.-Hyacinthe: Québec	13	46	73
St. Ignace: Michigan	20	46	85
St.-Ignace, Isle: Ontario	10	49	88
St.-Jacques: Québec	13	46	74
St.-James, C.: British Columbia	41	52	131
St.-Jean: Québec	13	45	73
St.-Jerôme: Québec	13	46	74
St. John: New Brunswick	9	45	66
St. John: *r.*, Maine/N.B.	8/9	46	68
St. John, C.: Newfoundland	9	50	55
St. John, L.: Québec	8	49	72
St. Johns: Michigan	20	43	85
St. John's: Newfoundland	9	48	53
St. Johns: *r.*, Florida	25	30	82
St. Johnsbury: Vermont	13	45	72
St. Johnsville: New York	13	43	75
St. Joseph: Louisiana	26	32	91
St. Joseph: Michigan	21	42	87
St. Joseph: Missouri	10	40	95
St.-Joseph: Québec	13	46	71
St. Joseph: *r.*, Indiana/Ohio	21	41	85
St. Joseph: *r.*, Michigan/Indiana	21	42	86
St. Joseph Bay: Florida	27	30	85
St. Joseph I.: Ontario	18	46	84
St. Joseph, L.: Ontario	31	51	91
St.-Jovite: Québec	13	46	75
St.-Lambert: Québec	2	45½	73½
St. Laurent: Québec	2	45½	73¾
St. Lawrence	8/9	49	68
St. Lawrence (St. Laurent): *r.*	12/13	—	—
St. Lawrence, Gulf of	9	48	63
St. Lawrence I.: Alaska	42	63	169
St. Lawrence Seaway: Qué./Ont.	12	44	76
St.-Lin: Québec	13	46	74
St. Louis: Missouri	10	39	90
St.-Louis, C. (C. Wolstenholme): Québec	45	63	78
St.-Louis, L.: Québec	2	45½	73¾
St.-Louis Park: Minnesota	3	45	93¼
Ste.-Marguerite: *r.*, Québec	9	51	67
Ste.-Marie: Québec	13	46	71
St. Martin I.: Michigan	20	46	87
St. Martin, L.: Manitoba	31	52	99
St. Martinville: Louisiana	26	30	92
St. Mary Bay: Nova Scotia	9	44	66
St. Marys: Alaska	43	62	163
St. Marys: Ohio	19	41	84
St. Marys: Ontario	19	43	81
St. Marys: Pennsylvania	14	41	79
St. Marys: *r.*, Georgia/Florida	25	31	82
St. Marys: *r.*, Ohio/Indiana	21	41	85
St. Mary's B.: Newfoundland	9	47	54
St. Matthews: South Carolina	24	34	81
St.-Maurice: *r.*, Québec	8	47	73
St. Michael: Alaska	42	63	162
St. Michaels: Maryland	17	39	76
St.-Michel: Québec	2	45½	73¾
St.-Michel: Québec	13	47	71
St.-Michel-des-Saints: Québec	13	47	74
St.-Pacôme: Québec	9	47	70
St. Paris: Ohio	19	40	84
St. Paul: Alberta	30	54	111
St. Paul: Alaska	60	57	170
St. Paul: Minnesota	10	45	93
St. Paul: *r.*, Nfld./Québec	9	57	58
St. Pauls: North Carolina	24	35	79
St. Peter: Minnesota	10	44	94
St. Petersburg: Florida	25	28	83
St.-Pie: Québec	13	46	73
St. Pierre: *i.*	9	47	56
St.-Pierre, Lac.: Québec	13	46	73
St.-Raymond: Québec	13	47	72
St. Regis: *r.*, New York	13	45	75
St. Rémi: Québec	13	45	74
St.-Remi-d'Amherst: Québec	13	46	75
Ste.-Rose: Québec	2	45½	73¾
St. Stephen: New Brunswick	9	45	67
St. Stephen: South Carolina	24	33	80
Ste.-Thérèse: Québec	2	45¾	73¾
Ste.-Thérèse, I.: Québec	2	45¾	73½
St. Thomas: Ontario	19	43	81
St.-Tite: Quebéc	13	47	73
Sakami: *r.*, Québec	8	53	76
Sakami L.: Québec	8	53	77
Salamanca: New York	19	42	79
Salamonie: *r.*, Indiana	21	41	85
Salem: Massachusetts	15	43	71
Salem: New Jersey	14	40	75
Salem: New York	13	43	73
Salem: Ohio	19	41	81
Salem: Oregon	39	45	123
Salem: Virginia	16	37	80
Salem: West Virginia	16	39	81
Salida: Colorado	28	39	106
Salina: Kansas	28	39	98
Salinas: California	37	37	122
Salinas: *r.*, California	34	36	121
Saline: Michigan	19	42	84
Saline: *r.*, Arkansas	26	33	92
Saline Bayou: *r.*, Louisiana	26	32	93
Saline Valley: California	35	37	118
Salineville: Ohio	19	41	81
Salisbury: Maryland	17	38	76
Salisbury: North Carolina	24	35	81
Salisbury I.: N.W.T.	45	64	77
Salkum: Washington	39	47	123
Sallisaw: Oklahoma	26	35	95
Salmo: British Columbia	41	49	117
Salmon: Idaho	32	45	114
Salmon: *r.*, Idaho	32	45	116
Salmon Arm: B.C.	38	51	119
Salmon Creek: *town*, California	37	38	123
Salmon Res.: New York	12	44	76
Salmon River Mts.: Idaho	32	45	115
Salt: *r.*, Arizona	33	34	111
Salt: *r.*, Missouri	10	40	92
Salt Creek: Illinois	21	40	89
Salt Creek: Illinois	4	41¾	88
Saltdale: California	35	35	118
Salt Fork: *r.*, Texas	29	33	100
Salt Lake City: Utah	33	41	112
Salton City: California	35	33	116
Salton Sea: California	35	33	116
Salt River: *sett.*, N.W.T.	30	60	112
Saltsburg: Pennsylvania	19	40	79
Saltville: Virginia	16	37	82
Salt Wells: Nevada	33	39	119
Saluda: South Carolina	24	34	82
Saluda: Virginia	17	38	77
Saluda: *r.*, South Carolina	24	34	82
Salvador, L.: Louisiana	27	30	90
Salyersville: Kentucky	16	38	83
Sam Ford Fiord: N.W.T.	45	71	71
Sammamish, Lake: *and State P.*, Washington	6	47½	122
Sam Rayburn Res.: Texas	26	31	94
Samson: Alabama	27	31	86
Sanak Is.: Alaska	43	54	163
San Andreas: California	37	38	121
San Andreas Fault: California	6	37½	122½
San Andreas Lake: California	6	37½	122½
San Angelo: Texas	29	31	100
San Antonio: Texas	22	29	99
San Antonio: *r.*, California	34	36	121
San Antonio: *r.*, Texas	22	27	97
San Antonio Res.: California	7	34	117¾
San Ardo: California	34	36	121
San Augustine: Texas	26	32	94
San Benito: *r.*, California	34	37	121
San Bernardino: California	35	34	117
San Bernardino Mts.: California	35	34	117
San Blas Bay: Florida	27	30	85
San Blas, C.: Florida	27	30	85
Sanbornville: New Hampshire	13	44	71
San Bruno: *& mtn.*, California	6	37¾	122½
San Carlos: California	6	37½	122¼
San Clemente: California	37	33	118
San Clemente I.: California	35	33	119
Sandberg: California	35	35	119
Sandersville: Georgia	24	33	83
San Diego: California	35	33	117
San Dimas Res: California	7	34½	117¾
Sandoval: Illinois	10	39	89
Sandpoint: Idaho	32	28	117
Sand Point: *sett.*, Alaska	43	55	161
Sand Point: Washington	6	47¾	122¼
Sandspit: British Columbia	41	53	132
Sand Springs: Oklahoma	29	36	96
Sandston: Virginia	17	38	77
Sandusky: Michigan	18	43	83
Sandusky: Ohio	19	41	83
Sandusky: *r.*, Ohio	19	41	83
Sandwich: Illinois	21	42	89
Sandwich Bay: Newfoundland	9	54	57
Sandy: Nevada	35	36	116
Sandy: Oregon	39	45	122
Sandy: Utah	33	41	112
Sandy: *r.*, Québec	9	55	68
Sandy Hook: *penin.*, New Jersey	1	40½	74
Sandy L.: Ontario	31	53	93
San Felipe: California	37	37	121
San Fernando: California	7	34¼	118
San Fernando Valley: California	7	34¼	118
Sanford: Florida	25	29	81
Sanford: Maine	11	43	71
Sanford: North Carolina	24	35	79
San Francisco: California	37	38	122
San Francisco: *r.*, N. Mex./Ariz.	29	33	109
San Francisco Bay: California	37	38	122
San Francisco State Fish & Game Res.: California	6	37½	122
San Gabriel: California	7	34	118
San Gabriel: *r.*, California	7	34	118
San Gabriel Mts.: California	35	34	118
San Gabriel Res.: California	7	34¼	117¾
Sangamon: *r.*, Illinois	21	40	88
Sanger: California	37	37	120
Sanger: Texas	26	33	97
Sangre de Cristo Range: Colorado/New Mexico	29	37	105
San Gregorio: California	37	37	122
Sanhedrin, Mt.: California	37	40	123
Sanibel I.: Florida	25	26	82
San Jacinto: California	35	34	117
San Jacinto: *r.*, Texas	26	30	95
San Jacinto Peak: California	35	34	117
San Joaquin: California	37	37	120
San Joaquin: *r.*, California	37	37	121
San Jose: California	37	37	122
San Jose: *r.*, New Mexico	29	35	108
San Juan: Puerto Rico	27	18	66
San Juan, Cabezas de: Puerto Rico	27	18	66
San Juan: *r.*	29	37	110
San Juan: *r.*, California	34	36	120
San Juan Bautista: California	34	37	122
San Juan Capistrano: California	35	34	118
San Juan Is.: Washington	38	49	123
San Juan Mts.: Colorado	29	38	107
San Leandro: California	6	37¾	122¼
San Lorenzo: California	6	37¾	122¼
San Lucas: California	34	36	121
San Luis Obipso: California	34	35	121
San Luis Obipso Bay: California	34	35	121
San Manuel: Arizona	33	33	111
San Marcos: Texas	22	30	98
San Martin: California	37	37	122
San Mateo: California	37	38	122
San Miguel: California	34	36	121
San Miguel I.: California	34	34	120
San Nicolas I.: California	34	33	119
San Onofre: California	35	33	118
San Pablo: California	6	38	122½
San Pablo Bay: California	6	38	122¼
San Pablo Res.: California	6	38	122¼
San Pasqual: California	35	33	117
San Patrico: Texas	22	28	98
San Pedro: California	7	33¾	118¼
San Pedro Bay: California	7	34	118¼
San Pedro Channel: California	35	33	118
San Rafeal: *& bay:* California	6	38	122½
San Rafael Mts.: California	34	35	120
San Ramon: California	37	38	122
San Simeon: California	34	36	121
Santa Ana: California	7	33¾	117¾
Santa Ana: *r.*, California	7	33¾	117¾
Santa Barbara: California	34	34	120
Santa Barbara Chan.: California	34	34	120
Santa Barbara I.: California	34	33	119
Santa Barbara Is.: California	34	34	120
Santa Barbara Res.: California	34	35	120
Santa Catalina, G. of: California	35	33	118
Santa Catalina I.: California	35	33	118
Santa Clara: California	37	37	122
Santa Cruz: California	37	37	122
Santa Cruz: *r.*, Arizona	33	32	111
Santa Cruz I.: California	34	34	120
Santa Cruz Mts.: California	37	27	122
Sante Fe: New Mexico	29	36	106
Santa Lucia Range: California	34	36	122
Santa Margarita: California	34	35	121
Santa Margarita: *r.*, California	35	33	117
Santa Maria: California	34	35	120
Santa Monica: California	7	34	118½
Santa Monica Mts: California	7	34	118½
Santa Paula: California	34	34	120
San Pedro, Pt.: California	6	37½	122½
Santa Rita Park: California	37	37	121
Santa Rosa: California	37	38	123
Santa Rosa: New Mexico	29	35	105
Santa Rosa I.: California	34	34	120
Santa Rosa I.: Florida	27	30	87
Santa Susana: California	35	34	119
Santa Ynez: California	34	36	120
Santa Ynez Mts.: California	34	34	120
Santa Ysabel: California	35	33	117
Santee: California	35	33	117
Santee: *dam & r.*, South Carolina	24	33	80

Addendum

Lists places named on thematic maps that are not shown on urban plans or topographic maps

	N	W
Big Sandy: *power stn.*, Ky.	38° 06′	82° 36′
Bigstone Creek: *sett.*, Alta.	49° 22′	116° 57′
Bird River: *sett.*, Man.	30° 31′	95° 17′
Bixby: Missouri	37° 39′	91° 07′
Black River Falls: *sett.*, Wis.	44° 16′	91° 00′
Blueberry: British Columbia	56° 44′	121° 48′
Blake Terrace: Atlantic Ocean	32° 00′	78° 00′
Boss: Missouri	37° 38′	91° 11′
Bowdoin: Montana	48° 23′	107° 36′
Bowron Prov. Park: B.C.	53° 10′	123° 00′
Brackenridge: Pennsylvania	40° 36′	79° 44′
Braeburn: Pennsylvania	47° 37′	79° 42′
Braithwaite: Louisiana	29° 51′	89° 56′
Brayton Point: *power stn.*, Massachusetts	41° 46′	71° 07′
Bridge River: *dam*, B.C.	50° 43′	122° 20′
Bridgeville: Pennsylvania	40° 21′	80° 07′
Brighton: Pennsylvania	40° 58′	74° 46′
Brilliant: British Columbia	49° 19′	117° 38′
Browns Bank: Atlantic O.	43° 00′	66° 00′
Bruce Lake: *sett.*, Ontario	50° 49′	92° 25′
Brunner Is.: *power stn.*, Pa.	40° 17′	76° 43′
Brunswick: Maine	43° 54′	69° 57′
Buhl: Minnesota	47° 30′	92° 46′
Bull Run: *power stn.*, Tenn.	36° 06′	84° 07′
Burgin: Utah	39° 56′	111° 37′
Burin: Newfoundland	47° 02′	55° 10′
Burke: Idaho	47° 31′	115° 48′
Burnham: Pennsylvania	40° 38′	77° 34′
Burns Habor: Indiana	41° 37′	87° 10′
Burnsville: N. Carolina	35° 03′	80° 21′
Burnt Mills: N. Carolina	36° 45′	76° 21′
Butler: Alabama	32° 05′	88° 13′
Buttle Lake: British Columbia	49° 52′	124° 48′
Cabrillo Nat. Mon.: Calif.	32° 38′	117° 14′
Cairo: Illinois	37° 00′	89° 10′
Calcite: Michigan	45° 24′	83° 47′
Calhoun: Tennessee	35° 17′	83° 45′
California, Gulf of: Mexico	27° 00′	111° 00′
Calumet: Michigan	47° 14′	88° 27′
Cameron: Louisiana	29° 47′	93° 19′
Cane Run: *power stn.*, Ky.	38° 14′	85° 45′
Canoga Park: *sett.*, Calif.	34° 07′	118° 37′
Cape Tormentine: *sett.*, N.B.	46° 08′	63° 47′
Caraquet: New Brunswick	47° 48′	64° 57′
Castle Hayne: N. Carolina	34° 21′	77° 54′
Catawba: S. Carolina	34° 51′	80° 54′
Catawba: *r.*, N.C./S.C.	34° 40′	80° 54′
Cave in Rock: *sett.*, Illinois	37° 28′	88° 09′
Cave Spring: Georgia	34° 06′	85° 20′
Cayce: S. Carolina	33° 58′	81° 03′
Cedar Springs: Georgia	31° 12′	85° 00′
Cessford: Alberta	51° 01′	111° 33′
Chamblee: Georgia	33° 53′	84° 18′
Chance: Yukon	66° 02′	138° 25′
Charleston Rise: Atlantic O.	30° 00′	75° 00′
Chatham: New Brunswick	47° 02′	65° 28′
Chauvin: Louisiana	29° 26′	90° 35′
Chesterfield: Virginia	37° 23′	77° 30′
Cheswick: Pennsylvania	40° 32′	79° 48′
Chetwynd: British Columbia	55° 40′	121° 30′
Chibougamau Prov. Park: Qué.	49° 30′	73° 30′
Chickamauga & Chattanooga N. Military Pk.: Ga./Tenn.	35° 00′	85° 20′
Chicoutimi Prov. Park: Qué.	49° 30′	70° 15′
Chileno Valley: California	38° 10′	122° 45′
Chino: Arizona	35° 20′	112° 56′
Chinook: Montana	48° 35′	109° 13′
Chisholm: Minnesota	47° 29′	92° 52′
Cimarron: Oklahoma	35° 22′	97° 48′
Clancy: Montana	46° 27′	111° 58′
Clarkdale: Georgia	33° 49′	84° 39′
Clarkesville: Georgia	34° 36′	83° 31′
Clatskanie: Oregon	46° 06′	123° 12′
Claverack: New York	42° 13′	73° 43′
Clayton: Idaho	45° 15′	114° 24′
Clear Creek: Yukon	63° 45′	137° 15′
Clearwater Prov. Park: Man.	54° 00′	101° 01′
Cleveland: Georgia	34° 35′	83° 45′
Clifty Creek: *power stn.*, Ind.	38° 44′	85° 22′
Clinton: Maine	44° 38′	69° 30′
Clinton Creek: *sett.*, Yukon	64° 28′	140° 31′
Coal Harbour: B.C.	50° 36′	127° 35′
Coalton: Kentucky	38° 23′	82° 47′
Coleraine: Minnesota	47° 16′	93° 26′
Collbran: Alabama	34° 22′	85° 46′
College Station: Texas	30° 36′	96° 20′
Colton: California	34° 04′	117° 56′
Come-by-Chance: Nfld.	47° 51′	53° 59′
Conda: Idaho	42° 44′	111° 33′
Contra Costa: *power stn.*, Calif.	38° 00′	121° 48′
Cooper: *power stn.*, Kentucky	36° 59′	84° 36′
Coosa Pines: Alabama	33° 27′	86° 06′
Copper Cities: Arizona	33° 24′	110° 52′
Copper Queen: Arizona	31° 26′	109° 55′
Cordero: Nevada	41° 58′	117° 44′
Corinna: Maine	44° 55′	69° 15′
Cornwall Is.: N.W.T.	77° 40′	95° 00′
Cove Fort: Utah	38° 36′	112° 20′
Croft: N. Carolina	35° 20′	80° 50′
Crossfield: Alberta	51° 04′	113° 52′
Crystal River: *power stn.*, Fla.	28° 54′	82° 38′
Cuba: New Mexico	35° 00′	107° 03′
Cumberland Hill: *town*, R.I.	42° 55′	71° 28′
Cumberland Pen.: N.W.T.	63° 00′	60° 00′
Curwood, Mt.: Michigan	46° 42′	88° 15′

	N	W
Dandridge: Tennessee	36° 00′	83° 24′
Darwin Mtn.: Calif.	37° 11′	118° 42′
Deception Bay: *sett.*, Québec	62° 10′	74° 45′
Delway: N. Carolina	34° 51′	78° 17′
Denmark Strait: Atlantic O.	67° 00′	25° 00′
Depot Harbour: Ontario	49° 19′	80° 06′
Delta: Utah	39° 21′	112° 34′
Detroit: *dam*, Oregon	44° 44′	122° 14′
Detroit: *r.*, Mich./Ont.	42° 12′	83° 08′
Digby: Nova Scotia	44° 37′	65° 46′
Drake Point: *sett.*, N.W.T.	76° 20′	108° 02′
Dresden: Illinois	41° 21′	88° 26′
Dresden: New York	42° 41′	76° 57′
Dryden: Ontario	49° 47′	92° 49′
Duck Mtn. Prov. Park: Man.	51° 40′	101° 00′
Dulac: Louisiana	29° 23′	90° 42′
Eagle: Colorado	39° 39′	106° 49′
Eagle Mtn.: California	33° 50′	115° 30′
East Crossfield: Alberta	51° 04′	113° 50′
East Stroudsburg: Pa.	40° 58′	78° 12′
Eden: N. Carolina	36° 28′	79° 40′
Effingham: Illinois	39° 07′	88° 32′
Eglin: Florida	30° 33′	86° 31′
Eielson: Alaska	64° 40′	147° 04′
Ellef Ringnes Is.: N.W.T.	78° 30′	102° 30′
Elmira: Prince Edward Island	46° 27′	62° 04′
Elmsford: New York	41° 03′	73° 49′
El Segundo: California	33° 55′	118° 24′
Emperius: Colorado	37° 50′	107° 20′
Empire: Colorado	39° 45′	105° 41′
Empire: Louisiana	29° 23′	89° 35′
Etiwanda: California	34° 07′	117° 27′
Eveleth: Minnesota	47° 27′	92° 32′
Ewa Beach: *sett.*. Hawaii	21° 18′	158° 00′
Faeroe Iceland Rise: Atlantic Ocean	67° 00′	10° 00′
Fairfax: Alabama	32° 47′	85° 11′
Fairfield: Alabama	33° 29′	86° 59′
Falcon: *dam*, Texas	26° 32′	99° 10′
Falconer: New York	42° 06′	79° 12′
Falls City: Texas	29° 59′	98° 01′
Faraday Seamount Group: Atlantic Ocean	50° 00′	28° 00′
Faro: Yukon	63° 14′	33° 03′
F. C. Gannon: *power stn.*, Fla.	27° 57′	82° 27′
Fernandina Beach: Florida	30° 40′	81° 27′
Festus: Missouri	38° 13′	90° 23′
Feuilles *see* Leaf: *r.*, Qué.	57° 45′	73° 00′
Filer City: Michigan	44° 12′	86° 19′
Five Corners: New York	42° 07′	77° 50′
Flat River: *sett.*, Missouri	39° 51′	90° 31′
Flemish Cap: Atlantic Ocean	47° 00′	43° 00′
Fontana: Tennessee	35° 27′	83° 47′
Forest Lawn: Alberta	51° 02′	113° 58′
Fort Donelson Nat. Military Park: Tennessee	36° 30′	87° 52′
Fort Loudon: *dam*, Tennessee	35° 47′	84° 16′
Fortune: Newfoundland	47° 04′	55° 51′
Four Corners: *power stn.*, New Mexico	36° 44′	108° 12′
Fox Islands: Alaska	53° 30′	167° 00′
Franklin: Kentucky	36° 43′	86° 34′
Fraser Mills: B.C.	49° 19′	122° 52′
Fredericksburg & Spotsylvania N. Military Pk.: Va.	38° 18′	77° 27′
Gabbs: Nevada	38° 52′	117° 55′
Gardiner: *dam*, Saskatchewan	51° 31′	107° 13′
Georges Bank: Atlantic O.	43° 00′	67° 00′
Gettysburg Nat. Cemetery: Pa.	39° 49′	77° 14′
Gibbs Fracture Zone: Atlantic Ocean	50° 00′	35° 00′
Gibraltar: California	34° 45′	120° 50′
Gimli: Manitoba	50° 39′	97° 00′
Glen Canyon Nat. Rec. Area: Ariz./Utah	37° 00′	110° 00′
Glenwood: Alabama	31° 39′	86° 10′
Gloucester: Ontario	45° 27′	75° 23′
Glover: Missouri	37° 29′	90° 42′
Gorda Escarpment: Pacific O.	40° 00′	127° 00′
Gordon Lake: Ontario	50° 00′	93° 35′
Gordon M. Shrum: *dam*, B.C.	56° 01′	122° 12′
Grand Banks: Atlantic Ocean	46° 00′	57° 00′
Grande Baleine *see* Great Whale: *r.*, Québec	55° 00′	76° 30′
Granite City: Illinois	38° 42′	90° 08′
Great Falls: *dam*, Tennessee	35° 48′	85° 36′
Grindstone: Québec	47° 22′	61° 56′
Gros Morne Nat. Park: Nfld.	49° 31′	57° 50′
Guild: New Hampshire	43° 15′	72° 08′
Guilford: Maine	45° 10′	69° 23′
Guilford Courthouse Nat'l Hist. Park: N.C.	36° 06′	79° 48′
Gulf Islands N.P.: Fla./Miss.	30° 15′	88° 30′
Hamilton: Mississippi	33° 44′	88° 27′
Hamshire: Texas	20° 51′	94° 18′
Happy Valley: Newfoundland	53° 18′	60° 18′
Harborside: Maine	44° 18′	68° 48′
Harpers Ferry Nat'l Hist. Park: W. Va./Md.	39° 19′	77° 44′
Harbour Grace: Nfld.	47° 42′	53° 13′
Harllee Branch: *power stn.*, Ga.	33° 05′	83° 14′
Harmattan: Alberta	51° 46′	114° 30′
Hawesville: Kentucky	37° 53′	86° 47′

	N	W
H. B. Robinson: *power stn.*, S. Carolina	34° 22′	80° 04
Henderson Creek: Yukon	63° 20′	139° 53
High Level: Alberta	58° 30′	117° 08
Hilton Mines: Québec	45° 36′	76° 29
Hogatza River: *sett.*, Alaska	66° 00′	155° 29
Holyrood: Newfoundland	47° 24′	53° 10
Hoolehua: Hawaii	21° 09′	157° 05
Horseshoe Lake: *power stn.*, Oklahoma	35° 29′	97° 09
Hoyt Lakes: *sett.*, Minnesota	47° 27′	91° 50
Hugh Keenleyside: *dam*, B.C.	49° 20′	117° 33
Hugoton: Kansas	37° 10′	101° 20
Huguley: Alabama	32° 51′	85° 18
Humboldt Bay: *power stn.*, Calif.	40° 46′	124° 09
Huntington: Oregon	44° 21′	117° 15
Hussar: Alberta	51° 03′	112° 41
Indiantown: Florida	27° 01′	80° 28
Intercoastal City: Louisiana	29° 43′	90° 58
Ironton: Missouri	37° 36′	90° 37
Iroquois Falls: *sett.*, Ontario	48° 46′	80° 40
Isle-Maligne: Québec	48° 34′	71° 38
Jefferson Nat. Expansion Mem. Nat'l Hist. Site: Mo.	38° 37′	90° 11
Joanna: S. Carolina	34° 24′	81° 48
Johnsonville: Tennessee	36° 03′	87° 58
J. D. Rockefeller Parkway: Wyo.	41° 00′	110° 30
Joppa: Illinois	37° 12′	88° 50
Joutel: Québec	40° 28′	78° 20
Jumping Pound: Alberta	51° 12′	114° 33
Kamsack: Saskatchewan	51° 03′	101° 54
Karnes City: Texas	28° 53′	97° 54
Kayob South: Alberta	54° 12′	117° 08′
Kearny: New Jersey	40° 45′	74° 09′
Keewatin: Minnesota	47° 23′	93° 04′
Kejimkujik Nat. Park: N.S.	44° 25′	65° 20′
Kelly Lake: *sett.*, Minnesota	47° 24′	93° 00′
Kelsey: California	38° 46′	119° 51′
Kennesaw Mtn. Nat. Battle-field Park: Ga.	34° 01′	84° 36′
Kentucky: *dam*, Kentucky	37° 00′	88° 15′
Kettle Rapids: *dam*, Manitoba	56° 19′	94° 40′
King Christian Island: N.W.T.	77° 45′	102° 00′
Kinkaid: *power stn.*, Illinois	37° 46′	89° 19′
Kinsella: Alberta	53° 00′	111° 32′
Kitsault: British Columbia	55° 44′	129° 35′
Kodiak Station: Alaska	57° 53′	152° 29′
Krannert: Georgia	34° 17′	85° 10′
Kyuquot: British Columbia	50° 02′	127° 23′
Labadie: Missouri	38° 31′	90° 48′
La Blanca: Texas	26° 20′	98° 02′
Labrador Sea: Can./Greenland	58° 00′	55° 00′
Lac de Renzy: Québec	45° 33′	75° 38′
Lackawanna: New York	42° 49′	78° 49′
La Grand *see* Ft. George: *r.*, Québec	53° 30′	77° 00′
Laguna: New Mexico	35° 03′	107° 24′
Lake Meredith Nat. Rec. Area: Texas	35° 40′	101° 40′
Landis: N. Carolina	35° 33′	80° 36′
La Sal: Utah	38° 19′	109° 14′
La Saire: Québec	48° 48′	79° 12′
Lawrenceville: Illinois	38° 44′	87° 41′
Lehi: Utah	40° 23′	111° 51′
Lisbon Valley: Utah	38° 10′	109° 05′
Little Gypsy: *power stn.*. La.	30° 00′	90° 27′
Lone Pine Creek: *sett.*, Alta.	51° 43′	114° 00′
Longhurst: N. Carolina	36° 25′	78° 58′
Long Island: *sett.*, New York	40° 44′	73° 52′
Louiseville: Québec	46° 16′	72° 57′
Louvicourt: Québec	48° 05′	77° 40′
Lowell: Vermont	44° 48′	72° 27′
Lowman: Idaho	44° 04′	115° 37′
Lyon: Colorado	40° 13′	105° 16′
Mackenzie King Is.: N.W.T.	78° 50′	113° 00′
McLeansville: N. Carolina	36° 05′	79° 45′
Magma: Arizona	33° 08′	111° 29′
Maiden Rock: Montana	45° 41′	112° 43′
Maple Grove: Ohio	30° 23′	83° 07′
Mapleville: Rhode Island	41° 57′	71° 39′
Marquette Range: Michigan	46° 35′	87° 25′
Marystown: Newfoundland	47° 11′	55° 10′
Mascot: Tennessee	36° 03′	83° 45′
Maspeth: New York	40° 43′	73° 55′
Maxville: Montana	46° 22′	113° 12′
Melville Island: N.W.T.	75° 40′	111° 00′
Mendocino Seascarp: Pacific O.	46° 00′	135° 00′
Metaline Falls: *sett.*, Wash.	48° 51′	117° 22′
Metropolis: Illinois	37° 09′	88° 43′
Mexico: Kentucky	37° 12′	88° 06′
Mica: *dam*, British Columbia	53° 24′	118° 20′
Mid-Atlantic Ridge: Atlantic Ocean	35° 00′	35° 00′
Midvale: Utah	40° 36′	111° 54′
Milltown: New Jersey	40° 27′	74° 26′
Mineral Park: *sett.*, Arizona	35° 10′	114° 01′
Mineral Point: Wisconsin	42° 51′	90° 10′
Moline: Illinois	41° 30′	90° 30′
Montana City: Montana	46° 31′	111° 57′
Montecello: *dam*, California	38° 30′	122° 07′

Place	N	W
Moose Mtn.: *sett.*, Ontario	46° 45′	80° 59′
Moreland: Georgia	33° 17′	84° 46′
Morgantown: Pennsylvania	40° 09′	75° 53′
Mosby: Montana	46° 59′	107° 53′
Moss Landing: *sett.*, Calif.	36° 48′	121° 47′
Mossyrock: *dam*, Washington	46° 31′	122° 29′
Mountain Iron: *sett.*, Minn.	47° 31′	92° 37′
Mt. Edzia Prov. Park: B.C.	57° 30′	130° 45′
Mount Storm: *sett.*, W. Va.	39° 16′	79° 14′
Mullans: Idaho	47° 28′	115° 48′
Mumtrak *see* Goodnews: Alaska	59° 47′	161° 35′
Muncho L. Prov. Park: B.C.	58° 50′	125° 45′
Muskegon Heights: *town*, Michigan	43° 11′	86° 15′
Murray Fracture Zone: Pacific Ocean	35° 00′	130° 00′
Nashwauk: Minnesota	47° 22′	93° 09′
Natchez Trace Parkway: Miss./Tenn./Ala.	35° 50′	88° 15′
Needham Heights: Mass.	42° 17′	71° 14′
Needville: Texas	29° 24′	94° 50′
Negaunee: Michigan	46° 30′	87° 36′
New Almaden: California	37° 12′	121° 47′
Newark: Texas	33° 00′	97° 29′
New Cornelia: Arizona	32° 23′	112° 53′
Newfoundland Basin: Atlantic Ocean	42° 00′	43° 00′
New Idria: California	36° 24′	120° 40′
New Madrid: Missouri	36° 34′	89° 32′
Newmarket: Tennessee	36° 06′	83° 36′
Newton: Massachusetts	42° 20′	71° 11′
Niagara Falls: Can./U.S.A.	43° 05′	79° 04′
Nickajack: *dam*, Tennessee	35° 00′	85° 42′
Nine Mile Pt.: *power stn.*, N.Y.	43° 23′	76° 44′
Niota: Tennessee	35° 30′	84° 32′
Nolichucky: *dam*, Tennessee	36° 05′	82° 52′
N. American Basin: Atlantic Ocean	33° 00′	60° 00′
N. Magnetic Pole 1970: N.W.T.	76° 02′	101° 00′
Northport: Alabama	33° 12′	87° 36′
North Sea	55° 00′	0° —
North Surrey: B.C.	49° 13′	122° 54′
North Tonawanda: N.Y.	43° 01′	78° 52′
Nunivak Nat. Wildlife Refuge: Alaska	60° 10′	166° 30′
Oak Creek: *power stn.*, Wis.	42° 52′	87° 54′
Oceanographer Fracture Zone: Atlantic Ocean	35° 00′	35° 00′
Octagon: Newfoundland	47° 34′	52° 40′
Olustee: Oklahoma	34° 33′	99° 25′
Orange City: Iowa	43° 00′	96° 03′
Orange Lake: *sett.*, New York	41° 30′	74° 06′
Osburn: Idaho	47° 30′	116° 00′
Oyster Creek: *power stn.*, N.J.	39° 50′	74° 11′
Ozark Nat. Scenic Riverway: Missouri	38° 10′	92° 40′
Pacific Crest Trail: Calif.-Wash.	—	—
Pacific Ocean	—	—
Palmer: Michigan	46° 26′	87° 35′
Patrick Air Force Base: Fla.	28° 13′	80° 47′
Payson: Arizona	34° 13′	111° 20′
Peachland: British Columbia	49° 46′	119° 44′
Pelton: *dam*, Oregon	44° 37′	121° 07′
Permanente: California	37° 04′	122° 00′
Petersburg Nat. Battlefield: Va.	37° 13′	77° 24′
Petit-Mécantina *see* Little Mecantina: *r.*, Qué.	52° 55′	61° 30′
Pharr: Texas	26° 11′	98° 11′
Philadelphia: Tennessee	35° 40′	84° 24′
Philip Sporn: *power stn.*, West Virginia	38° 56′	81° 56′
Phillipsdale: Rhode Island	41° 50′	71° 22′
P. H. Robinson: *power stn.*, Texas	29° 30′	94° 58′
Pickering: *power stn.*, Ontario	43° 52′	79° 02′
Pictou: Nova Scotia	45° 41′	62° 43′
Pinchi Lake: British Columbia	54° 30′	124° 20′
Pine Bend: Minnesota	44° 46′	93° 01′
Pine Creek: *sett.*, California	37° 10′	118° 38′
Plainview: New York	40° 46′	73° 28′
Platteville: Wisconsin	42° 44′	90° 28′
Plymouth Meeting: Pa.	40° 06′	75° 16′
Point Barrow: *sett.*, Alaska	70° 42′	156° 25′
Point Beach: *power stn.*, Wis.	44° 18′	87° 33′
Pointe-Noire: *sett.*, Québec	50° 10′	66° 27′
Point Tupper: *sett.*, N.S.	45° 36′	61° 20′
Port-Cartier-Sept-Iles Prov. Park Québec	50° 30′	67° 10′
Porterdale: Georgia	33° 36′	83° 54′
Port Hawkesbury: N.S.	45° 37′	61° 21′
Port Isabel: Texas	26° 04′	97° 12′
Port Manatee: Florida	27° 28′	82° 30′
Port Reading: New Jersey	40° 34′	74° 15′
Potosi: Missouri	37° 56′	90° 47′
Powder River Basin: Wyo.	43° 03′	106° 58′
Prince Patrick Is.: N.W.T.	76° 30′	119° 00′
Queensboro: British Columbia	49° 09′	122° 29′
Quirk Creek: *sett.*, Alberta	50° 50′	114° 10′
Radersburg: Montana	46° 11′	111° 37′
Ram River: *sett.*, Alberta	52° 07′	114° 50′
Ray Point: *sett.*, Texas	28° 30′	98° 13′
Red Bird: Nevada	40° 10′	118° 30′
Remac: British Columbia	49° 01′	117° 22′
Rexdale: Ontario	43° 43′	79° 35′
Reykjanes Ridge: Atlantic O.	60° 00′	27° 00′
Riceboro: Georgia	31° 44′	81° 26′
Riegelwood: N. Carolina	34° 22′	78° 14′
Rimouski Prov. Park: Qué.	48° 00′	68° 10′
Robbins: N. Carolina	35° 25′	79° 34′
Robert E. Ginna: *power stn.*, New York	43° 15′	77° 16′
Robinson: Illinois	39° 00′	87° 44′
Rocanville: Saskatchewan	50° 22′	101° 45′
Rockall Bank: Atlantic Ocean	57° 00′	17° 00′
Rockfield: Kentucky	36° 46′	86° 36′
Rogers: Arkansas	36° 20′	94° 07′
Romulus: N.W.T.	79° 40′	84° 00′
Round Butte: *dam*, Oregon	44° 37′	121° 07′
Rowley: Utah	32° 43′	100° 54′
Sable Is. Bank: Atlantic O.	44° 00′	61° 00′
St. Andrews: New Brunswick	45° 05′	67° 03′
St. Charles: Québec	45° 41′	73° 10′
St. Jean, L. *see* St. John, L.: Québec	49° 25′	72° 30′
St. Marys: Georgia	30° 43′	81° 32′
St. Mary's: *r.*, Mich./Ont.	46° 10′	84° 00′
St. Paul Park: Minnesota	44° 50′	92° 59′
Sakakewa, L. *see* Garrison Res.: N.D.	47° 30′	102° 00′
Sand Lake: *sett.*, Alaska	60° 30′	148° 57′
Sand Lake: *sett.*, New York	42° 32′	73° 31′
Sandon: British Columbia	49° 58′	117° 14′
San Pedro: New Mexico	35° 58′	106° 20′
Sargassa Sea: Atlantic Ocean.	27° 00′	67° 00′
Sault Ste. Maire Canal: Ont.	46° 32′	84° 22′
Savannah Creek: *sett.*, Alberta	50° 20′	114° 38′
Schumacher: Ontario	48° 21′	81° 16′
Scottsville: Virginia	37° 48′	78° 29′
Secaucus: New Jersey	40° 48′	75° 50′
Seguin: Texas	29° 34′	97° 58′
Sequoyah: Oklahoma	36° 22′	95° 33′
Shallow Water: Kansas	38° 22′	100° 55′
Sharonville: Ohio	39° 16′	84° 24′
Sharpsville: Pennsylvania	41° 15′	80° 28′
Shawinigan Falls *see* Shawinigan: Québec	46° 33′	72° 45′
Shawmut: Alabama	32° 48′	85° 12′
Shirley Basin: Wyo.	42° 20′	106° 25′
Shoshone: *r.*, Washington	44° 48′	108° 10′
Shullsburg: Wisconsin	42° 34′	90° 15′
Sierrita: Arizona	32° 00′	112° 58′
Siloam Springs: *sett.*, Ala.	36° 11′	94° 32′
Sinclair: Wyoming	41° 46′	107° 06′
Sixtymile: *r.*, Yukon	63° 58′	140° 45′
Southeast Newfoundland Ridge: Atlantic Ocean	42° 00′	48° 00′
South Shore (Taylor): *sett.*, Kentucky	38° 43′	82° 59′
Spelter: W. Virginia	39° 21′	80° 20′
Spokane: *r.*, Idaho/Wash.	47° 54′	118° 20′
Spor Mountain: Utah	39° 50′	113° 15′
Spring City: Pennsylvania	40° 10′	75° 33′
Springfield: Tennessee	36° 30′	86° 53′
Springvale: Maine	43° 27′	70° 50′
Star: N. Carolina	35° 24′	79° 46′
Star Lake: *sett.*, New York	44° 10′	75° 04′
Steep Rock Lake: *sett.*, Ont.	48° 50′	91° 39′
Stellarton: Nova Scotia	45° 34′	62° 40′
Stevenson: Alabama	34° 52′	85° 50′
Stillwater Range: Nevada	39° 35′	118° 10′
Stone Mtn. Prov. Park: B.C.	58° 40′	124° 30′
Strachan: Alberta	52° 40′	115° 04′
Stratford Centre: Québec	45° 48′	71° 08′
Sturgeon Lake: *sett.*, Ontario	45° 27′	78° 42′
Sullivan: Missouri	38° 12′	91° 09′
Sverdrup Islands: N.W.T.	79° 30′	90° 00′
Sweetwater: *sett.*, Missouri	37° 10′	90° 50′
Swepsonville: N. Carolina	35° 58′	79° 23′
Taconite: Minnesota	47° 13′	93° 22′
Tanners Creek: *power stn.*, Ind.	39° 05′	84° 51′
Tasu Harbour: B.C.	52° 45′	132° 07′
Tempe: Arizona	33° 24′	111° 55′
Theodore: Alabama	30° 32′	88° 10′
Thomas H. Allen: *power stn.*, Tennessee	34° 07′	90° 03′
Three Rivers: *sett.*, Texas	28° 28′	98° 11′
Tilden Township: Michigan	46° 26′	87° 44′
Toglu: Northwest Territories	69° 20′	133° 10′
Tomah: Wisconsin	43° 59′	90° 30′
Townsville: N. Carolina	36° 29′	78° 25′
Trading House Cr.: *power stn.*, Texas	31° 33′	97° 09′
Treadway: Tennessee	36° 23′	83° 16′
Tremonton: Utah	41° 42′	112° 10′
Troy: Michigan	42° 36′	83° 09′
Tungsten: N.W.T.	63° 08′	128° 08′
Tungsten Queen: N. Carolina	36° 29′	78° 25′
Twin Buttes: *sett.*, Arizona	31° 52′	111° 03′
Tyrone: New Mexico	32° 40′	108° 22′
Uchi Lake: *sett.*, Ontario	51° 04′	92° 35′
Umpqua: *r.*, Oregon	43° 15′	122° 40′
Union Bridge: Maryland	39° 34′	77° 10′
Upper Fraser: B.C.	54° 07′	121° 56′
Uravan: Colorado	38° 22′	108° 44′
Valencia: New Mexico	34° 48′	106° 43′
Vallecitos: California	37° 20′	121° 53′
Valliant: Oklahoma	34° 01′	95° 07′
Vanadium: New Mexico	32° 47′	108° 05′
Vananda: British Columbia	49° 45′	124° 33′
Vancoram: Ohio	40° 20′	80° 31′
Vanscoy: Saskatchewan	52° 00′	106° 58′
Veta Grande: Nevada	39° 00′	119° 30′
Viburnum: Missouri	37° 43′	91° 08′
Viscount: Saskatchewan	51° 57′	105° 41′
W. A. C. Bennett: *dam*, B.C.	56° 10′	122° 29′
Wallace: Idaho	47° 28′	115° 56′
Walters: *dam*, N. Carolina	35° 46′	83° 06′
W. A. Parrish: *power stn.*, Texas	29° 34′	95° 45′
Waterton: Alberta	49° 08′	112° 44′
Watertown: Connecticut	41° 36′	73° 07′
Wattenberg: Colorado	40° 01′	104° 50′
Wawa: Ontario	48° 00′	84° 46′
Wax: Georgia	34° 08′	84° 59′
W. C. Beckjord: *power stn.*, Ohio	38° 57′	84° 17′
Welland Canal: Ontario	43° 00′	79° 30′
Wessington Springs: *sett.*, S. Dakota	44° 05′	98° 34′
Westbrook: Maine	43° 40′	70° 21′
West European Basin: Atlantic Ocean	46° 00′	15° 00′
West Fork: *r.*, Missouri	37° 25′	91° 00′
West Green: Georgia	31° 36′	82° 44′
West Homestead: Pennsylvania	40° 24′	79° 56′
West Monroe: Louisiana	32° 32′	92° 10′
West Point: Alabama	34° 17′	86° 57′
West Valley: New York	42° 26′	78° 37′
White Pine: Michigan	46° 45′	89° 35′
Whiteshell Prov. Park: Man.	50° 00′	95° 25′
White Springs: *sett.*, Florida	30° 20′	82° 45′
W. H. Sammis: *power stn.*, Ohio	40° 32′	80° 41′
Wilder: Kentucky	39° 05′	84° 30′
Willmore Wilderness Park: Alberta	53° 40′	119° 00′
Wilson: *dam*, Alabama	34° 45′	87° 40′
Wilson Spring: *sett.*, Ark.	34° 33′	93° 20′
Wilton: Iowa	41° 34′	91° 02′
Winborne: Alberta	51° 52′	113° 48′
Windsor: *dam*, Massachusetts	42° 18′	72° 21′
Winton: Minnesota	47° 55′	91° 48′
Woodlawn: N. Carolina	35° 47′	82° 02′
Wood River Junction: R.I.	41° 26′	71° 42′
Woodville: S. Carolina	34° 37′	82° 24′
Woodward: Alabama	33° 26′	86° 59′

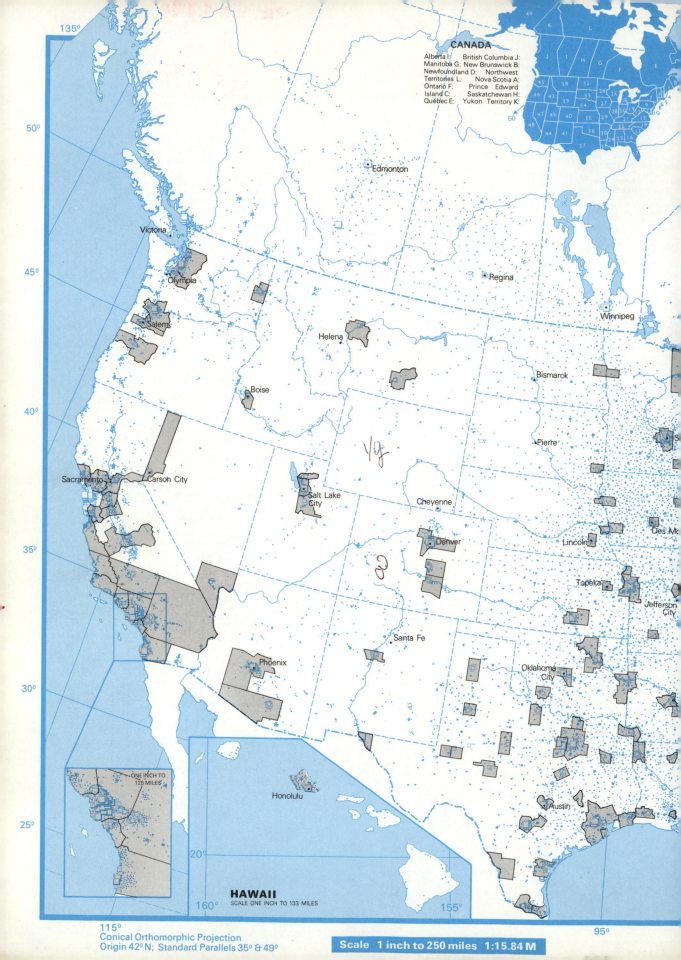

Edmonton

Victoria

Olympia

Salem

Helena

Boise

Regina

Winnipeg

Bismarck

Pierre

Sacramento   Carson City

Salt Lake City

Cheyenne

Denver

Lincoln

Des Mo

Topeka

Jefferson City

Santa Fe

Phoenix

Oklahoma City

Honolulu

Austin

ONE INCH TO 125 MILES

HAWAII
SCALE ONE INCH TO 133 MILES

115°
Conical Orthomorphic Projection
Origin 42° N; Standard Parallels 35° & 49°

Scale   1 inch to 250 miles   1:15.84 M